TIM SOUTPHOMMASANE

I'M NOT RACIST *but*...

Tim Soutphommasane is Australia's Race Discrimination Commissioner, a role he commenced in 2013. Prior to joining the Australian Human Rights Commission, he was a political philosopher at the University of Sydney and Monash University. He is the author of *Don't Go Back To Where You Came From* (2012, winner of a NSW Premier's Literary Award), *The Virtuous Citizen* (2012) and *Reclaiming Patriotism* (2009), and co-editor of *All That's Left* (2010). He has been an opinion columnist with *The Age* and *The Weekend Australian*. His radio series about Australian multiculturalism, *Mongrel Nation* (ABC Radio National), won a UN Media Peace Award in 2013.

TIM SOUTPHOMMASANE
I'M NOT RACIST *but...*
40 YEARS OF THE RACIAL DISCRIMINATION ACT

MAXINE BENEBA CLARKE, BINDI COLE CHOCKA,
BENJAMIN LAW, ALICE PUNG, CHRISTOS TSIOLKAS

A NewSouth book

Published by
NewSouth Publishing
University of New South Wales Press Ltd
University of New South Wales
Sydney NSW 2052
AUSTRALIA
newsouthpublishing.com

© Australian Human Rights Commission 2015
First published 2015

10 9 8 7 6 5 4 3 2 1

This book is copyright. While copyright of the work as a whole is vested in the Australian Human Rights Commission, copyright of individual chapters is retained by the chapter authors. Apart from any fair dealing for the purpose of private study, research, criticism or review, as permitted under the Copyright Act, no part of this book may be reproduced by any process without written permission. Inquiries should be addressed to the publisher.

National Library of Australia Cataloguing-in-Publication entry
Creator: Soutphommasane, Tim, author.
Title: I'm not racist but ... forty years of the Racial Discrimination Act / Tim Soutphommasane; with contributions by Maxine Beneba Clarke, Bindi Cole Chocka, Benjamin Law, Alice Pung and Christos Tsiolkas.
ISBN: 9781742234274 (paperback)
       9781742242057 (ePub/Kindle)
       9781742247342 (ePDF)
Notes: Includes index.
Subjects: Australia. Racial Discrimination Act 1975.
  Race discrimination – Australia.
  Racism – Australia.
  Freedom of speech – Australia.
  Tolerance – Australia.
  Australia – Race relations.
Other Creators/Contributors: Clarke, Maxine Beneba, author; Cole Chocka, Bindi, author; Law, Benjamin, author; Pung, Alice, author; Tsiolkas, Christos, author.
Dewey Number: 305.800994

Design Josephine Pajor-Markus
Cover design Xou Creative

Published in association with the Australian Human Rights Commission.

CONTENTS

Acknowledgments viii

Contributors x

Timeline: 40+ years of race and related issues in Australia xii

Introduction 1

1 Race in Australia: a short historical account 11

2 The Racial Discrimination Act: equality and dignity in the law 48

   Christos Tsiolkas: A mongrel multiculturalism 88

3 Freedom of speech and its limits: is there a right to be a bigot? 98

   Alice Pung: The reasonable man 137

4 Casual racism and bigotry: the many faces of prejudice and discrimination 142

   Maxine Beneba Clarke: Calling out casual racism 176

5 Empathy and privilege: putting yourself in another's shoes 183

   Bindi Cole Chocka: Thick skin 208

6 Friendship: the civic bonds of patriotism	214
Benjamin Law: It's easy to make friends with white people	*244*
Afterword	249
Appendix: *Racial Discrimination Act 1975* (extracts from the Act)	255
Notes	267
Index	290

In memory of Gough Whitlam and Malcolm Fraser, whose leadership on human rights, racial equality and multiculturalism remind us what Australia can be when it is at its best.

ACKNOWLEDGMENTS

Writing this book afforded me many opportunities to test and reflect on arguments I have put forward in various speeches. Chapters 3–6 are based on speeches I delivered at Australian National University (Alice Tay Lecture in Law and Human Rights, 3 March 2014), University of South Australia (Centre for Research in Education Annual Oration, 13 November 2014), B'Nai B'rith NSW (B'nai B'rith Annual Human Rights Address 2014, 3 November 2014), and Sydney PEN (Sydney PEN Lecture, 23 August 2013). Chapters 1 and 2 draw upon my opening remarks to the RDA@40 conference I convened on 19–20 February 2015, and an article I wrote for the *LSJ: Law Society of NSW Journal* (February 2015).

I am grateful for the advice and suggestions of Phillipa McGuinness, Nick Bryant, Nick Dyrenfurth and Simon Rice. Katie Ellinson, Rivkah Nissim, Padma Raman, Jeremy Spinak and Tony Kitchener also provided comments on chapters. Stephanie Fowler and Lucian Tan assisted in finalising references. The editing talents of Averil Moffat have improved the text. I feel privileged to include in

Acknowledgments

this volume contributions from writers and artists I admire and respect: Maxine Beneba Clarke, Bindi Cole Chocka, Benjamin Law, Alice Pung, Christos Tsiolkas. I owe special thanks to Sarah Hepworth for her love, patience and encouragement.

CONTRIBUTORS

Maxine Beneba Clarke is an Australian writer of Afro-Caribbean descent. She is the author of the critically acclaimed short fiction collection *Foreign Soil* (2014), and the poetry collections *Gil Scott Heron is On Parole* (2009), and *Nothing Here Needs Fixing* (2013). Her memoir, *The Hate Race*, about growing up black in white, middle class Australia, is due for publication in 2016.

Bindi Cole Chocka is an award winning, Melbourne-born photographer, curator, new media artist and writer. Her work often references her life story and experiences, such as her Wadawurrung heritage and the importance of Christianity in her life. Her deeply personal and powerful artistic practice questions the way people circumscribe and misconstrue contemporary identity and experience. She was one of the plaintiffs in the *Eatock v Bolt* case.

Benjamin Law is a journalist, columnist and screenwriter based in both Brisbane and Sydney. He is the author of two books – *The Family Law* (2010) and

Contributors

Gaysia: Adventures in the Queer East (2012) – both of which were nominated for Australian Book Industry Awards. He is the co-author of the comedy book *Shit Asian Mothers Say* (2014) with his sister Michelle and illustrator Oslo Davis, and is currently writing the TV adaptation of *The Family Law* for SBS and Matchbox Pictures. Benjamin is a frequent contributor to *Good Weekend*, *frankie* and *The Monthly*, and has also written for more than than 50 publications, businesses and agencies in Australia and worldwide.

Alice Pung is the author of the award-winning books *Unpolished Gem* (2006), *Her Father's Daughter* (2011) and the acclaimed novel *Laurinda* (2014). She also edited the anthology *Growing Up Asian in Australia* (2008).

Christos Tsiolkas is a novelist, playwright, essayist and screen writer. His novels include *Loaded* (1995), *The Jesus Man* (1999), *Dead Europe* (2005), *The Slap* (2008) and *Barracuda* (2013). He released an anthology of short stories, *Merciless Gods*, in 2014. He was the co-author, along with Sasha Soldatow, of *Jump Cuts: An Autobiography* (1996). Christos is the film critic for *The Saturday Paper*.

TIMELINE
40+ YEARS OF RACE AND RELATED ISSUES IN AUSTRALIA

1973   Whitlam Government completes the dismantling of the White Australia policy and indicates that all international agreements relating to immigration and race are to be ratified.

1973   Immigration Minister Al Grassby makes the first official reference to the word 'multicultural' in an address in Melbourne.

1975   The *Racial Discrimination Act 1975*, Australia's first federal human rights and anti-discrimination legislation, comes into effect.

1976   The first boat carrying Indochinese refugees arrives in Darwin.

Timeline

1977 Fraser Government adopts a formal humanitarian policy for the resettlement of refugees from Southeast Asia.

1980 SBS TV begins full-time transmission.

1984 Historian Geoffrey Blainey delivers a speech in Warrnambool, Victoria, warning of the Asianisation of Australia and sparking a national debate.

1986 With the establishment of the Human Rights and Equal Opportunity Commission, the office of Community Relations Commissioner becomes that of Race Discrimination Commissioner.

1988 Opposition leader John Howard speculates upon the level of Asian immigration that Australian society could accommodate.

Late 1980s Asian restaurants are firebombed by the Australian Nationalist Movement.

1991 Report of the National Inquiry into Racist Violence in Australia is released.

1991	Royal Commission into Aboriginal Deaths in Custody National Report is released.
1992	The High Court's decision in *Mabo* recognises native title in Australia for the first time.
1992	Mandatory detention is introduced for non-citizens who arrive in Australia without a visa.
1993	AFL footballer Nicky Winmar responds to racial abuse at a match, in what becomes an iconic episode.
1994	The Commonwealth Parliament passes the Native Title Bill.
1995	Racial Discrimination Act is amended to include provisions against racial hatred/racial vilification.
1997	Pauline Hanson's One Nation Party is founded.
1998	The Howard Government amends native title legislation in response to the *Wik* judgment.

Timeline

2001 The Howard Government introduces the 'Pacific Solution'.

2004 Redfern riots take place, triggered by the death of Thomas 'TJ' Hickey.

2004 Australian population hits 20 million.

2005 A race riot occurs in Cronulla, Sydney, involving a 6000-strong mob targeting people of Middle Eastern background.

2007 Northern Territory intervention measures come into effect, including a suspension of the Racial Discrimination Act.

2008 Prime Minister Kevin Rudd offers an apology to the Stolen Generation.

2010 Expert panel on the Constitutional recognition of Aboriginal and Torres Strait Islander peoples appointed.

2010 Gillard Government reinstates the Racial Discrimination Act's operation in the Northern Territory.

2011	Federal Court finds Herald-Sun columnist Andrew Bolt contravened section 18C of the Racial Discrimination Act.
2011	People's Republic of China overtakes United Kingdom as the main source country of permanent migrant arrivals.
2012	Final report of the expert panel on Constitutional recognition is published.
2013	Newly elected Abbott Government pledges to repeal section 18C of the RDA.
2014	Prime Minister Tony Abbott abandons move to repeal section 18C.
2015	Australian Bureau of Statistics confirms that 28 per cent of Australia's population (6.6 million people) were born overseas – the highest proportion of overseas-born in 120 years.

INTRODUCTION

Is Australia a racist country? During my time as Race Discrimination Commissioner, I have been posed this question constantly. Almost every time, I find the invitation to comment puzzling, albeit predictable. Australians appear alone in asking such a question about themselves; other nationalities seem not to expose themselves to such routine scrutiny. It is as though some of us hope for ready confirmation of some moral flaw in the national character, while others are only too eager to find an affirmation of our egalitarian tolerance. Perhaps because of this, my answers to the question tend to be met with an air of disappointment. Not everyone is satisfied with the thought that, while racism warrants our condemnation, we should resist defining our country by its worst aspects. For that matter, not everyone is comfortable with the proposition that racism may be more prevalent than they believe.

But if we are asked about racism and national identity so often, it is because there are so many reminders of racism's persistence. It is rare to find a week when issues surrounding race are not reported in the news. Most notably, a distinctive genre of racial controversy has emerged. For example, in July 2014, legal secretary Karen Bailey gained international notoriety when she launched into an anti-Asian tirade against another passenger on a Sydney train – an attack filmed and replayed in news bulletins around the world. That episode is one of many that have been prominently reported, usually accompanied by video footage captured by bystanders on their mobile phones. For those who have ever suffered racial abuse, the scenes are familiar. The perpetrators are loud, often threatening, always revelling in their verbal violence. There are the uncomfortable bystanders who avert their gaze and imagine they have seen nothing.

Increasingly, though, more and more are standing up for those on the receiving end. Media reports about racist incidents highlight that bystanders are fighting back on public transport. At sporting events, traditionally safe havens for anyone who wanted to vent racial prejudices, spectators are also reporting acts of racist abuse to authorities. There is no simple explanation for such developments. The attention that media are giving to racism may have something to do with it: the airing of confronting video footage of racism appears to have stiffened people's spines against bullies and bigots. The example set by public figures such as AFL footballer and 2014 Australian of the Year Adam Goodes – who took dramatic

Introduction

exception to being called an ape at the Melbourne Cricket Ground in 2013 – seems also to have empowered people to challenge abuse and insult. It is only right that we take public acts of racism seriously, as they are deeply subversive of our values. It may be one thing to harbour some racist thoughts in one's own mind, thoughts that may never be disclosed. It is another thing to voice the sentiment in public or to someone's face. This is where the civic harm of racism lies. When unchecked, it can allow people to believe they are entitled to harass, belittle and intimidate others because of their race, ethnicity or origin. Those who suffer a racist taunt or threat can feel like a second-class citizen or less than a person. Racism is repugnant because it wounds dignity and damages equality.

Any vigilance must extend into the banality of our everyday lives. Racism can be insidious. It resides not only in overt acts of disdain or discrimination, but also in subtle expressions of prejudice. It exists in the form of what Martin Luther King Jr first described as the 'soft bigotry of low expectations', the assumptions that people can make of others based on unfavourable stereotypes. It can exist as well in the form of seemingly harmless humour, passed off as affectionate jesting, or disguised by appeals to ironic sophistication. Often, among friends and acquaintances, its airing is preceded by that curious disclaimer: 'I'm not racist but ...'

This book reflects upon the Australian experience of racism, on the occasion of the fortieth anniversary of the *Racial Discrimination Act 1975*. Introduced by the Commonwealth Parliament, the Act (or 'the RDA') was this country's first national human rights legislation. It was a landmark achievement that punctuated the dismantling of the White Australia policy and the inception of Australian racial equality. As demonstrated by recent debates about free speech and racial vilification – prompted by the Abbott Government's proposed repeal of section 18C of the Act in 2014, and by attempts in January 2015 to revive the repeal following the *Charlie Hebdo* massacre in Paris – the law has had its share of controversies. Its history has been marked by contesting visions of the law, justice and Australian society. Yet the Act's presence means that there is, in the national life, an unambiguous public commitment to eliminating racism and to maintaining cultural harmony.

My attention in this book is not confined, however, to the legislation alone. The Act's forty years of operation have been proof that laws can only ever be fully understood in context. The law, as it exists, reflects historical debates and expresses society's collective aspirations. And as much as laws can help to clarify a society's values, they can also point to its shortcomings in living up to them.

We should appreciate the cultural background to any discussion of racism and our legislative response.

Introduction

There is a very Australian way to talk about race, as I have alluded. Whenever bigotry, prejudice or discrimination is revealed on the national stage, all of us can agree: we would never dream of endorsing it. We can all say, hand on heart, that racism is abhorrent. But before long, doubt emerges. Someone will ask: Is Australia a racist country? Is this evidence of some essential racist character, some ineradicable racist stain, in Australian society?

One response is that of parochial defensiveness. According to this stance, Australians are not nearly as racist as others around the world. We should, it is argued, reserve the word 'racism' for only those instances when there has been racial violence or professions of racial superiority. Moreover, we are entitled to take offence when racism is alleged, as racism is the lowest judgment you can make of another person's character. For the parochialist, to contemplate charging that a fellow Australian is racist is a mark of someone who likes to think the worst of their country and compatriots.

Others take the path of self-flagellation. This is the position of those who believe Australian nationhood is inseparable from racism. It is asserted that even modern sensibilities cannot obliterate old biases and assumptions rooted in notions of racial superiority. On this view, national myths about fairness and egalitarianism – and about the happy harmony of multiculturalism – serve to conceal the true nature

I'm not racist but ...

of the national psyche. So long as there is an Australian national identity, the argument runs, there will be racial exclusion. The only way to overcome this is to renounce nationalism in all its forms; we should instead embrace a cosmopolitanism in which people belong to a single community based on their common humanity.

There is an alternative to these two extremes. After all, why should we accept the premise of questioning whether Australia is a racist country? Such a question may miss the point. Every country has its bigots, its prejudices and its problems with discrimination. It is unhelpful to turn every incident involving racism into a test that demands of us a wholesale judgment about the Australian national character.

A more objective view would recognise that today's Australia is relatively free from the racial tensions and discrimination that afflict other societies. We should be able to take pride in our achievements as a multicultural, immigrant society since the demise of the White Australia ideal. Whereas places like the United States and Britain have periodic race riots, such episodes here are rare: the Cronulla riot of 2005, for instance, stands as an aberration. We have largely been untarnished by organised racism. Thankfully, we do not have the equivalents of the Ku Klux Klan, the Front National or the English Defence League. Australia has also avoided the contagion of extremist movements that have gained significant

Introduction

popularity across Europe in response to immigration and the supposed 'Islamification' of the West. When anti-Muslim activists organised 'Reclaim Australia' rallies in April 2015 they were able to muster only small numbers in most of the capital cities.

Australia has been a country defined by social cohesion. Such qualities were evident in December 2014, in the wake of the deadly Martin Place siege in Sydney. In what most regarded as a 'lone wolf' terrorist attack, self-styled sheikh Man Haron Monis took 18 people hostage in a Lindt chocolate café. Hours into the siege, a large number of Australians demonstrated their solidarity with Muslim Australians through the viral 'I'll ride with you' social media campaign. Commuters from around the country offered to ride public transport with Muslims who may have felt vulnerable to any anti-Islamic sentiment stirred by the siege. The dominant response was one of unity – of Australians coming together and not allowing Muslims to feel unwelcome.

None of this means we should be in denial about the challenge of maintaining cultural harmony and racial tolerance. A significant number of people are affected by racism: about 20 per cent of Australians have experienced verbal racial abuse, and about 5 per cent have experienced racial violence in physical form.[1] There remains room for improvement. But any progress requires that racial issues be the subjects of serious public debate. For this to happen, we should understand that racism is never as simple as it appears: it can be as much a product of ignorance or innocence as it is of anxiety and antagonism. And rather than always leaving us with moral clarity, racism can leave us with a sense of contradiction. For example, I have experienced occasions, even in my current role, when well-intentioned people have expressed to me their support for racial equality and multiculturalism, only to proceed to compliment me on how well I speak English given my Asian heritage. I have been subjected to threatening racial abuse in Sydney while travelling with a member of staff – by a taxi driver who was himself an immigrant from a non-European background. A few years ago in Canberra, within the space of a few hours, I went from feeling patriotic pride while attending an Australia Day event to being taunted by a car full of flag-draped youths making slit-eyed gestures while jeering, 'Go home!'

As for public debate itself, we would do well to avoid ideological posturing. When people raise questions about racism, there should be no rush to make cynical excuses: to say that calling something 'racist' only serves to makes things worse and unfairly victimises those who have caused the offence in the first place. By the same token, criticising racism need not mean criticising each and every Australian for being racist, as though we are implicated in every instance of ignorance or bigotry. We can condemn racism when

Introduction

it occurs, without needing to draw sweeping conclusions about the moral character of the nation or to answer the charge that we are being 'un-Australian'. In this book, I adopt a stance that can be described as a humane and critical patriotism. It avoids both parochialism and cultural self-loathing, in declining to see racism as either a figment of a politically correct imagination or an inevitable by-product of nationhood. It is patriotic in believing that our society should always strive to be at its best. Within such a patriotic view, racism is to be regarded as an affront to notions of egalitarianism and a fair go, as well as an impediment to our society reaching its full potential.

This book brings together a number of chapters, which began their life as speeches and articles during my first year-and-a-half as Commissioner. It seeks to provide historical and philosophical context for discussions about race, and to provide an account of the history and impact of the Racial Discrimination Act. It deals with a number of specific issues in detail. Given recent public debate about section 18C of the Act, this book explores questions about free speech and racial vilification. It reflects on the evolving nature of contemporary racism, especially its increasingly 'casual' nature. It considers the challenge of building racial tolerance and cultural harmony – in particular, the need for us to affirm our common ground as fellow citizens and the moral bond we share as members of Australian society.

This volume also features a number of short essays from contributors. Christos Tsiolkas, Alice Pung, Maxine Beneba Clarke, Bindi Cole Chocka and Benjamin Law each provide some personal reflections about racism in Australia. These essays, touching on many of this book's themes and written from a variety of perspectives, serve to remind us that considerations about race must not be separated from lived experience. Fighting racism can never just be about high philosophy or legal interpretation; it is ultimately about people treating each other as equals and with dignity, in every part of their lives.

1
RACE IN AUSTRALIA
A SHORT HISTORICAL ACCOUNT

Countries are like people: every nation wishes to be liked or approved by others. As revealed by our so-called cultural cringe, a sense of anxiety has always featured in the Australian national identity. On racial matters, some would argue that such anxiety is well-founded. After all, Australia appears to enjoy some international repute for racism. In his book about Australia, British journalist Nick Bryant describes us as a 'story of multicultural success', but nonetheless a country that 'still had some way to go before it could bury its reputation as a redneck nation'.[1] On American television's popular *Daily Show* program in 2014, presenter John Oliver called Australia 'one of the most comfortably racist places I've ever been in', with a population that has 'settled into their intolerance like an old resentful slipper'.[2] Barely after he left Australia in 2009, the former chief executive of Telstra, American Sol Trujillo,

I'm not racist but ...

made international headlines telling the BBC that Australia was a racist and backward country where doing business felt like 'a step back in time'.[3]

Such international images of Australia unfairly depict us as something of a white Anglo-Celtic outpost in Asia, a place whose hostility towards non-whites and non-Europeans is derived from the national DNA. This does not seem to square with one undeniable reality. Our society is a dynamic and diverse one, in which more than a quarter of the population was born overseas. In each of the past seven decades, Australia has taken in more than a million immigrants, increasingly from Asia. If racism were as comfortably entrenched in our society as some suggest, it seems odd and miraculously unlikely that Australia has managed such a significant program of immigration without experiencing profound social discord.

Of course, racism continues to cause collective discomfort from time to time. In this, Australia is by no means alone. There are many countries where race has played a central role in defining the national identity. Many others also have national histories bound up in the experience of colonialism. It is just that, as Australians, we in many ways continue to grapple with our history and issues around race. We may well be described as a country with an ancient Aboriginal heritage, British political foundation and contemporary multicultural character; yet those components may not always sit easily together.⁴

This is revealed every summer leading into Australia Day. Few countries mark their national day with such extensive collective introspection. Particularly in recent years, 26 January has been as much a day of ambivalence as it is of celebration. For some, Australia Day – commemorating the day that Arthur Phillip and the First Fleet established the colony of New South Wales in Sydney Cove – has a fundamentally racist nature. It is inappropriate, they argue, to have a national day that rejoices in the event that amounted to the dispossession and destruction of Indigenous peoples under the British Crown. Others argue that Australia Day has descended into jingoistic celebration, which excludes many from our multiracial, multicultural society. For others, perhaps most, Australia Day is an occasion for benign patriotic revelry, even if it demands some measure of national reflection.

Clearly, much of our cultural sensitivity to racial matters is implicated in our history. British colonisation of Australia was built on the presumption that civilised humanity was achievable only by Europeans. When the colonies federated as a Commonwealth in 1901, the organising principle was that of racial unity in the form of a White Australia. A sense of white superiority was regarded as thoroughly compatible with enlightened social views, both liberal and radical.⁵ Such notions about race may no longer be widely accepted, but their legacies continue to shape debates about Australian identity and nationhood. This is true not only with respect to our understanding of Indigenous history and culture, but also of the place of immigrants in our national life. Yet to what extent does the present draw upon the assumptions of the past? How exactly have we been shaped by the history of European colonialism and White Australia? And, perhaps more basic, how should we understand race and racism?

THE NOTION OF RACE

We speak often about race. Few us of bat an eyelid when we refer to someone's race or racial characteristics. It is self-evident that someone's physical appearance will reflect their racial background. We also accept that such differences can be consequential. How people understand their identity may reflect their membership of a racial group. Bearing such membership may, in turn, affect the manner in which people are treated by others – in some cases, in a negative way. The majority of us recognise that racial prejudice and discrimination exist.

The very term 'race' can be confusing, though. Many scientists and anthropologists deny that race exists in any meaningful sense. They argue there is no biological entity that warrants the use of the term.

Race in Australia

In his landmark 1972 study of the human genome, Harvard University geneticist Richard Lewontin contended that, 'human racial classification is of no social value and is positively destructive of social and human relations'.[6] His study found that the differences between what we regard as racial groups are far smaller than what such groups have in common. In genetic terms, there is little that separates us, regardless of our racial backgrounds. We all share more than 99 per cent in our genetic makeup. The difference between an Englishman and an Egyptian, between an Indian and an Irishman is miniscule. There is a basic unity to humankind.

Nonetheless, race matters. The suggestion that race does not exist seems to contradict people's encounters with different groups of people who look different. Racial characteristics serve as markers of geographic origin or social identity. When we meet a person who appears to be, say, Chinese, and they are indeed born in China, what explains it, if not race? As Christine Kenneally explains in her history of DNA, there can be a conflation of race with *ancestry* – an idea of which we need not be afraid. 'Ancestry is real', as Kenneally notes, 'and it can't just be defined away. You can see it on people's faces, and you can definitely identify it in their DNA. The *it* that makes letters of the genome fall into different patterns in different groups is in fact the *ancestry* of the people carrying them'.[7]

Race has, in any case, always featured in the modern understanding of identity. In the late 17th and early 18th centuries, race emerged as a key concept in Enlightenment thinking about human nature. In contrast to the traditional view during the Middle Ages, which saw humanity as creatures of God, the Enlightenment saw a new emphasis on the physical aspects of human nature. Thus, in its early usage, the notion of race was frequently bound up in discussions about climate, soil, social habits and political liberty. It was considered part of the law of nature. As explained by French philosopher Charles de Montesquieu, climate shaped the tempers of the mind and the passions of the heart. In turn, these determined the spirit of a country's laws and governments. Whereas the heat 'enervates the strength and courage of men', those in cold climates 'have a certain vigour of body and mind, which renders them patient and intrepid, and qualifies them for arduous enterprises'.[8] Such differences explained the 'servile spirit' of Asia as opposed to the 'genius for liberty' in Europe.

Race quickly became a characteristic that helped to explain why civilised humanity was something only Europeans could supposedly achieve. To be white and European was the very meaning of being civilised. This notion of superiority provided the ideological basis for the European dominion over the rest of the world, a state of affairs that has characterised global affairs for most of the past 500 years.

Europeans had the power to determine the standing of non-Europeans, and they did so by dividing the world between 'men' and 'natives'.[9] Native peoples were conquered or subjugated, their cultures extinguished; otherwise occupied lands were 'discovered'.

In the Australian case, British colonisation was justified by the doctrine of *terra nullius*. In claiming sovereignty over the land, the British Government acted as if Australia were uninhabited. They regarded the land as being without civilised habitation – without law, government or history. The British had treated the Indigenous inhabitants 'as people too low in the scale of social organisation to be acknowledged as possessing rights and interests in land'.[10] For some, British sovereignty depended on discriminatory denigration of Indigenous peoples. For others, such as historian John Hirst, it was more the case that the British, 'had a very poor understanding of the connection between Aborigines and the land', and had, 'by their own lights' acted correctly and without malice.[11]

Whatever view one may take, the historical development of the Australian state followed a similar trajectory to that of other white settler states. Whether it was the United States, Canada, New Zealand, Rhodesia or South Africa, the pattern was consistent: territory would be taken from inhabitants, there would be displacement of aboriginal populations. There would be deaths caused by the colonial enterprise. Some native peoples died because of warfare or because settlers wished to exterminate them. Some died after being removed from land that was being 'settled'. Others would die from disease.

All this was regarded as inevitable features of colonial progress. There was little lament for such human costs, as the march of European colonialism across different continents proceeded unimpeded. By 1914, the powers of Europe held roughly 85 per cent of the earth as colonies, protectorates, dominions and commonwealths.[12] Within this colonial world, there emerged a transnational European polity, in which colour bars separated Europeans from others. For the white European, there was secure knowledge of one's membership of a superior race, and tranquil consciousness that one's skin amounted to special admittance into the ranks of civilisation.[13]

There remains considerable debate among historians and scholars about how we should characterise European colonisation of Australia. The bitterness of the so-called 'history wars' in Australia – debates about the writing and interpretation of the history of European settlement in Australia – shows how such matters can provoke partisan division.[14] Yet the colonisation of Australia did involve cultural and physical destruction of Aboriginal people and culture. There may not have been a dedicated state project aimed at the genocide of Aboriginal people – colonial policies included ones aimed at 'protecting' Aboriginal people – but the inevitable result of colonisation was something approaching extermination. As Indigenous advocate Noel Pearson has recently observed, 'frontier destruction and protection served the same colonial logic ... [a] logic that envisaged *no future* for the native peoples, whose homelands were to be usurped and societies swept aside by the expanding colonies'.[15]

There can be no doubt that racial notions underpinned the British colonising experience. According to Pearson, accounts of the death of Aboriginal people on the frontier:

> speak to me of the profoundest moral problem of this history: the heavy accounting of the humanity of the Aborigines. It is not the horrific scenes of mass murder that are most appalling here; it is the mundanity and casual parsimony of it all. No people on earth were considered lower. No people rated lower on the ruling scales of human worth, and their deaths elicited the least level of moral reproval.[16]

Such thinking was a consistent feature of colonial thinking. Yet in subtle ways, racial ideas were never totally fixed. By the mid-19th century, Montesquieu's prototypical ideas about race, climate and geography had evolved. Buttressed by colonial experience of conquest and occupation, discussions of race assumed a more feverish quality. Most notably, in the 1850s, the French aristocrat Count Arthur Gobineau wrote his four-volume work *The Inequality of the Human Races* – arguably the first attempt at a systematic expression of 'scientific racism'.

For Gobineau, the different races sat in a hierarchy. The black race was characterised by an 'intensity of desire' but by 'dull, or even non-existent mental faculties'. The yellow race demonstrated 'feebleness of desire, little physical energy, tendencies to mediocrity in everything'. As for the white race, its members were defined by 'energetic intelligence, perseverance, physical power, instinct for order and love of liberty'. Gobineau was in no doubt about the superior race: 'Everything great, noble and fruitful in the works of men belongs to one family alone – the Aryan race … When the Aryan blood is exhausted, stagnation supervenes.'[17] With Gobineau's theories, race was no longer merely part of some vaguely grasped 'law of nature'. It became a category with apparent biological validity.

RACE AS A CIVIC PRINCIPLE

In Australia, racial ideals grew in prominence from the 1830s onwards. By 1837, with convict labour in declining supply, pastoralists in the colony of New South Wales began searching for new sources of cheap labour. With continuing frontier violence ruling out Aboriginal peoples, pastoralists focused their attention initially on indentured labour from India.

There was little enthusiasm for the idea. British colonial officials feared that indentured labourers from India would become a permanent degrading presence in the colony. They would obstruct the mission 'of reserving the continent of New Holland as a place where the English race shall be spread from sea to sea unmixed with any lower caste'.[18] Much as 'we now regret the folly of our ancestors in colonising North America from Africa, so should our posterity have to censure us if we should colonise Australia from India'.[19]

These arguments were later transferred to the prospect of imported Chinese labour. But the public concern was amplified. Whereas indentured Indian labour was merely a hypothetical, Chinese labour entered the colonial economy in significant numbers during the gold-rush years mid-century. On the goldfields, miners agitated against Chinese prospectors. Anti-Chinese riots erupted on many goldfields, including at Hanging Rock (1852), Bendigo (1854) and Buckland River (1857). Following riots at Lambing Flat in 1861, a bill to restrict Chinese immigration was passed in the New South Wales parliament. Few believed that races could successfully mix.

Often, the incendiary rhetoric of the time resorted

to crude depictions of the Chinese as an inferior, grostesque and contemptible race. According to the *Bathurst Free Press*, Anglo-Saxon or European diggers were justified in objecting to 'a race with whom they have little more in common than with a race of baboons or a tribe of ourang-outangs'.[20] An editorial in the *Illustrated Sydney News* in 1878 noted that, 'we cannot get over our repugnance to the race, whose tawny, parchment coloured skins, black hair, lank and coarse, no beards, oblique eyes and high cheek bones distinguish them so widely from ourselves, and place them so far beneath our recognised standards of manliness and beauty'.[21]

Opponents of Chinese immigration also argued there were economic reasons for restriction: coolie immigration would lead to unfair competition of Asian labour against European labour. Yet, 'once the Chinese were perceived as an economic threat, the belief in Anglo-Saxon superiority quickly turned Chinese customs into conclusive proof of Oriental infamy'.[22] The presence of Chinese immigrants, almost all of whom were male, was quickly regarded as leading to bad moral tendencies. Chinese were associated with vice, filth and treachery – with opium dens and degeneracy. In the public mind, this immorality was tied to a fear of contamination: the effect of allowing Chinese immigration would be to diminish the character of the colonies. The Chinese, many argued, could never be assimilated into a civilised

British society. Were they to marry and mix with white women, they would pollute racial purity. Some of the anti-Chinese racial feeling reflected the inherent fragility of the convict period of colonial history. 'Behind many of the debates', as historian Ann Curthoys notes, 'was that older argument against convictism, that the importation of a lower, immoral, and unfree class degraded the upper classes and indeed the whole society'.[23]

What was arguably most striking about anti-Chinese feeling during the 19th century was that race was used as a *civic* principle. If the Chinese could never be accepted as equals, the thinking went, it was better that they were not accepted into society at all. Liberal reformers were loudest in declaiming the prospect of a permanent Chinese population, often pointing to experiences of the Californian gold rush in America as a warning. Their objection was that the presence of an inferior class would be prejudicial to equality and undermine the liberty of the entire community. One leading critic in the New South Wales assembly, Henry Parkes, expressed his concern that an influx of Chinese would lead to 'future discord, anarchy and civil war'.[24] Feelings of racial animosity were given a peculiarly egalitarian flavour.

Again, there was in this something that was also present in other fledgling European liberal democracies. Recent scholars have highlighted that liberalism has within it the potential for exclusion. For all of its principled celebration of liberty and equality, liberalism can harbour the view that portions of humanity will not be ready for freedom. Indeed, by the mid-19th century, prominent liberal thinkers in Europe vigorously supported imperial colonialism and its accompanying ideas of racial superiority. Even that impeccable liberal John Stuart Mill believed that 'nations which are still barbarous have not got beyond the period during which it is likely to be for their benefit that they should be conquered and held in subjection by foreigners'.[25]

In the Australian context, such ideological concerns with race had less to do with imperial expansion and conquest. By the mid-1800s, the task of 'taming' the frontier was largely accomplished. But there remained the task of excluding non-Europeans from the colonial project. The strength of anti-Chinese sentiment intensified towards the end of the 19th century, notwithstanding legislation passed in the colonies restricting immigration. The colonial imagination believed Australia faced a physical threat from Asia, something demonstrated by the popularity of invasion narratives rehearsed by writers.

In one well-known example, in 1888 the Labor intellectual William Lane fictionalised a possible war between the white and yellow races. Set in 1908, Lane's story featured farmers and workers in Queensland who fought off an insidious incursion from Chinese immigrants. The message of Lane's serialised fiction was clear: there could be no complacency about the survival of the white British race. Were the Chinese given the opportunity, they would become the dominant race in the land, and surviving whites would become a subjugated people. The vast, 'empty' Australian continent had to be protected from the teeming hordes of the north.[26]

What was fiction for Lane assumed the form of serious historical prophecy for Charles Pearson, a leading liberal political and scholarly figure in Victoria. Pearson's 1893 book, *National Life and Character: A Forecast*, provided the definitive statement of colonial Australia's racial thinking, lending intellectual authority to some of the cruder ideas expressed by Lane and others. The book would have a profound effect in Britain, North America and even Europe. 'The reading world at large was startled', the Regius Professor of Law at Oxford wrote, 'as by the apparition of a literary meteor'. Pearson's admirers included the future American president Theodore Roosevelt, who wrote to tell Pearson that no book 'has excited anything like as much interest or has caused so many men to feel that they had to revise their mental estimates of facts', and the British prime minister William Gladstone, who sang Pearson's praises to guests at Downing Street.[27] The German Kaiser Wilhelm was reportedly engrossed in *National Life and Character* when he invented the phrase 'yellow peril'.[28]

I'm not racist but ...

According to Pearson, white Europeans needed to anticipate a not far distant future when they would find themselves under challenge from the coloured races:

> The day will come, and perhaps is not far distant, when the European observer will look round to see the globe circled with a continuous zone of the black and yellow races, no longer too weak for aggression or under tutelage, but independent ... The citizens of these countries will then be taken up into the social relations of the white races, will throng the English turf or the salons of Paris, and will be admitted to inter-marriage ... We shall wake to find ourselves elbowed and hustled, and perhaps even thrust aside by peoples whom we looked down upon as servile and thought of as bound always to minister to our needs. The solitary consolation will be that these changes have been inevitable.[29]

Not many agreed that this scenario was inevitable, or with Pearson's stance of accepting change with stoic fortitude.[30] Pearson's forecast in fact had the very opposite effect. It spurred many into believing that the racial character of the Australian was a matter of fundamental importance, not only to these far-flung colonies but also to the future of metropolitan Europe. Australia needed to aspire to be a global monument to European racial virtue and fitness. In Pearson's own words, Australians were 'guarding the last part of the world, in which the higher races can live and increase freely, for the higher civilisation'.[31] Pearson had created Australia as the last hope of a European race, a prospect that appealed to many other intellectuals who saw modern civilisation as anaemic. European racial excellence was to be reborn in the antipodes.[32]

WHITE AUSTRALIA

Such intellectual thought during the 1880s and 1890s was reinforced by more popular cultural influences such as *The Bulletin*, Australia's first national newspaper. Radical and republican, it was also an uncompromising advocate of racial morality. In its famous statement on who is an Australian, *The Bulletin* articulated the unity of racial identity and political liberty. All men who leave the 'tyrant-ridden lands of Europe', who may flee from 'odious military conscription', who may repudiate 'the worm-eaten lie of the divine right of kings to murder peasants' could be regarded as Australians even 'before they set foot on the ship which brings them hither'. Yet political liberty was something only for the white man: 'No nigger, no Chinaman, no lascar, no kanaka, no purveyor of cheap coloured labour, is an Australian.'[33]

Through the federation of the colonies, Australians had their seminal opportunity to legislate for their racial identity. Those responsible for the drafting of the Australian Constitution were mindful of the experience of slavery and civil war in the United States. For Alfred Deakin, a Victorian protégé of Charles Pearson and among the leading voices behind Federation, 'our Constitution marks a distinct advance upon and difference from that of the United States', in providing Parliament with powers to deal with race.[34] Through section 51, the Australian Parliament was empowered to legislate with respect to immigration and emigration, relations with the islands of the Pacific, as well as 'the people of any race, for whom it is deemed necessary to make special laws'.[35]

The Commonwealth Parliament was quick to give expression to a policy of White Australia. The first legislation passed was the *Pacific Island Labourers Act 1901*, which expelled all Pacific Islanders working in Australia. Henry Bournes Higgins – best remembered as the president of the Commonwealth Court of Conciliation and Arbitration who ruled on a 'living wage' in the *Harvester* case – spoke in support of the legislation as 'the most vitally important measure on the programme which the government has put before us'.[36] Higgins believed that the Commonwealth of Australia was taking justified steps to avoiding the kind of slave trade that emerged in the

Race in Australia

United States. According to this view, the deportation of the approximately 10000 Pacific Islanders working in Australia (mostly in sugar plantations in Queensland) at the time would ensure the living standards of Australian workers would not be undermined by cheap coloured labour.

This was soon followed by the enactment of the *Immigration Restriction Act 1901*, which introduced a new administrative requirement for immigrants. At the time, other territories had in place dictation tests designed to screen non-European arrivals: most notably, in Natal, South Africa, immigrants were required to fill out a form in a European language. The dictation introduced by the Australian parliament went much further. Any coloured person seeking entry into Australia was required to write out, at dictation, a passage of 50 words in *any* European language. To the disappointment of some parliamentarians, the Act did not introduce a direct ban on 'coloured' migration. This reflected objections by the British Colonial Office to explicit legislative disqualifications based on race: British authorities upheld the imperial tradition of making no formal distinction based on race or colour. Yet the Immigration Restriction Act empowered customs officers with almost absolute freedom to exclude anyone they regarded as undesirable by virtue of their race or nationality. A non-European immigrant may have possessed fluent English, but if they could not write a passage dictated in, say, Finnish or Gaelic, they could be prevented from disembarking in Australia.

There would be other notable public expressions about race in the early life of the Federation. The first Commonwealth Parliament also passed the *Post and Telegraph Act 1901*, which stipulated that the Commonwealth government could issue mail contracts only to ships that employed white labour exclusively. The Australian Labor Party enshrined in its early policy platform an overarching principle: 'The cultivation of an Australian sentiment based upon the maintenance of racial purity.'[37] For the architects of the White Australia policy, however, it was the Immigration Restriction Act and the Pacific Island Labourers Act that were foundational. According to Deakin, the two pieces of legislation were 'the necessary complement of a single policy'.[38]

The White Australia policy was a matter of some international concern. The Japanese took grave offence that they were considered racially inferior to Europeans, and resented being considered alongside blacks, Pacific Islanders, Indians and other Asian peoples. There was also disquiet about the ostensibly anti-Imperial nature of White Australia. The first non-whites to be rejected by the dictation test were two Pathan men from northern India, who were both British subjects and former soldiers in the Imperial Army. Indian residents in Victoria petitioned the British Colonial Office, posing some thorny

Race in Australia

questions: What was the difference between an Indian and any other British subject? And why were those fighting Britain's wars being excluded from Australia when Germans, Russians and Italians were not subject to the dictation test?[39]

In time, the exclusionary power of the White Australia policy became more apparent. It extended to other white European peoples deemed hostile as a result of the First World War. German, Austrian, Hungarian and Bulgarian nationals were excluded from migrating to Australia until 1926. In the 1920s, quotas had also been extended to Greeks, Albanians, Yugoslavs, Estonians, Poles and Czechs. In 1930, two boatloads of Italians received dictation tests, which led to a number of already naturalised Australians being debarred. The inter-war years represented 'a high-water mark in racial and ethnic exclusion, as the push for white Australian "purity" increasingly implied a British Australia as well'.[40]

Public and political support for White Australia continued through to the Second World War. Prime minister John Curtin affirmed in wartime that, 'this country shall remain forever the home of the descendants of those people who came here in peace in order to establish in the South Seas an outpost of the British race'.[41] Yet the end of the war would bring with it the first steps towards the eventual dismantling of a racially discriminatory immigration policy. The Japanese encroachment upon New

Guinea, and the bombing of Darwin and Broome, led many to conclude that Australia had to 'populate or perish'. Under the Chifley Government, immigration minister Arthur Calwell embarked on an ambitious program of postwar immigration. By 1950, almost 200 000 immigrants had arrived, primarily from Europe. One million more would arrive in the decade that followed. The aim was nothing less than national reconstruction, though the influx of migrants was paradoxically accompanied by an ongoing commitment to White Australia. There remained the firm belief that Australia should be maintained as a white, British nation – and that national prosperity and unity depended on racial and cultural homogeneity.

Through all this, one particular aspect of the White Australia doctrine went largely unchallenged and unnoticed. Parallel to immigration policies, White Australia also involved the exclusion and assimilation of Aboriginal people. The assumption of policymakers – and the Australian public – was that the Aboriginal 'race' would over time wither into extinction. Yet it was not until the 1990s that the true extent of official practices was revealed. The Human Rights and Equal Opportunity Commission's landmark *Bringing them home* Inquiry, led by Sir Ronald Wilson and Mick Dodson, provided the first systematic picture of how governments separated Aboriginal children from their families by compulsion, duress or undue influence. The Inquiry revealed that removing these children – now referred to as the stolen generations – was aimed at making Aboriginal cultural values and identities pass out of existence. It found that separate laws for Indigenous children breached the international prohibition of racial discrimination. Reflecting on the report in 2001, Dodson wrote, 'never before had Australia's history – its laws, practices and policies pertaining to the treatment of my people – been portrayed as so overtly racist'.[42]

By the 1960s, the White Australia policy became increasingly untenable. Australia found itself increasingly subjected to international criticism for racial discrimination, at a time when many countries were beginning to endorse universal principles of racial equality. Civil rights movements against racial segregation influenced a younger generation of Australians. Inspired by the freedom riders of the United States, student leader Charles Perkins organised the Freedom Ride of 1965, bringing racial discrimination against Aboriginal people to a national audience. Australians were confronted by the fact that, in many country towns, Aboriginal people were barred from pubs, cinemas and swimming pools. In 1967, Australians voted resoundingly in a referendum to ensure Aboriginal people would be counted in the national census for the first time.

The White Australia policy was losing its primacy on the immigration front as well. In 1957, non-Europeans with 15 years residence in Australia were allowed to become citizens. The introduction of the *Migration Act 1958* replaced the controversial dictation test with a new system of entry permits. A review of immigration policy also led to a decision in 1966 to accept well-qualified immigrants, including non-Europeans. Change was occurring, though elements of discrimination remained. For instance, while British and European immigrants continued to enjoy assisted passage, immigrants from Asia and elsewhere were not extended the same benefit.

It was not until 1973 that the White Australia policy was completely abolished. The Whitlam Government moved to remove race as a criterion in Australia's immigration policies. All immigrants, regardless of their origin, were made eligible for citizenship after they had lived in Australia for three years. Instructions were made to overseas posts to disregard race entirely as a factor in the selection of immigrants. International agreements relating to immigration and race, including the *Convention on the Elimination of All Forms of Racial Discrimination*, were to be ratified. In the words of the Whitlam Government's immigration minister Al Grassby, the White Australia policy was now 'dead and buried'. In its place was a new vision for Australian society: a multiculturalism that sought to celebrate ethnic and racial difference rather than suppress it.[43]

THE LEGACIES OF WHITE AUSTRALIA

Race continues to shape Australian public culture. Ideas about race influence our government, our media, our language, our national debates. This is not to say that doctrines of a White Australia have the same power in 2015 as they did in 1915. It is no longer tenable to speak of excluding non-Europeans, and no longer respectable to proclaim the urgency of protecting a superior British civilisation from cultural sources of corruption. Australian society has changed so dramatically over the past seven decades that a resurrection of White Australia is impossible. Only within the company of racist extremists would such notions be entertained with seriousness.

But the ideology of racial unity continues to infuse public thinking about nationhood. This is to a large extent a reflection of history. During the colonial era and for the majority of the Federation's history, White Australia provided an explicit doctrine for determining who could be admitted into Australian society and who could not. It included a comprehensive political vocabulary and cultural repertoire. The mere mention of phrases such as *terra nullius*, the teeming hordes or cheap labour is enough to trigger mental images of what the national project involved.

Multicultural Australia lacks the symbolic power boasted by its ideological predecessor. The White

I'm not racist but ...

Australia policy was inaugurated as an official statement of nationhood, but its renunciation was never granted the same moment. It was largely through sheepish embarrassment rather than proud conviction that White Australia was gradually dismantled from the 1950s to the 1970s. Its passing was not marked with any national sense of fanfare or finality. There was 'no climactic legislative act by the national parliament to bring closure, no widely recognised prime ministerial declaration, no event to match the clarity of 1901'.[44] As well, there was no seminal moment for the advent of multiculturalism. The transition from White Australia to its successor national myth, in some senses, remains ongoing.

It is striking that the language of contemporary debates echoes that of the past. Arguments about Aboriginality, for example, replicate colonial discourses about colour and blood quantum. Many of the colonial parliaments enshrined notions of 'half-caste' Aborigines into legislation that purported to protect Aboriginal children – legislation that was used to remove 'half-caste' children for the purpose of letting 'full-blooded' Aborigines die out. Within some public commentary about race and Aboriginal identity today, there remains a disproportionate attention paid to the 'whiteness' of some Aboriginal people's appearance. From the perspective of many Aboriginal people, there is a troubling reprisal of attitudes that presumed the end of an Aboriginal 'race' and prescribed assimilation as the definitive solution for 'half-castes'.[45]

This is compounded by an all too frequent failure of compassion and understanding of historical injustices endured by Aboriginal Australia. During the 1990s, debates about native title added an abrasive quality to the national conversation. Efforts to counter a 'black-armband' view of Australian history encouraged the reassertion of a white settler narrative of Australian development. For many Aboriginal Australians, there was limited realisation that 'the tolerance of disrespect and the denial of our history maintains racism as a core value of Australian society'.[46]

Equally revealing is the public and political concern with border protection. Some have noted the apparent symmetry in the Immigration Restriction Act passed by the first Commonwealth parliament and the *Border Protection Act 2001* passed by the parliament during its centenary year. Since that time, Australian immigration policy has been dominated by border protection: specifically, the goal of preventing boats carrying asylum seekers from landing in Australian territory and avoiding the resettlement of boat-borne refugees on the mainland. Just as immigration restriction aimed to exclude all non-Europeans from Australia, many believe the politics of border protection has been aimed at keeping Australia free of asylum seekers.[47] According to cultural scholar

Suvendrini Perera, fear of asylum seekers exists because 'secreted in the crevices and dark, invisible spaces of these illegalised bodies and intruding small craft lurk the invading germs and threatening micro-organisms of the tropics – that generous geography that the very construct of insular Australia strives to hold at bay'.[48]

To be sure, the role of race in debates about asylum seekers is contested. A hardened stance towards the arrival of asylum seekers by boat has not meant a return to White Australia. Australia maintains an immigration program that does not discriminate among potential entrants on the grounds of race. Public endorsement of tougher measures against asylum seekers has been accompanied by continuing support for a substantial immigration program, one that has increasingly involved permanent and temporary arrivals from countries in Asia. Proponents of a more hardline approach on boat arrivals also frame their arguments not in racial terms, but in terms of fairness and humanitarianism. If there is resistance to accepting asylum seekers, the reasons justifying it appeal to ideas about restoring order to a refugee process that has been hijacked by 'people smugglers', or to the proposition that turning back boats in Australian waters prevents lives from being lost at sea.

The ideology of White Australia was, though, one in which racial ideas were inseparable from obsessive attention to border control. Could it be that contemporary concerns about border security represent a recurrence of such anxieties? Political historian Robert Manne considers it naive, if not disingenuous, to believe that race has played no part in asylum seeker policy. Punitive policies pursued against asylum seekers may be understood as the proper assertion of national sovereignty: a self-determining political community, through its elected representatives, has the right to decide who is admitted into membership. But, according to Manne, were the majority of asylum seekers white Zimbabweans fleeing from the regime of Robert Mugabe, rather than Afghan Hazaras or Iraqis, it would be 'improbable, or so it seems to me, that public opinion would have tolerated their detention behind razor wire or their transportation to the hellhole in Nauru'.[49] Support for harsh asylum seeker policies has been 'quite clearly an expression of a subliminal or unselfconscious racism, triggered by the profound "otherness" of the swarthy and exotic strangers from Iraq, Iran and Afghanistan'.[50]

The continuing influence of race is also revealed in the everyday realm of Australian society. Its contemporary expression is not only political but also social. It can concern how people think Australian life ought to be, or how it ought to be represented. Often what we may ordinarily regard as racism concerns the 'national space'. It is about people's belief that they have the power to decide who is 'more' Australian, or what is 'really' Australian. As anthropologist

I'm not racist but ...

Ghassan Hage explains, the marker of national belonging is possession of forms of 'cultural capital' – certain linguistic, physical and cultural dispositions that are shared by members of the dominant national group. In the Australian case, whether one belongs may depend on one's conformity to the national images associated with the culture of white Australia:

> Being 'male', 'European', 'of British descent', 'of Irish descent', 'Protestant', 'Catholic', 'rich in economic capital', or a 'good sportsperson', or having 'a white skin', 'an Aussie accent' or 'blond hair', all of these operate as national capitals in the sense that their possession allows the person who owns them to claim certain forms of dominant national belonging.[51]

There is a need to distinguish here between the official terms of national citizenship and the unofficial. In formal terms, citizenship does not depend on cultural characteristics, at least if culture is understood as being tied to race, ethnicity or ancestry. One's background does not disqualify one from being eligible for formal citizenship. Hage's point concerns those unwritten rules of national identity. These are the rules that explain why the child of an immigrant may be told that they speak perfect English, even if they were born in the country and have known no other home. Or why some people who may not look 'typically Australian' can be presumed to be from elsewhere. Like many Australians who are not Anglo-Celtic in background, I am often asked, 'Where are you from?' Usually, it is an expression of curiosity: people are simply interested in knowing about my heritage (or in which part of the country I live). Yet there are also times when a questioner's tone may come across as less benign – as in the case of, 'No, where are you *really* from?'

As such exchanges illustrate, not everyone makes the distinction between the political and cultural conditions of nationality. If nothing else, a recent resurgence in nationalism has blurred the line between the official and unofficial requirements of citizenship. During the past decade, particularly since the Cronulla riot of December 2005, symbols such as the national flag have sometimes taken on unedifying implications. Expressions of Australian nationhood have become associated with assertive, at times even belligerent, nationalism directed at immigrants: 'We grew here, you flew here', to quote one slogan with currency. In less dramatic terms, the reinjection of ethnic character into Australian citizenship was perhaps best symbolised in 2006, when questions about Don Bradman were inserted into the pool of questions in the citizenship test for immigrants who wished to naturalise.[52]

To cite another example, the language of 'Team Australia' that has been used since 2014 in discussions about community harmony and home-grown terrorism has had a similar effect. If 'Team Australia' is simply shorthand for an Australian liberal democratic community, for a community of equal citizens, there would be nothing controversial about it. Yet its use seems to beg the very question about whether there may be some groups – perhaps those who may not be regarded as 'really' one of us – who may need to make a special effort to demonstrate their national loyalty. In speaking to various Muslim and Arab communities, I have detected a troubling sentiment of alienation: many, including those born here, have concluded they are being told that membership of an Australian political community might not be enough to qualify for 'Team Australia'. But if formal citizenship is not enough, what is?

RACE AND RACISM

It remains to consider in more detail the relationship between race and racism. As a starting point, race exists as a concept denoting a person or group's ancestral background – namely, ethnic or national origins, but also features such as colour that may be associated with those origins. Racism, meanwhile, refers to a social phenomenon. It begins with assumptions or stereotypes that attribute permanent traits or qualities to an entire group of people.[53] It is manifested in discrimination and expressions of contempt. Thus understood, racism refers not only to acts of discrimination and vilification, but also to those ideas, language, institutions, practices and behaviours that feed such conduct.

Contemporary racism in Australia reflects, to some extent, the deeply ambivalent nature of the nation's historical treatment of race. The days of White Australia may be behind us, but this does not mean that we are any better at talking about racism. There can be a reflexive defensiveness to conversations about race. Some maintain, for instance, that while you may call out racist acts or behaviour, you should refrain from calling someone a 'racist', as this amounts to a moral denunciation of a fellow member of society.[54] At the same time, the charge of racism can be thrown around too readily. An incident of racial discrimination or vilification can often prompt a blanket condemnation of society for its complicity – with the unhelpful consequence of further entrenching divided attitudes.[55]

It is important that we are able to have honest conversations about racism. While it may be tempting to tread warily around race, we should not be apologetic. Nor should we entertain the idea that we can somehow strip from discussions of racism any hint of controversy. This is because there *is* a fundamentally moral quality to them. There is something moral, because the question of racism involves how we treat others. When an act of racism occurs, it harms the social standing that another person or group of people enjoy. It can also harm the freedom and well-being of its target. Any society concerned with combating racism will necessarily be interested in promoting certain dispositions among its members: tolerance and decency, respect and fairness.

Part of the problem with racism is that it is commonly understood as a belief. In my work as Commissioner, I am still frequently asked in media interviews and in conversations about whether racism exists in contemporary Australia in any significant form. When people think about racism, some picture only the kind of racism you would associate with the Klu Klux Klan or neo-Nazi thugs. Some continue to understand racism either in terms of a belief about racial superiority or organised persecution of minorities. Racism should not be defined so narrowly. In its ordinary usage today, racism refers to anything that has the effect of unfairly disadvantaging or privileging someone on the basis of their racial background. This can be expressed through both belief and behaviour. It is not only about philosophy but also about practice. And it need not assume the form of vile extremism.

In order to talk honestly about racism, we must first understand it. What are the sources of racism? What are some of the assumptions and motivations behind stereotypes, prejudice and discrimination?

Typically, we have understood the basic structure in terms of hatred. But, as with other social ills, not all racism stems from hatred. Sometimes it can be born of fear and anxiety. Though fear in its most immediate sense involves a heightened concern about the immediate safety of one's own body and life, it can extend to one's community. It can involve cultural anxiety. This has been one thread that has run consistently through the historical fabric of racism: the fear that a certain other poses a danger to a national identity or way of life.

Then there is envy and resentment. Racial hostility can be connected with feelings that members of some groups may possess goods that one does not. This seems to be a particular danger during periods of economic downturn. But even in more prosperous times, feelings of resentment about the perceived advantages of others can arise. To name one example, it is striking that many of the negative stereotypes rehearsed about Aboriginal and Torres Strait Islander people involve a view about the injustice of perceived special treatment that they receive.[56]

Racism can also be the product of ignorance and arrogance. It may not necessarily be the case that those who say or do things with racist implications mean to inflict malicious harm on others. Psychologists have helpfully explained that racism can sometimes be motivated by a concern about belonging to one's own racial or social group. It can be as much about bonding with one's friends or colleagues, as it is about venting antipathy towards a racial group that one finds objectionable.[57] Sometimes the damage can be done innocently or incidentally – because one simply may not know better. This is the case with so-called casual racism, where someone can make a throwaway comment or nonchalant insult that has the effect of denigrating someone because of their race (see chapter 4). What one person may regard as harmless may in fact inflict some injury on another.

Fear and anxiety; envy and resentment; ignorance and arrogance – these are some of the psychological roots of racism. But they all have one thing in common. They all involve, to varying degrees, a withholding of sympathy or compassion from those who are subjected to racist behaviour. At times, this can involve an inability or unwillingness to see things from the perspective of another. At other times, it can involve a readiness to deny that racism exists in the first place. Those who declare, 'I'm not racist but …' are also the ones most likely to point out that 'real racism' is what exists in other countries – to suggest that any egregious racism that exists elsewhere in Asia, Africa or the Middle East somehow excuses any racism here.

Such deflections of racism reflect a significant obstacle to more mature conversations about race and racism in contemporary Australia. Too often, we end up with a perverse debate where sometimes calling out racism is regarded as a bigger moral crime than the perpetration of racism itself. Those who deign to speak up about racism are labelled purveyors of grievance politics, as though people would revel in the victimhood of racism. This is ironic: the same people who would dismiss racism in such terms are also those who accuse others of bad faith and assuming the worst of their fellow citizens. But there is also a moral blindness at play. Those who are inclined to regard complaints about racism as mere identity politics fail to understand one thing. For those on the receiving end of racism, the experience of racism is not an excuse for political posturing; it is an experience that wounds and diminishes one's quality of life. Those who experience racism would prefer not to be talking about it at all. They would prefer that it never happened in the first place.

2

THE RACIAL DISCRIMINATION ACT

EQUALITY AND DIGNITY IN THE LAW

Consider the following scenarios. A man of Sri Lankan background works at a warehouse but finds other employees of Anglo-Celtic background receiving better hours and pay rises; his co-workers frequently subject him to derogatory racial comments and harassment. An Aboriginal man makes arrangements to rent a room in a boarding house but is told by the caretaker when he arrives: 'We don't take anyone who is Aboriginal because there have been problems in the past. This is management policy.' A woman of Asian background comes across an anti-immigration website on the internet: using inflammatory language involving racial epithets, it encourages people to abuse and attack Asians they encounter on the street.

These are drawn from actual complaints made

The Racial Discrimination Act

under federal law concerning racial discrimination. In each case, those who lodged a complaint enjoyed some form of remedy agreed to by the respondent party. The abused worker resigned from his employment but was paid his entitlement and damages. The rejected boarder was provided with an apology and compensation. The distressed woman succeeded in having the internet service provider concerned disable the racist website.[1]

Prior to the enactment of anti-discrimination laws, there was little that those on the receiving end of racial discrimination or hatred could do about their mistreatment. True, a citizen subjected to racial discrimination or harassment could, in theory, turn to the criminal code or to civil actions under the common law. Yet in reality this was cold comfort. In the absence of an actual physical assault or immediate specific threat, racial hatred is typically beyond the reach of the criminal law. As for the common law, the targets of racism had very few legal remedies available for interference with the person, reputation and property. The general right to be free from being discriminated against on racial grounds – indeed on any ground – has never been developed in common law.[2]

It would be the task of legislation to establish that right. That development came in the form of the *Racial Discrimination Act 1975*. The Act makes it unlawful for a person to discriminate on the basis of race, colour, descent, ethnicity or national origin. It guarantees equal opportunity across a range of activities in society. It makes unlawful acts of racial vilification in public, including through print, broadcast and internet media. It also provides legal remedies against acts of discrimination, through conciliation and a right to civil action in the courts.[3]

The enactment of this law has special claim to being an administrative innovation. It was the first human rights and anti-discrimination legislation passed by the Commonwealth Parliament. Its introduction represented the rejection of White Australia. Racism would no longer have the explicit backing of the law. Yet what kind of impact has legislation had in reducing racial prejudice and discrimination?

RACE AND THE LAW

The Racial Discrimination Act (RDA) has been described as 'akin to the Civil Rights Act 1964 in the US'.[4] It is the law that secures for all Australians, whatever their racial background, equality before the law. Yet its significance can easily be overlooked. Those who have never experienced the pangs of prejudice and the degradation of discrimination can discount its importance. Even when the Act was passed by the Parliament in 1975, it was greeted with only a muted sense of historical gravity.

The Racial Discrimination Act

This was understandable. Whereas in the United States civil rights legislation was enacted as the culmination of a rights struggle, the push for Australian racial equality was never accompanied by the emergence of a social movement, at least of equivalent scale. The American national conscience would be awakened by moments such as the Supreme Court's decision in *Brown v Board of Education* (1954) overruling racial segregation in schools, the brutal Mississippi murder of 14-year-old Emmett Till (1955) and the refusal of Rosa Parks in Montgomery, Alabama, to surrender her bus seat to a white woman (1955). There were sit-ins, protests and freedom rides. There was the great march on Washington DC in 1963, in which 250 000 people converged on the Lincoln Memorial to hear Martin Luther King Jr's clarion call for racial justice. A nation came to believe that it could fulfil a certain dream.

In Australia, the forces behind the introduction of racial equality laws appeared to come from the international sphere more than from the domestic. The RDA gave effect to Australia's commitment as a signatory to the *International Convention on the Elimination of All Forms of Racial Discrimination* (CERD). Adopted by the international community in 1966, CERD reflected the heightened global concern at the time about racial discrimination and its consequences. They were heady times. In addition to the civil rights movement in the United States, the horrors of the Holocaust, outbursts of anti-Semitism and the advent of apartheid in South Africa gave impetus to the recognition of racial equality. Speaking in favour of CERD's adoption in 1965, then President of the UN General Assembly Amintore Fanfani would characterise the fight against racial discrimination as 'one of the most urgent and crucial problems that have arisen in the matter of protecting fundamental human rights'.[5]

Insofar as there was local urgency to racial equality, this did not become clear during the 1960s. Almost a decade elapsed from Australia's signature to CERD to the introduction of legislation lending it domestic force. The formal demise of the White Australia policy, and the transition to a multicultural society, did not occur until the 1970s. But by that time, the conditions for change were met. Mass immigration meant it was no longer tenable to expect that newcomers could be assimilated into an Australian way of life defined by ethnic and racial homogeneity. Australia's own Freedom Ride and the 1967 referendum pointed to a new awareness about including Aboriginal people in the national life. Sport was also to play a role in changing public consciousness. In 1971, anti-apartheid protests occurred around the country, coinciding with a six-week tour by the South African Springbok rugby team (Queensland premier Joh Bjelke-Petersen infamously declared a month-long state of emergency).

The Racial Discrimination Act

The introduction of laws prohibiting racial discrimination in 1975 was an important political development. As explored in chapter 1, Australian society was historically structured on notions of race. Colonial governments openly sanctioned discrimination on racial lines; racial integrity was a defining aspiration of Australian nationhood. The ethos of 'Australia for the white man' was maintained without serious dissent or demurral.

Indeed, for most of the period since Federation, Australia displayed features of what historian George Frederickson calls an 'overtly racist regime'. In such regimes, racist principles were 'fully codified into laws effectively enforced by the state or made a central concern of public policy'.[6] The domestic application of racist beliefs to non-white Australians was admittedly limited in one sense: since unwelcome aliens were prevented from entering the country for much of the 20th century, there was relatively little active expression of racism against foreigners. Yet a racist regime was precisely what existed for Aboriginal people, at whom policies of protection and assimilation were directed. In its treatment of Aboriginal people, Australian public life upheld formal exclusion and racial regulation.

Legalised racism, when it exists, finds expression within institutional patterns or social practices. At its most extreme, such patterns and practices are revealed in brutal violence, dogmatic persecution and controlled hostility. Consider the lynching and segregation of African Americans in the South during the Jim Crow era, the Nazis' demonisation and extermination of Jews in Europe, or the second-class citizenship of South African blacks under apartheid.[7] Many would argue the systematic mistreatment of Aboriginal Australians could be added to such a catalogue. Frontier violence was succeeded by state protection laws that excluded Aboriginal and Torres Strait Islander people from voting in elections, restricted their movement and denied their rights to the lands of their birth. Authorities were empowered under state laws to forcibly remove Aboriginal children and to control Aborigines' earnings and bank accounts. For all intents and purposes, during most of Australia's colonial period and history as a Federation, Aboriginal Australians have been treated as less than full citizens.

The enactment of the RDA may be understood as a significant redress of such history, but such redress has been incomplete. It remains an anomaly that the Australian Constitution – the supreme law of our liberal democracy – continues to permit racial discrimination. Section 25 countenances the states disqualifying people from voting in elections (a recognition, at the time of Federation, of legislation in Queensland and Western Australia that disqualified Aboriginal men from voting). Section 51 (xxvi), the so-called race power, also authorises the Common-

The Racial Discrimination Act

wealth to make racially discriminatory laws. The framers of the Constitution regarded this power as being of immense importance to the new Australian nation. In the constitutional conventions of the 1890s, there had been prolonged debate about a clause guaranteeing equal protection of the laws, modelled on the Fourteenth Amendment to the Constitution of the United States. The original Commonwealth Bill of 1891, and the Adelaide Convention in 1897, in fact adopted a provision to that effect. At the Melbourne Convention of 1898, however, delegates rejected a proposal that:

> The citizens of each State and all other persons owing allegiance to the Queen and residing in any territory of the Commonwealth, shall be citizens of the Commonwealth and shall be entitled to all the privileges and immunities of the citizens of the Commonwealth in several States and a State shall make or enforce any law abridging any privilege or immunity of the citizen of the Commonwealth nor shall a State deprive any person of life, liberty or property without due process of law or deny to any person within its jurisdiction the equal protection of its laws.[8]

The failure to adopt this clause, combined with the endorsement of section 51 (xxvi), meant the Parliament could deal with people of any race much as it pleased. The Commonwealth was empowered, in the words of constitutional experts John Quick and Robert Garran, 'to localise them within defined areas, to restrict their migration, to confine them to certain occupations, or to give them special protection and secure their return after a certain period to the country whence they came'.[9] Against this background, Australian law's stance on race is at best ambiguous: the RDA exists under a Constitution whose text still tolerates racial discrimination.

LEGISLATING FOR EQUAL DIGNITY

The RDA nonetheless introduced something new to Australian law and society. As well as being a statement of political commitment to multiculturalism, in more philosophical terms the RDA was an attempt to legislate for human dignity. Such a thrust becomes apparent from the Act's provenance in human rights law. Dignity is the closest thing we have to an internationally accepted foundation for modern justice and equality.[10] Article 1 of the *Universal Declaration of Human Rights* (1948) states that, 'All human beings are born free and equal in dignity and rights'.[11] The treaty considered as the pre-eminent statement of human rights law, the *International Covenant on Civil and Political Rights* (1966), has in its preamble a recognition that human rights 'derive from the inherent dignity of the human person'.[12] The preamble of CERD cites 'the principles of the dignity and equality inherent in all human beings'.[13]

The aspiration of racial equality, in particular, has been one expressed through the repertoire of dignity. In the United States, we saw it in the righteous determination of the civil rights movement for justice through non-violent protest. In South Africa, we saw it in Nelson Mandela: the personification of nobility and generosity in the face of apartheid injustice. In Australia, we saw it best in 1975, when then prime minister Gough Whitlam offered the first recognition of Aboriginal land rights. There was the poignancy of Whitlam pouring red dirt into the hands of Vincent Lingiari, an act that signified the passing of ownership of lands back to his Gurindji people. We remember Lingiari's response: 'We're all friendly now. We're all mates. We're all mates.' As the writer Martin Flanagan reflects, it was 'a moment of natural grace and dignity without repeat in Australian history'.[14]

Such examples point to the different meanings of dignity and their implications on race. There is dignity as dignified manner: the aesthetic quality, which we associate with a certain upright bearing. But dignity is more than just 'moral orthopaedics'.[15] Dignity also concerns status and value. To uphold human dignity is to believe that all human beings have an intrinsic value – that every person, regardless of social rank or importance, is entitled to consideration. It is to accept that every human being should command respect because we have a status as rational agents, possessing the freedom to choose. There is, in this sense, an imperative to treat someone *with dignity*: to treat them with a certain respect as a person.[16]

If laws can be considered as statements of public morality, legislation such as the RDA is one way a society can broadcast its recognition of dignity. Philosopher Jeremy Waldron argues that the advent of human rights and anti-discrimination legislation can be understood as part of the democratisation of status. The modern notion of human dignity involves a levelling up of rank, such that 'we now try to accord to every human being something of the dignity, rank, and expectation of respect that was formerly accorded to nobility'.[17] Every man is a king, every woman a queen. For Waldron, laws prohibiting racial discrimination, insult and abuse are a modern manifestation of law's concern with protecting individuals of rank against degrading treatment. Just as English law, for example, protected nobles against imputations against their dignity, so it is that many liberal democracies today protect ethnic and racial groups from acts that defame them or bring them into public contempt.

Racial discrimination is not merely about hurting sensibilities, however. This is one difficulty with following Waldron's 'levelling up' thesis on dignity to its conclusion. It implies that dignitary harms are merely symbolic harms.[18] But given the foundational role assigned to dignity – demonstrated by the importance accorded to it within international human rights documents – it is open to ask whether we believe that all violations of fundamental human rights are therefore only symbolic. As political philosopher Michael Rosen argues, it should be evident that this cannot be so. An emphasis on dignity's symbolic harms can make us lose sight of the big picture: 'the worst of what the Nazi state did to the Jews was not the humiliation of herding them into cattle trucks and forcing them to live in conditions of unimaginable squalor; it was to murder them.'[19]

There is another reason for being cautious about levelling up. If we embrace dignity as being about exalted rank – that everyone is a king or a queen – we should understand the aristocratic standard it implies. The privileges attached to the dignity of nobility sit uncomfortably with modern egalitarianism. At the heart of the dignity enjoyed by aristocrats was the claim, 'I don't have to answer to the likes of you'. This was why, for example, in England peers of the realm could not be arrested except for high offences such as treason or felony, why they could not be forced even to appear in court on most writs. If dignity is to play a role in our law and morality, we have to reconstruct it. We should have no interest 'in casting dignity as the haughty business of behaving badly and refusing to be held accountable for it'.[20]

We should be clear, then, about the nature of the harm caused by acts injuring human dignity on racial grounds. Arguably, it goes to the very nature of rights. This is because those who bear rights are regarded by the law as rational, self-controlling agents who have the power to stand up for themselves. A right is something that can be 'demanded, claimed, insisted upon without embarrassment or shame'.[21]

Racial prejudice and discrimination can certainly have profound effects on a person (as with any prejudicial or discriminatory conduct based on attributes such as sex, disability or sexual orientation). It may involve not just a lack of due respect; it may inflict more grievous wounds. As the philosopher Charles Taylor observed in his influential essay on multiculturalism and 'the politics of recognition':

> our identity is partly shaped by recognition or its absence, often by the misrecognition of others, and so a person or group of people can suffer real damage, real distortion, if the people or society around them mirror back to them a confining or demeaning or contemptible picture of themselves. Nonrecognition or misrecognition can inflict harm, can be a form of oppression, imprisoning someone in a false, distorted, and reduced mode of being.[22]

If we take this view, we see that ostensibly symbolic

The Racial Discrimination Act

harm may in fact run deeper. The indignity of racial discrimination can cause harm to someone's ability to be a bearer of rights – to be able to defend and assert one's rights on terms of equality with others, to participate and have standing in one's society as a full member. A right to equal dignity is not only a moral and universal one, but also a civic one: it is about equality and the rights of citizenship.

THE RACIAL DISCRIMINATION BILL 1975

Federal legislation on racial discrimination did not enjoy an easy birth. As attorney-general in the Whitlam Government, Senator Lionel Murphy introduced a Racial Discrimination Bill in the Senate on three occasions, in November 1973, April 1974 and October 1974. At the first attempt, the legislative intention was made clear. According to Murphy, 'the Bill proposes that racial discrimination should be made unlawful in Australia' and 'proclaims the equality and essential dignity of all human beings which is the foundation of all instruments relating to human rights'.[23] Murphy did not succeed in getting the legislation passed (his various bills lapsed). It required a fourth attempt by his successor as attorney-general, Kep Enderby, in the final year of the Whitlam Government. Introduced into the Parliament in February 1975, the Racial Discrimination Bill was passed in June 1975 with amendments made by the Senate.

The debate surrounding the bill revealed divided opinion between the Labor government and the Coalition opposition. In his second reading speech introducing the bill, Enderby again returned to Australia's obligations under CERD, arguing that his fellow parliamentarians would surely agree that 'all human beings are born free and equal in dignity and rights and that any doctrine of superiority based on racial differentiation is scientifically false, morally condemnable, socially unjust and dangerous and without any justification'.[24] The attorney-general argued that, as common law provided few effective remedies against discrimination, it was necessary for the Parliament to legislate. But having legal sanctions enacted was about more than just remedies. It was also about social change:

> The proscribing of racial discrimination in legislative form will ... make people more aware of the evils, the undesirable and unsociable consequences of discrimination – the hurtful consequences of discrimination – and make them more obvious and conspicuous. In this regard the Bill will perform an important educative role. In addition, the introduction of legislation will furnish legal background on which to rest changes reflecting basic community attitudes. The fact that racial discrimination is unlawful

The Racial Discrimination Act

will make it easier for people to resist social pressures that result in discrimination.[25]

The bill had both general and particular provisions. In addition to a broad prohibition of racial discrimination, it made it unlawful to refuse or deny access to public places by reason of race. A principle of equal opportunity would also apply to dealings in land and housing, the provision of goods and services, the provision of employment, the membership of trade unions and in the realm of advertising. In giving the law effect, the bill provided for remedies including an injunction restraining the doing of discriminatory acts, an order requiring remedial acts, and an order for damages. It also provided for an office of Community Relations Commissioner, who would have powers to mediate and conciliate instances of racial discrimination, as well as to commence legal proceedings before a court.

There was agreement, on both sides of Parliament, about the laudable goals of the proposed legislation; no one disputed the abhorrence of racial discrimination. But there was still vehement opposition expressed in some quarters. Queensland National senator Glen Sheil predicted that, far from eliminating racial discrimination, the bill would have 'the most dangerous effect' of creating 'an official race relations industry with a staff of dedicated anti-racists' intent on persecuting white Australians.[26] Another Queenslander,

Liberal senator Ian Wood, fulminated that, 'it is a lot of utter nonsense and rubbish to bring such a Bill before this Parliament', since 'racialism in this country probably is practised less than it is in the big majority of countries'.[27] The views of Sheil and Wood were in stark contrast to their Coalition colleague from the north, Senator Neville Bonner, the first Aboriginal person elected to parliament. After recalling one personal experience when denied a job because an owner of a farm told him, 'I could not have an Aborigine working on my farm', Bonner tersely noted: 'There is no discrimination, according to some people.'[28]

Other Coalition members were more measured in their reservations about the bill, though their objections revealed ideological or philosophical resistance to legislating for dignity. For backbencher John Howard, the Member for Bennelong, it was important to recognise that race was an 'extremely tender' subject.[29] There was room in the debate for differences of opinion about 'the best method by which the problem of racial discrimination in our society can be handled', and for doubts to be expressed about using 'legislative coercion' to promote tolerance.[30] Senator Fred Chaney had doubts about some of the machinery associated with the proposed office of Community Relations Commissioner, but expressed fundamental agreement with the Government that legislation can set a standard for behaviour and change attitudes over time on race.[31]

The Racial Discrimination Act

Shadow attorney-general Ivor Greenwood gave the lengthiest critique. While acknowledging that the bill 'gives expression to a desirable and acceptable principle', Greenwood then proceeded to cast doubt about the constitutionality of using the external affairs power to legislate. There was even doubt about the very existence of racism: 'We in Australia have been singularly free of racial discrimination', the senator would say, and it was only in recent times that instances of racial disharmony had been 'created by persons who claim there is a racism which … does not exist'.[32] In any case, governments should be wary of legislating to change human conduct, since its effect may even be to undermine race relations. There was, according to Greenwood, 'a tendency for laws of this character to exacerbate the tensions which they were expressly designed to avoid', and to 'be used as a source of provocation, a focal point for professional agitators who wanted to stir up trouble'.[33]

Such sentiments led many on the Government benches to charge that the Opposition, while not opposing the bill outright, was damning it with faint praise. At the conclusion of the parliamentary debate on the bill, attorney-general Enderby acknowledged that one could neither legislate for morality nor expect that community behaviour would change instantaneously. Yet, Enderby argued, it was important to recognise that laws also exist to express the feelings of a civilised society. And, perhaps more importantly,

I'm not racist but ...

his fellow legislators should refrain from stoking fear about anti-discrimination laws exacerbating racial tensions:

> Do not blame legislation like this that has appeared around the world for the rising tide of racial anger that exists in the world. The legislation has been in response to that rising tide of racial anger. My God, racial relations in the United States of America have been transformed, and transformed for the better, as a result of legislation in that country. I can remember my boyhood days when films portrayed negroes as monkeys. Those days are gone and negroes now stand in large measure with a certain dignity largely because of the Warren court and the way in which it was able to interpret the United States Constitution and apply that interpretation to legislation. With great respect, Mr Speaker, I ask honourable members opposite not to talk that nonsense.[34]

Enderby's bill would pass, but not without some concessions. To assuage Opposition concerns, the powers of the Community Relations Commissioner were limited largely to education, advocacy and conciliation. While aggrieved parties could institute civil proceedings before a court, this was not a power granted to the Commissioner.

The Racial Discrimination Act

The RDA received its royal assent on 11 June 1975 and came into force on 31 October 1975. Former immigration minister Al Grassby was announced as the inaugural Community Relations Commissioner – recognition of his standing as the 'father of Australian multiculturalism'. At a ceremony for the proclamation of the Act, the prime minister Gough Whitlam reflected that 'the main victims of social deprivation and restricted opportunity' have been 'the oldest Australians on the one hand and the newest Australians on the other'. The legislation was 'a historic measure' in the struggle for human rights, Whitlam said, forecasting that it may signal the eventual removal of discriminatory laws on the statute books of at least one State (namely, Queensland). Yet Whitlam saw the importance of the law as not only specifically about redress of present abuses and past injustices. It was also about setting standards for the future: to build, as he put it, 'a climate of maturity, of goodwill, of cooperation and understanding at all levels of society'.[35]

The very parliamentary debate about the RDA's enactment, however, seemed to highlight the magnitude of this challenge. Everyone could agree that racial discrimination warranted condemnation; who would disagree? But such common ground only went so far. Whether it was ideological disagreement about the role of legislation in eliminating discrimination, or the passionate defensiveness about racism expressed by some Coalition members, it was clear that racial discrimination was indeed 'an extremely tender' area of concern.

THE RACIAL DISCRIMINATION ACT, 1975–2015

Australian society has changed significantly since the RDA came into force. From a population of 13.8 million in 1975, Australia today is home to 23.8 million. Ethnic and racial diversity has increased over that time, as a result of immigration from countries in Asia and the Middle East. In addition, there has been a softening of attitudes on race and multiculturalism. Public surveys demonstrate strong public support for cultural diversity. For example, the most recent Scanlon Foundation study of social cohesion in Australia found that 85 per cent of respondents agreed that multiculturalism was a good thing and 58 per cent agreed that immigration intake in Australia is 'about right' or 'too low'.[36] For the most part, the story of Australian multiculturalism since the 1970s has been one of extraordinary success. The RDA has played an important role in this, providing the legislative architecture of racial equality.

There have been a number of amendments to the original legislation. The office of Community Relations Commissioner lost its autonomy in 1981 when it was made part of the newly founded Human Rights

The Racial Discrimination Act

Commission. It became the office of Race Discrimination Commissioner in 1986, with the establishment of the Human Rights and Equal Opportunity Commission (since renamed the Australian Human Rights Commission). Subsequent amendments also removed from the Commissioner the function of inquiring into and conciliating complaints alleging infringements of the Act – something that is now conducted by the Australian Human Rights Commission (AHRC) independently of the Commissioner.

A number of amendments to the legislation were made in 1990. In addition to the original provision prohibiting explicit racial discrimination (section 9), a new clause was inserted into the Act concerning 'indirect' racial discrimination. This meant that the imposition of any term, condition or requirement, unless reasonable, would be treated as discriminatory if it impairs the equal enjoyment of any human right by persons of a racial group. Two other clauses were also added: one to include vicarious liability for racial discrimination and one to extend unlawful discrimination to acts where race was a reason for doing the act (whether or not it was the dominant reason).

The most significant changes, though, came as a result of the *Racial Hatred Act 1995*. Responding to rising concern about racial violence and community harmony, and seeking to give more complete effect to Australia's obligations under CERD, the Parliament introduced to the Act provisions dealing with racial vilification (see chapter 3). A new section 18C made it unlawful to do a public act that is reasonably likely to offend, insult, humiliate or intimidate someone because of their race, colour, ethnicity or national origin. This section was accompanied by free speech exemptions (section 18D) for a number of defined acts concerning the public interest. These provisions on racial vilification and free speech have recently been subject to intense debate, following an unsuccessful proposal for amendment in 2014.

Throughout, the legislation has retained its civil character. Contrary to popular perception, no one can be prosecuted or convicted for breaching the Act. Racial discrimination may be unlawful, but it does not constitute a criminal offence attracting penalties. A contravention of the law is neither a misdemeanour nor a felony, but a statutory civil wrong. Where someone believes they have experienced racial discrimination under the law, they are free to make a complaint to the AHRC and seek a remedy.

It may not involve the criminal law, but the RDA has provided an important mechanism for redress. Since it commenced operation, more than 6000 complaints about racial discrimination have been successfully conciliated, with fewer than 300 reported decisions made by a court or tribunal over that time.[37] To give some indication of how the law currently operates, in 2013–14 the AHRC finalised 443 complaints under the RDA: of those

The Racial Discrimination Act

14 complaints proceeded to court (3 per cent of complaints).

The relatively small number of litigated cases highlights the conciliatory and educative character of the legislation. Having in place a conciliation framework allows for a complaint-handling process that is accessible, private and flexible. It aims to provide an informal resolution of a complaint in way that avoids the lengthiness and expense of litigation. The conciliator, in the form of the AHRC as a third party, seeks to uncover evidence to show the parties where they stand with regard to their rights and obligations. A successful conciliation is one where both parties agree on the resolution, and which prevents a repetition of the act that was cause for complaint – as in those examples of complaints previously mentioned (other examples also follow later in this chapter).[38]

This framework reflects some of the debates about the character of the legislation in the 1970s. The initial Racial Discrimination Bill proposed by then attorney-general Lionel Murphy in fact created a number of *offences*, including in relation to acts of racial incitement and racial violence. Yet later revised versions of the bill stepped back from creating offences and, as noted above, pared back some of the powers of the Community Relations Commissioner. Such changes were warmly welcomed by some critics in 1975, including John Howard: 'The Opposition believes that the amendments will have the effect of replacing the blunt instrument of the Racial Discrimination Bill as originally presented with a process of conciliation and education which we believe will do a great deal more effectively to reduce the incidence of racial discrimination in Australia than would have been the case'.[39] Similar objections were made in 1995 in the debates about the Racial Hatred Bill, which contained provisions making racial hatred a criminal offence, forcing the Keating Government to legislate only for a civil provision.

Conciliation enjoys numerous advantages over adversarial forms of enforcing the legislation. The confidential nature of the conciliation process enables negotiations to be conducted freely and openly. Those familiar with the process highlight that complainant parties enjoy an opportunity to explain to respondent parties how they have been affected by an alleged contravention of the law. They can also hold a respondent party to account without that party incurring public opprobrium (as could happen in a determination by the courts). At the same time, the option of going to court is not removed from the equation: it remains an avenue that can ultimately be pursued if a complaint does not result in a satisfactory resolution.

Agreements achieved at conciliation vary in nature. Some include monetary settlements. In one complaint, a young Aboriginal man who was refused employment because he was considered by management to be 'too

The Racial Discrimination Act

Aboriginal' received $15 000 damages for loss of dignity, and received a public apology placed in two metropolitan newspapers. Often remedies include more systemic responses to discrimination. For example, in one complaint by two workers of Nigerian ethnic background, it was alleged that their factory supervisor had subjected them to racist remarks and victimisation. Following conciliation, the company agreed to provide the complainants with written apologies and with a payment of $17 550 to each complainant. The company also agreed to establish an anti-discrimination policy, provide anti-discrimination training to all staff members, and encourage the supervisor in question to attend counselling. In other cases, a resolution can simply be found through an apology and a gesture of goodwill. One complaint alleging that a local club had refused to serve beer to Aboriginal men was resolved with the club owner offering a verbal apology and an invitation to the complainants to have a drink with him at the club.[40]

The type of agreements reached in successful conciliations mirror the kind of remedies obtained following formal determination by the courts. Take, for example, one case concerning discrimination in accommodation, which involved a caravan park business refusing to rent to Aboriginal persons 'under any circumstances whatsoever'. A complaint about this resulted in a finding that 'blatant racial discrimination' had occurred and an order that the caravan park owner pay compensation of $20 700.[41] Another case concerning racial discrimination in employment resulted in the award of $30 000 for economic loss, damages of hurt and costs.[42] Insofar as there appear to be differences in remedies, it is that the resolutions reached through successful conciliation are more likely to include action by respondents aimed at preventing future instances of discrimination. This is because the remedial powers of the federal courts are concerned only with redressing the situation of the complainant in the particular case.[43]

THE IMPACT OF THE RDA

Let us now consider in more detail a fundamental question: What overall impact has the RDA had in reducing racial discrimination? Few would dispute that significant progress has been made in race relations since 1975. Yet, the extent to which this can be attributed to legislation is open to question. As anti-discrimination law scholar Simon Rice observes, it is the 'holy grail' of law reform to be able to say when and how a law is effective in achieving social change.[44] Identifying cause and effect on such matters is a notoriously inexact science.

Some of Rice's academic colleagues have drawn sceptical conclusions about the RDA's contribution. Reflecting on the RDA a decade ago, on its 30th anniversary, law professor Beth Gaze wrote that, 'on any assessment, the RDA has not lived up to its symbolic promise'. For the most part, 'it has proved to be weak as an instrument in fighting racial discrimination'.[45] Another scholar, Margaret Thornton, in a well-known critique of the false 'liberal promise' of anti-discrimination law, decried the 'atomism' of instruments such as the RDA.[46] In Thornton's view, the law's concern with individual complaints about acts of racial discrimination means that it can only make a dent on the more general problem of racism. It fails to sanction the institutionalised prejudice and deeply entrenched social attitudes from which acts of discrimination originate:

> Racism ... by its very nature, is endemic, that is, it is diffused throughout the social fabric. There is no clearly identifiable [person] who can be held liable for a harm that is buried deep within the social psyche and that has developed the status of a self-serving 'truth' as a result of replication and longevity. The disjuncture between racism and an act of racial discrimination is a major limitation of the RDA or, indeed, any legislative schema based on an individual complaint-based model, as a mechanism for effecting change.[47]

It is true that the legal mechanism of complaint handling must be put into a larger social context. The presence of the RDA has not eradicated racial discrimination. The law did not prevent the rise during the 1990s of anti-immigrant racism and xenophobia. Nor has it prevented the significant rise in the incidence of racial and religious discrimination recorded in recent surveys on social cohesion.[48]

Yet it seems unfair to expect that a single piece of legislation could, on its own, transform a political culture – particularly if there may be other elements in that political culture that work to undermine its goals. It seems also unfair to be judging legislation against a standard that legislators never originally set themselves and which their successors have never accepted. For example, in introducing the Racial Discrimination Bill, then attorney-general Kep Enderby recognised that while 'laws proscribing discrimination are vital', they are 'not in themselves sufficient' and should be complemented by the promotion of education and research.[49] Speaking on the proclamation of the RDA, the prime minister Gough Whitlam sounded a similar note of caution: 'Social attitudes and mental habits do not readily lend themselves to codification and statutory prohibitions.'[50] On the occasion of the 20th anniversary of the RDA, then prime minister Paul Keating also observed that no one should be 'under the illusion that we could legislate to abolish prejudice', reiterating that 'legislation alone is not enough'.[51]

There are a number of respects in which the RDA has made a significant impact. As the first Commonwealth legislation concerning human rights and discrimination, the RDA set a precedent. In the time that has elapsed since 1975, all states and territories have enacted anti-discrimination legislation. The Commonwealth parliament has enacted legislation concerning sex discrimination, disability discrimination and age discrimination. The High Court case of *Koowarta v Bjelke-Petersen*, which concerned the RDA, was also the first instance the courts recognised that domestic laws could be considered valid exercises of the external affairs power in the Constitution.[52] The judgment in that case would provide authority for the development of the external affairs power in subsequent cases such as the celebrated *Tasmanian Dams* case.[53]

More specific to matters of race, the RDA has been a significant instrument in prohibiting racial discrimination. Former chief justice of the High Court, Sir Harry Gibbs, once described the legislation as providing a qualified 'bill of rights'.[54] Through the provisions under section 10, and by virtue of section 109 of the Australian Constitution, the RDA can override any state or territory legislation that discriminates on the basis of race.[55] This guarantee of equality before the law has established a national standard of racial non-discrimination. As constitutional lawyer George Williams notes, however, the effect of this standard should not be overstated. There have been 26 occasions when an Australian court has considered an alleged inconsistency of a state or territory law with the RDA. But only on *seven* occasions have such cases succeeded, demonstrating the unfulfilled potential of the legislation.[56]

Even so, the RDA has been used to assist in securing land rights for Indigenous people, something foreshadowed in *Koowarta*. In that case, John Koowarta, a Wik man from Cape York, brought an action alleging that the Queensland Government had breached the RDA. The Queensland Government had blocked the sale of land to Koowarta and other members of the Wik community, in line with cabinet policy that Aboriginal people should not be able to acquire large tracts of land. Ruling on the matter, the High Court endorsed the constitutional validity of the RDA (although Koowarta and his family's claims to their land would be stymied by political manoeuvres for some 30 years). In his Ninian Stephen Lecture of 2014, the High Court's current chief justice, Robert French, reflected that the case 'had the practical consequence that the RDA survived to become an important aspect of Australia's domestic human rights architecture'.[57]

The role of the RDA in underpinning native title would be confirmed in the 1988 High Court judgment in *Mabo v State of Queensland (No. 1)*.[58] There, the majority of the High Court held that Queensland legislation, which sought to extinguish native title in the Murray Islands of the Torres Strait, was

The Racial Discrimination Act

constitutionally invalid because it was inconsistent with the RDA. The judgment meant that no state law could validly extinguish or acquire native title rights in a way that discriminated on the basis of race. *Mabo (No. 1)* also meant, of course, that *Mabo (No. 2)* would proceed – a case in which the High Court would recognise native title at common law and the rejection of the doctrine of *terra nullius*.[59] But, as former High Court justice Michael Kirby has observed, without the earlier decision in *Koowarta*, it is doubtful that the *Mabo* decision would have had much impact:

> If, in *Koowarta*, the Racial Discrimination Act 1975 (Cth) had been held constitutionally invalid, the protection of federal law against the threatened 'bucket loads' of extinguishment of native title would have been missing. The general principle in *Mabo* ... would probably have been rendered nugatory. State and Territory laws, and State executive action, would quickly have swept the dreams of native title into the dust can of lost hopes. Unless prevented by federal laws, State laws and actions might have attempted to restore the *status quo ante*, before the suggested 'heresy' of Eddie Mabo's native title had arrived on the scene and spread like a wildflower in the Australian legal desert.[60]

It is true that the RDA has also had its limitations,

even in the area where it has enjoyed greatest impact. Following the High Court's ruling in the *Wik* case, in which a majority of judges held that native title could co-exist with the granting of pastoral leases, the Howard Government introduced the *Native Title Amendment Act 1998*. This was legislation that restricted claims for native title and had the effect of rolling back the protections provided by the RDA. Without prohibitions against racial discrimination embedded in the Constitution, the integrity of the RDA is subject to the vicissitudes of national politics. The principle of racial non-discrimination remains vulnerable to the possibility of suspension or repeal by the Commonwealth Parliament.[61]

This would be most dramatically illustrated when the Howard Government implemented the Northern Territory Emergency Response, following a report on child abuse in Aboriginal communities in the territory (commonly known as the NT Intervention). In order to implement the policy – which included bans on the sale and distribution of alcohol and compulsory income management of residents in prescribed communities – the Government suspended the RDA. It did this by excluding the Intervention from the RDA's prohibitions on racial discrimination and by providing that acts done during the Intervention were 'special measures' under the RDA. The Gillard Government reinstated the RDA in 2010, but continued the NT Intervention, on the basis that acts conducted for its purpose were 'special measures'. These moves affirmed the RDA on the one hand, but highlighted for many its ambiguous potential on the other.

PUBLIC VALUES AND CIVIL SOCIETY

We see, then, that the RDA's impact needs to be assessed in a number of ways. There is, most obviously, the instrumental level at which the legislation works – namely, in providing redress for acts of racial discrimination. Some commentators have argued there are shortcomings in this regard, particularly in the area of employment, given the small number of cases that have been litigated in the federal courts. One possible reason is that in legal proceedings courts require allegations of racism to be proven by complainants, with evidence of the highest probative value. This is an area that warrants consideration of reform, particularly since countries such as the United Kingdom have anti-discrimination laws where it is adequate that racial discrimination could be inferred from the facts (the onus then being on the respondent to prove that race was not the ground).[62]

But any assessment should recognise that the bulk of the RDA's operation exists in the realm of conciliation rather than litigation. It is revealing that the area that attracts the most complaints in race discrimination has consistently been that of employment. Equally significant is that the majority of complaints conciliated by the AHRC result in an agreed outcome among parties. Much like a duck's feet furiously paddling under water, the real work of the legislation may not be evident at first glance.

Part of the RDA's contribution also lies in human rights advocacy and education. As discussed, in providing a philosophical foundation for the recognition of native title, the RDA has been an important tool for the advancement of Indigenous rights. There is also the legislation's creation of the office of the Community Relations Commissioner, which would later become that of the Race Discrimination Commissioner. There was explicit recognition at the legislation's inception that it would never be sufficient to provide a legal mechanism for complaints about discrimination – that education and policy initiatives would be vital to achieving social progress on racial matters. The RDA thus provides for a Race Discrimination Commissioner, whose functions include working 'to develop, conduct and foster research and educational programs' and to 'prepare, and to publish […] guidelines for the avoidance of infringements'.[63]

An important part of my current work as Commissioner, for example, involves leading the National Anti-Racism Strategy, which was launched in 2012.[64] The strategy aims to improve public understanding of racism, and to empower Australians to respond to prejudice and discrimination. Educational work conducted as part of the strategy covers the workplace, schools, sport, public services and the internet. There has, for example, been curricular material developed for primary and high school students in history and physical education, as well as guidance for employers on dealing with cultural diversity in their workplaces.

The strategy also includes a campaign called 'Racism. It Stops with Me', which invites individuals and organisations to pledge a stand against racism. At the time of writing, more than 340 organisations across the country are formal supporters of the campaign (AFL footballer Adam Goodes is also a prominent ambassador of the campaign). Some organisations join because of local incidents involving bigotry and hatred. In country Victoria, Bendigo council supported the campaign as part of the community's response to anti-Muslim protests over the building of a mosque in the town. In the case of Ventura Bus Lines, the company responded to a much publicised incident on one of its buses in Melbourne, where a passenger racially abused and threatened another passenger who had been singing a song in French: as part of its support for 'Racism. It Stops with Me', the company introduced new training for bus drivers about how to deal with racist abuse. Others, such as the 20-odd universities across the country who are campaign members, join because they believe it is a powerful way to build a more welcoming atmosphere within their organisation. Whatever the context, membership of the campaign has proven to be a means of expressing public commitment to racial tolerance and cultural harmony.

Returning to the law, there is one respect in which the value and impact of racial discrimination legislation are exceedingly difficult to measure. Laws serve to express a community's political morality. They set rules for how people should conduct their lives together; they articulate a community's aspirations for fairness and justice. The very presence of the RDA is itself of importance, because it reflects a statement from Australian society that it does not accept racial discrimination and is committed to the equal dignity of its members. It gives people the assurance that they will not be treated unfavourably or with contempt because of their race. In light of Australia's history of racial discrimination, this is no trivial feat for our legal and political culture.

At the same time, by existing as rules, the law may shape people's behaviour. On the matter of race, one early American legal scholar of anti-discrimination laws put it in the following terms:

> … the mere existence of the law itself affects prejudice. People usually agree with the law and internalise its values. This is because considerable moral and symbolic weight is added to a principle when it is embedded in legislation.

The Racial Discrimination Act

> Additionally, most people are conformists, and the law usually represents the prevailing attitudes in the community. The law, embodying as it does the societally acceptable norm, constantly holds before people an image of what their feelings should be. Over an appreciable period, this cannot help but influence them in their private attitudes. As a result, while we may not be able to repeal prejudice by law, [it] ... is an essential part of the enterprise of education which alone can end prejudice.[65]

There is one area where the RDA has had particularly significant impact on prejudice and attitudes. The introduction of racial vilification provisions in 1995 took the law beyond acts of discrimination in areas such as employment, accommodation and the provision of goods and services. In covering public acts that abused or degraded others because of their race, the provision of section 18C attempted to do more than protect people against unfair treatment. The section has sought 'to ensure that people are not actually caused mental harm because of their race'.[66] By making acts of racial vilification unlawful, the RDA has set a norm for civility in a multicultural society. Many communities affected by racial vilification have consciously used section 18C as an instrument of advocacy – for instance, to put a perpetrator or publisher of racial hate speech on notice.[67] As highlighted to me by various community representatives and organisations, there is utility in being able to invoke the RDA when making representations about racially offensive conduct. Having the law on your side can assist in securing some redress, even if you may not end up pursuing a formal complaint about racial vilification. Such experience demonstrates the powerful educative effect of legislation.

All this must inform any assessment of the RDA's contribution to eliminating racial discrimination. It should go without saying that we cannot rely upon legislation – and legislation alone – to achieve social change. It is unrealistic to expect that law can deal exhaustively with the causes of social phenomena, for the law is more typically equipped to deal with the symptoms. If we are interested in educating people for social change, it must be at the level of policies and programs, and be done in schools and communities. As well as through the power of the state, through our parliaments and our laws, such work must be conducted through the habits of civil society.[68] Changing attitudes and values is work we must do in our family, our work, our churches, our sporting clubs, our neighbourhoods. 'Perhaps', as Simon Rice reminds us, 'we can aim no higher than to pursue Zeno's paradox, forever halving the distance to our goal, destined never to achieve it.'[69] But there are also good reasons to be celebrating the presence of legislative protections against racial discrimination.

The Racial Discrimination Act

Today, public expressions of racial contempt and hatred are greeted almost universally with disapproval. Would we be in the same position were the RDA not to exist at all?

A MONGREL MULTICULTURALISM
CHRISTOS TSIOLKAS

'*They are perversions, they are sick. Those poofters rape children. This country is sick, this is why they are all divorced, all are ignorant, it is because they allow such perversions to exist.*'

The response is violent, he spits out his words in a rage. He turns to me again, seeking affirmation.

'*This country is sick.*'

He is a young man, who migrated from East Africa as a teenager. He is maybe 20 years younger than I am and we are both members of the same sports complex in the northern suburbs of Melbourne. Our interactions have been minimal. At first we merely nodded at each other, remaining in cordial silence. But one morning, when we were the only two members in the spa, we began a tentative conversation and found shared agreement in our opposition to the wars in Iraq and in Afghanistan. From then on, our interactions became more amiable. We exchanged names and the most rudimentary of biographies. On this occasion I had just showered after doing laps and had entered the steam room. He was in there and I greeted him warmly with *Salaam*. There was another young man there, an Anglo-Celtic Australian with pierced nipples and a lattice of tattoos over his arms and up his legs. This youth smiled at me as I took a seat on the other end of the bench and he attempted to begin a conversation with both of us. He mentioned the heat of the day, the upcoming footy games on the weekend. His mannerisms and speech were flamboyant. I answered good-naturedly but I was aware of how the other man refused to engage: he stared stonily in front of him. The tattooed youth rose, pointedly farewelled both of us, and left the steam room. As soon as the door had shut, the man turned to me, and let loose with his invective.

I will admit to cowardice, that though there was a part of me that desired to tell him that I was homosexual myself, I was anxious at how that would make our future casual interactions awkward and possibly hostile. I also recalled a previous conversation in which we had shared our mutual suspicion for the atomised relationship of Australians to family. Had I, inadvertently, given him reasons to assume I would share his viewpoint on sexuality? I wasn't necessarily deeply offended at his language. The words and the content reminded me of outbursts my father, my uncles and their friends, used to make about what they understood as the lax morality and extreme individualism of mainstream Australian culture. I was a child then, and my father and his peers had been young migrant men trying to come to terms with a radically different culture to the one they had known in rural mid-20th-century Greece and Yugoslavia. But I also didn't want his remarks to pass unchallenged. I coughed, interrupting his diatribe, and said, 'Please, I don't want to hear such things, my sister is lesbian and she is not perverted, she is not evil.' He was taken aback, there was even a moment of his trying to form words in response, but he decided to remain silent. The discomfort in that steam room felt like a physical weight, I had to breathe in deeply. Thankfully at that moment a middle-aged woman entered and I took my opportunity to escape.

We no longer talk to each other. We nod and acknowledge each other but we don't pretend anymore that we are at all like-minded.

The incident I have described above occurred over three years ago now but I have mused on it from time to time whenever arguments around the question of multiculturalism flare up in the media or in the general culture. Both local and international events can bring the moment back to me, whether it is the debate around changes to the Racial Discrimination Act or, more recently, the shock I experienced hearing of the fascist killings of the staff working at *Charlie Hebdo* in France. I immediately think back to it when I hear of how some poor soul has had to endure racial insults on the street or on a train or bus.

A mongrel multiculturalism

I think what I find both fascinating and perplexing about that incident in the steam room is that it is an example of the tensions arising from living within a multicultural society but an incident in which the expression of hate comes from the usually marginalised figure, in this case a young Muslim refugee from eastern Africa. Certainly I understand that it was a small and arguably trivial exchange but nevertheless it still disturbs me for the way it challenges my faith in the achievements of Australian multiculturalism and of how it reminds me of the difficulty in sometimes standing up to hate speech. I was humiliated in that moment, from both my gutlessness in response to his diatribe but also ashamed in recognising that this young man saw me as a sickness and an evil. But I was also saddened, disappointed in his ignorance, but more importantly, let down by his lack of civility. I felt let-down, betrayed.

Civility, the assumption of mutual respect across differences, strikes me as a core for the success of contemporary multicultural democratic societies. It is a word that seems anodyne, a concept that eschews the partisanship and enmity of ideological difference. It is also a term that might seem to be counter-intuitive for the way in which many of us understand Australian political and cultural history. I am not only referring to recent history, to the acrimonious and toxic parliamentary politics of the last decade, to the failure of leadership by all sides of politics to face the challenge of the asylum seekers debate in a humane and courageous manner. We are a country founded on a colonial dispossession that still blights the aspirations and sovereign goals of Indigenous Australians. We were set up as penal colonies that were to be the site of a further injustice, the transportation of the dispossessed of the British Isles and Ireland to serve as convict labourers. One of the first acts of the new national parliament in 1901 was legislation introducing the White Australia policy, which enshrined a racially determined understanding of citizenship as intrinsic to what it means to be Australian. Whether mythologised as a country of egalitarian and anti-class and anti-caste battlers or condemned as a nation of racist and parochial underachievers – God's Earth or the sardonically inflected the 'Lucky Country' of Donald Horne's pivotal book – the notion of civility seems to fly in the face of our history, our demographic constitution, of who we are, how we understand ourselves and how we are understood in the world. Courtesy, politeness, the mutuality of respects, these are values which would seem to underscore the ethical and social expression of civility. They are also characteristics that are seemingly at odds with both national and international understandings of the Australian national character. Positively, the Australian traits are larrikinism, bluntness and directness of speech, a suspicion of pretension and self-aggrandisation; more negatively, we are

A mongrel multiculturalism

seen as reactionary in our anti-political correctness, as anti-intellectual, coarse and vulgar in our speech and expression.

My sense is that both readings of the Australian character are valid, but that neither does justice to the complexity of what it is to be Australian in the early 21st century. The horror of Aboriginal dispossession, and then the subsequent violence of the colonial penal colonies certainly are intrinsic to understanding this country and its culture: no history or critique of Australia can ignore these national foundational truths. But there is a third moment to our history – the moment that I wish to call multiculturalism – that disrupts both the conservative's optimism and the radical's pessimism of what this country is. The economic need for Australia to industrialise post-WWII, and the intertwined need to increase its population, was the fertile ground for the transformation of Australian identity. The opening up of the country to Eastern and Southern European immigrant labourers inevitably led to a chipping away of the White Australia policy, a policy only abandoned in 1973 but a reality that was already becoming void a decade before that. Just as important as the coming of non-English speaking Europeans was the bipartisan acceptance of Vietnamese refugees at the end of the 1970s. If the acceptance of the first wave of immigrants arose from economic reasons, this second wave arose in part from a Cold War ideological

I'm not racist but ...

commitment from Malcolm Fraser's Coalition government to intercede on humanitarian grounds and offer asylum to people fleeing Communist dictatorship. With the settlement and absorption into the body politic of the Vietnamese, a long-standing isolationist fear from Anglo-Celtic Australians of Asia slowly began to dissolve.

There was conflict, there was hatred expressed, there was fear and there was always the poignant melancholy of exile that is always part of the immigrant and refugee experience. Antagonism to Multiculturalism, as government policy and national direction, was expressed on the ground – in schools, in pubs, in shopping malls and across backyard fences – and it also found expression politically, whether through John Howard's anxieties about the Asianisation of Australia when he was leader of the Opposition in the late 1980s or most urgently with the rise of Pauline Hanson's One Nation party in the early 1990s. Resentment to multiculturalism, as is evident throughout the world, is most acute at times of economic recession, when unemployment is increasing; and multiculturalism is always more identified as integral to our cities than it is to the rural. In no way do I want to argue that our becoming multicultural is a fait accompli or that it is something universally accepted by Australians. But slighting the truly transformative impact of multiculturalism is to ignore the reality of how the majority of us now live in its moment, that we accept the multi-ethnic, multi-lingual, multi-sexual and multi-identity of our public and private spaces.

I think it is in how we share those private and public spaces with one another that a civility at work in multicultural Australia can be gleaned. It is in how we can ride on a bus or on a train and assume the shared national identity of one another regardless of our heritage. It is in how we accept the differing religious traditions of our childrens' friends, or are not shocked that they have lesbian mothers or that a parent might be avowedly athiest. It is expressed in the casual camaraderie of our workplaces, and most intimately and I think importantly, in how within our extended families we accept the increasing diversity of our nieces and nephews, of our brothers and sisters and parents-in-law. The marker of our civilian contract is that those moments that disrupt the multicultural consensus – the riot on Cronulla Beach, racist hate spewed from a drunk on a bus and caught on a smartphone and uploaded onto social media – are greeted largely with disbelief. The outrage is never universal but I think it is close to collective and it isn't a shock only expressed in the cosmopolitan inner-city. These are incidents that outrage students at high schools at the creeping edges of our cities; it is named a moral failure in Australian Buddhist households, in Australian Christian households, in Australian Muslim households and in Australian atheist households. We are all in the moment of multiculturalism, even those who wish to deny it. This denial is often expressed in a rage that is poisonous, and it is so because they know that in refuting the moment they have now become the outsider.

That young man in the steam room had forged my acquaintance through a shared civility. But he betrayed that civility when he hissed at me, 'This country is sick'. As we now know there are always consequences to things we say, the martyrs of *Charlie Hebdo* have taught us that. But it is not the editors and cartoonists and publishers of that satirical magazine that betrayed multiculturalism, it was the fascist thugs who killed them. Civil behaviour, our sharing of social space, is part of what constitutes the health and vitality of the multicultural society. In a mutation that no-one could envisage when multiculturalism was first formulated as government policy in the early 1970s, the term has come to embrace ways of being and living and understanding one's identity that have gone beyond the limits of race and religion. For all the recurrence of the xenophobia or racism that still stains this nation, for all the despairing political venality of our treatment of asylum seekers, for all our failure across the political spectrum to have a mature and productive conversation about the centrality of immigration to our long-term cultural and economic well-being, mostly, on the level of our interactions in and of the every day, we treat each other with an

A mongrel multiculturalism

accepting civility. How we express it might seem at times crude or vulgar, rough and impolite, but that is part of the vitality of our Australian English, an English formed through the violent dispossessions that occurred on this land, to both blackfellas and the convict whitefellas, and the fact that so many of us are the descendants of the unwanted and the unwashed of Europe and Asia, and increasingly of Africa. We are rude, in our language and we are rude in our multiculturalism. I know now what I should have said to that bloke in the steam room, *'Shut it, mate, that's just ignorant and bloody stupid.'*

3

FREEDOM OF SPEECH AND ITS LIMITS

IS THERE A RIGHT TO BE A BIGOT?

Do we have a right to be bigots? The question has defined recent debates about racial vilification and freedom of speech. It gained currency after Attorney-General George Brandis claimed in March 2014 that, 'people do have a right to be bigots you know'. As he told the Senate, 'in a free country people do have rights to say things that other people find offensive or insulting or bigoted'.[1]

The invocation of this right to bigotry was made during a parliamentary exchange about the Abbott Government's proposal to amend the Racial Discrimination Act. Arguing that it stifled free speech, the Abbott Government sought in 2014 to repeal Part IIA of the Act. The key provision, section 18C, makes it unlawful to offend, insult, humiliate or intimidate another person on racial grounds. This was the section used in a civil action against newspaper columnist Andrew Bolt, in relation to a series of articles he had written about fair-skinned Aboriginal people.

Debates about race can often divide more than unite. Yet throughout 2014, the contest over section 18C united Australians in one sense. There was an emphatic affirmation of our commitment to racial tolerance. Indeed, there was widespread opposition to the proposed reform of the RDA: by multicultural and Aboriginal communities, members of the legal profession, human rights experts, psychologists, public health advocates, churches and civil society. Most were worried that amending the law would have the dangerous effect of licensing racial hatred.

Faced with such widespread concern, the Abbott Government abandoned its legislative proposal in August 2014. Announcing the retreat, Prime Minister Tony Abbott said he had made a 'leadership call'. The issue had become a 'needless complication' in his government's relationship with the Australian Muslim community, at a time when it was seeking to introduce new national security legislation. 'When it comes to counter-terrorism', Abbott said, 'everyone needs to be part of Team Australia'.[2]

The issue was briefly revisited in January 2015. Following the Islamist massacre of staff at satirical magazine *Charlie Hebdo* in Paris, some commentators called for an urgent reconsideration of section 18C. It was argued that, were the magazine's provocative cartoons about the prophet Mohammed and racial groups to be published in Australia, it would be 'banned' or 'shut down' because of the RDA.[3] The Federal Government quickly rejected such calls. Prime Minister Tony Abbott confirmed there would be no changes: it remained his government's position that it would not proceed with a repeal. While the Prime Minister said he 'would prefer that 18C were not in its current terms', he also acknowledged that he believed 'we do have very robust free speech in this country'.[4]

Matters of free speech have always attracted passionate disagreement. The life of the RDA has been marked by frequent debates about the balancing act between legislating against racial discrimination and protecting fundamental liberal freedoms. Such debates raise important questions about freedom and racial equality. What must freedom mean in a multicultural society? What, for instance, should be the proper limits of free speech consistent with racial tolerance? And what must freedom involve if it is to be enjoyed by all the members of our society, not just some?

Clearly, these are not idle questions. While the debate over section 18C was resolved with the right result – existing legal protections against racial vilification have been retained – at times it also generated too much heat and not enough light. There was, and is, considerable misunderstanding of how the vilification provisions of the RDA operate. And unfortunately there remains a great deal of confusion about the liberal concept of freedom, a concept at risk of being debased by ideological polemic and uninformed sloganeering. We need to do more to clarify what is implicated in any contest over freedom of speech. On matters concerning race, there are in fact two freedoms at stake: not just freedom of speech, but also freedom from racial vilification.

LIBERTY AND FREEDOM

When I studied political theory at the University of Oxford, the first topic we were taught was that of liberty or freedom. You can understand why. Freedom is integral to any discussion of the good life, the good society and the role of the state. Yet there is also something about freedom that is conducive to intellectual stimulation. Every autumn at the start of the academic year, familiar debates would resonate around the sandstone quads of Oxford's colleges. Does a tramp without money have the freedom to dine at the Ritz? Are rich and poor equally free to sleep under bridges? Is one truly free if one is not also autonomous? Can one be forced to be free, if one is held back by one's own will?

Much of the conversation about freedom continues to be shaped by the work of philosopher Isaiah

Berlin. In his lecture on 'Two Concepts of Liberty', Berlin made his famous distinction between negative and positive freedom.[5] According to Berlin, many understood liberty in its 'positive' sense. It meant 'freedom to', that is, being free to live according to the purposes set by one's own reason and conscience. In Berlin's view, however, liberty's true meaning was confined to its 'negative' conception. Negative liberty meant that one enjoys freedom when one is free from interference from others. To be free is to have an absence of constraint or coercion imposed by another human being.

This distinction had understandable appeal in providing clarity to the meaning of freedom. Berlin delivered his Two Concepts of Liberty lecture in 1958, at the height of the Cold War, when there was obvious political concern with communist totalitarianism. As he explained, the trouble with positive liberty was that it posited a higher or ideal self as the true end of freedom. If this higher self were to be conceived as something larger than the individual – as, say, a race, a Church, a Nation or a State – freedom could easily become a term of oppression. It would become possible for one to be coerced by another, and for that to be justified as necessary for one to be 'truly free'.[6]

Philosophical insights can, over time, lose some of their original nuance. In the case of Berlin's conceptions of liberty, too many have cited them as the final words on freedom. They have often been regarded as philosophical proof that any positive theory of freedom must be morally flawed. Yet, as the Canadian philosopher Charles Taylor has argued, the Berlinian view had its own deficiency.[7] The problem is that it rules out much of the modern understanding of freedom. Most of us would regard freedom as something that we *exercise* so as to determine the direction of our lives. By implication, this is a view that leaves room for the possibility that one can experience inner constraints on freedom, as well as external coercion from others.

This is something that a negative conception of freedom cannot contemplate. All that matters, on the negative view, is that one can do something in the absence of an obstacle imposed by someone else. Is the tramp free to dine the Ritz? The negative view would say that, yes, he has the formal opportunity to do so – even if it is of no value to him, and even if it is a freedom that he will be unable to exercise.

The trouble is this. Following Berlin's view can lead us to divorce freedom from human desires and motives. Defining freedom as simply an absence of external obstacles leaves little room for making judgments about obstacles. For example, the state's insistence that people wear seatbelts in cars can be regarded as a diminution of our freedom. But in that case the infringement is trivial. It does not deprive us of our freedom of movement; the only real price is that it may impose some aesthetic nuisance or trifling discomfort. Contrast this with, say, a law that restricts people from joining certain associations. In that case, we could all agree that there is a more significant infringement, one which may affect people's ability to exercise their moral freedom.

We will always make discriminating judgments about freedom. Its exercise is bound up in our understanding of dignity, individuality and happiness – bound up in our human purposes. We will value different kinds of freedom based on the significance of the purposes to which they are attached.

Of freedom, we can say this. It is difficult, if not also foolish, to reduce a discussion of it to any simple formula. It is not a one-dimensional concept. And yet, the cult of Sir Isaiah can lead people to believe that freedom can be defined exhaustively through a negative conception. Surely it is possible for us to speak about 'freedom to' as well as 'freedom from'; about freedom as something people exercise and not merely as an opportunity; and about people being held back from being fully free by inner as well as outer obstacles. Surely it is possible for us to do all this without lapsing into the insidious totalitarianism against which Berlin rightly cautioned.

FREEDOM OF SPEECH

That we need to draw upon both negative and positive conceptions of freedom becomes clear when we examine the liberal justifications behind freedom of speech.

The typical defence of free speech follows a predictable course. More frequently than not it begins with Voltaire: 'I may disagree with what you say, but I will defend to the death your right to say it.' The great *philosophe* never in fact said these words. Rather, they came from the writer E Beatrice Hall's fictionalised account of how Voltaire responded to the burning of a friend's book. Perhaps if the spirit of Voltaire could speak, he would say, 'I may disagree with what you quote me as saying, but I will defend even in death your right to misquote me'.

In substance, the case for free speech can appear to rest on a negative conception of freedom. Consider the justification of a constitutional guarantee of free speech in the United States. Arguably, the legal and political culture that has developed there provides the paradigmatic model for an absolutist defence of free speech. As the First Amendment to the US Constitution states, 'Congress shall make no law ... abridging the freedom of speech, or the freedom of the press'. While the force of these words appears unambiguous, it was not until the 20th century that they would be interpreted as offering a strong guarantee of free speech. In the earliest days of the American Republic, for example, Congress passed the Sedition Act of 1798, making it an offence to bring the president or Congress into disrepute or 'to excite against them ... the hatred of the good people of the United States'. Even as late as 1952, the Supreme Court declined to overturn a fine imposed on the president of the White Circle League of America concerning racist leaflets he had been distributing on Chicago streets urging people to 'protect the white race from being mongrelized' by the negro.[8]

The reinterpretation of the First Amendment only occurred following the First World War with the various judgments of Oliver Wendell Holmes Jr and Louis Brandeis. According to Holmes' dictum, the key principle of the Constitution is 'not free thought for those who agree with us but freedom for the thought of those we hate'.[9] The best test of ideas lies in 'the competition of the market', where their truth can be scrutinised and ultimately judged. The only restriction that a state is justified in imposing upon speech is when it can create 'a clear and present danger'.[10] Such sentiments would find an additional authority in Louis Brandeis, for whom 'sunlight is ... the best of disinfectants; electric light the most efficient policeman'.[11] Where there is noxious speech, Brandeis believed that society should avert the evil by exposing falsehoods and fallacies through discussion. Bad speech, as it were, can be remedied by more speech – that is to say, by good speech.[12]

The First Amendment-inspired defence of free speech, beginning with Holmes and Brandeis, involves three animating thoughts: that we must tolerate the expression of all nasty ideas, though not necessarily all dangerous actions; that there is some sphere within which individuals must be free to pursue their thoughts, without interference from government regulation; and that the best weapon for combating bad ideas is the persuasive power of good ideas.

In more philosophical terms, much of this has roots in the arguments of 19th-century British philosopher John Stuart Mill. As Mill stated in his famous essay *On Liberty*, there ought to be the fullest liberty in discussing any doctrine, however immoral it may be: 'If all mankind minus one were of one opinion, and only one person were of the contrary opinion, mankind would be no more justified in silencing that one person, than he, if he had the power, would be justified in silencing mankind.'[13] For Mill, we should not suppress an opinion because we may be mistaken about the truth. We can have no assurance that we were right about our opinions unless we have the liberty to discuss it: any opinion arrived at through other means would be held as a 'dead dogma', not as 'a living truth'.

At first glance, this appears to emphasise the importance of leaving individuals free from interference from state regulation of thought and speech. Certainly, those who identify as 'classical liberals' would regard Berlin, Mill, Holmes and Brandeis as kindred spirits on the matter of free speech. Yet it is worth delving deeper into the philosophical basis of their arguments.

It is interesting that Holmes appeared to find a certain glory in the idea of contest and battle. The competition of the marketplace may be harsh, but Holmes appeared to believe in the strenuous life.[14] By contrast, Brandeis had the perspective of a Romantic liberal progressive. In his interpretation of the First Amendment and the philosophy he felt it embodied, Brandeis saw the role of the state as being to empower individuals through the democratic process. Like Holmes, Mill also valued rigorous contest and rancorous controversy. Yet this was qualified by a view that conflict serves as 'an aid to the intelligent and living apprehension of a truth'.[15] In this respect, Mill was more alike to Brandeis than to Holmes: he was a Romantic liberal, rather than a brutal realist. For him, freedom of expression mattered not just because it enabled the discovery of truth. It ultimately mattered because it was necessary for people to develop their individuality.

The classic defence of free speech is not, then, a simple argument about negative freedom. With its resort to notions of individuality and self-realisation, what we see is clearly an argument that draws upon a positive conception of freedom. Moreover, ideas about the free exchange of ideas as the defining quality of a democratic polity point to the value of collective self-determination. In all, it is a view that has more in sympathy with a positive conception of freedom than it does with a negative one.

FREEDOM FROM RACIAL VILIFICATION

Let us turn to a second freedom – a freedom from racial vilification. Some may quibble that it makes limited sense to speak in such terms. When we think of freedom, we may typically have in mind things such as freedom of conscience, freedom of expression, freedom of assembly, freedom of association. We may refer to an interest in being protected from racial discrimination, the argument runs, but this strictly does not mean a freedom from racial vilification. The intention behind speaking in terms of a freedom from racial vilification is simply to highlight one thing: any right to protection from such behaviour has at its heart a concern with the fundamental interest of freedom. When racial vilification occurs, those on the receiving end of abuse and harassment can have a diminished enjoyment of their individual freedom.

I'm not racist but ...

Admittedly, it is more common to refer to the *harms* of racial abuse. There is now a considerable volume of research that highlights the serious health effects racism can have on individuals. Cruelty and fear need not be inflicted only through direct physical assault: you do not need to be hit on the head by a bigot to be hurt by bigotry. The stress of racial abuse can trigger physiological symptoms such as fear in the gut, rapid pulse rate and difficulty in breathing. Repeated exposure to it can undoubtedly contribute to conditions such as hypertension, nightmares, post-traumatic stress disorder, even psychosis and suicide.[16]

Racist speech can cause undetected harm, too. In a modern society, our identity – our sense not only of who we are, but also of our worth and dignity – is shaped by its recognition by those around us. Where society reflects back to someone a demeaning or contemptible picture of themselves that can inflict profound harm.[17] As described by one early study of race during the 1940s, a rebuff due to one's colour puts the victim 'in very much the situation of the very ugly person or one suffering from a loathsome disease'.[18] Those on the receiving end of abuse can feel more than just indignation, but also humiliation, self-reproach and even self-loathing.[19] Victims of racial abuse, no matter how much they resist it, can themselves begin to absorb the messages of hate and inferiority.[20] When the messages are pervasive, even well-meaning members of society can begin to entertain the idea that 'those people' – whomever they may be – are not worthy of our trust and respect.[21]

Those who are unfamiliar with the wounding power of racism may dismiss this as superficial complaints about words. There remains what can be called the 'thick-skin brigade': those who would declare, 'sticks and bones may break my bones, but words can never hurt me'. These are the people who believe the only racism that warrants our public attention is the kind that involves physical violence. Racial vilification is, according to this view, an ersatz racism that troubles only effete citizens incapable of dealing with their injured sensibilities.

Members of the 'thick-skin brigade' belong to the Middle Ages, to a time when the law was confined to offering remedies only for physical interference with life and property. This was a time when the law recognised that liberty meant only a protection from battery, and when property would still be referred to as land and chattel. Here, it is interesting to note the writings of the younger Louis Brandeis. Long before he became a Justice of the US Supreme Court, he co-wrote a celebrated article with Samuel Warren about 'The Right to Privacy'. Writing on that topic, Warren and Brandeis provide a revealing statement about the law's development in acknowledging our spiritual nature:

> This development of the law was inevitable. The intense intellectual and emotional life, and the heightening of sensations which came with the advance of civilization, made it clear to men that only a part of the pain, pleasure, and profit of life lay in physical things.[22]

So much for sticks and stones. And this was in the 1890s.

It is worth reiterating the nature of the psychological harm that may be experienced by those subjected to others' exercise of racist speech. In 2010, the Australian Human Rights Commission conducted a consultation involving a survey of Australians' perceptions and experiences of racism. It was commonplace for many respondents to reflect on how sad and angry the experience of racism made them feel, and how racism diminished their sense of worth. One respondent said, 'it makes me feel like I am a lesser human being'. Another mentioned its impact on emotions and health: 'I feel so much revulsion that I sometimes feel physically ill. It is a major contributor to the anxiety I experience in everyday life'.[23] Some were more explicit about the injury that racism inflicted on their freedom. One respondent, a male from China in his late 30s, said, 'I came to Australia for freedom. However, racism makes me feel my liberty is incomplete'.[24]

Other respondents highlighted how racism had

the effect of intimidating or inhibiting them. As described by one person, 'I feel like I am being treated as a second-class citizen. I cannot speak up against any unfair treatment in the workplace'. 'Racism', one man of African-American background said, 'makes me feel like I have to always be cognizant of what I say', in case he were to encounter bigotry.[25] Many others also described how racism made them feel unsafe, especially at night or in public places.

Such testimony – reflected in the conversations I have with communities across the country – demonstrates the impact that racism has on how Australians enjoy their freedom. There is the impact that racism can have on someone's self-perception. Where people begin to accept a picture of their own inferiority, this can get in the way of them exercising their freedom, in the positive sense. It is difficult to see how someone can reach their potential, or be a truly self-determining individual, if they constantly second-guess themselves or if they feel constantly without power or hope. And insofar as those who dispense racist abuse can intimidate others, it is open to consider them as interfering with others' freedom, in the negative sense. If those on the receiving end are no longer moving in certain circles because of fear, it must surely follow that their realm of non-interference has been violated.

If we do not always make the connection between racism and its curtailment of freedom, it is because we are more likely to regard the harm as one involving dignity. Racism reduces the standing of another to that of a second-class citizen. But dignity is also connected to freedom. Where there is an injury to dignity, there is an impact as well on someone's ability to exercise freedom. In the case of racism, the experience undermines the assurance of security to which every member of a good society is entitled. It undermines the sense of confidence that everyone will be treated fairly and justly – that everyone can walk down the street and conduct their business, without fear of abuse or assault.[26]

BALANCING FREEDOMS: THE RACIAL DISCRIMINATION ACT

How, then, are we to reconcile freedom of speech and freedom from racial vilification? From the perspective of international human rights law, Article 19 of the *International Covenant on Civil and Political Rights* (ICCPR) states that, 'everyone shall have the right to freedom of expression; this right shall include freedom to seek, receive and impart information and ideas of all kinds'. But Article 19 recognises that freedom of expression is not absolute: it 'carries with it special duties and responsibilities' and 'may therefore be subject to certain restrictions'. It is well established in human rights law that there is a right to be protected from racial vilification.[27] Article 20 of the ICCPR states that, 'any advocacy of national, racial or religious hatred that constitutes incitement to discrimination, hostility or violence shall be prohibited by law'. Article 4 of the *International Convention on the Elimination of All Forms of Racial Discrimination* (CERD) also requires State Parties to criminalise all dissemination of ideas based on racial superiority or hatred and incitement to racial discrimination, as well as all acts of violence or incitement to such acts against any racial or ethnic groups.

Australia has ratified both treaties. Through Part IIA of the RDA, introduced in 1995 as a civil prohibition of racial vilification, Commonwealth law has sought to give fuller effect to CERD (although Australia continues to have in place a reservation concerning the criminalisation of racial hatred and incitement). Australian courts have found that Part IIA involves a permissible limitation in light of an implied constitutional right of freedom of political communication. They have found the enactment is a reasonable, necessary and proportionate means for pursuing the interest of racial tolerance and social cohesion in a multicultural society.[28] The case law has also established that Part IIA is consistent with Australia's obligations under CERD: 'it is entirely consistent with the provisions of the Convention ... that a State Party should legislate to "nip in the bud" the doing of offensive, insulting, humiliating or intimidating public acts which are done because of race ... before such acts grow into incitement or promotion of racial hatred or discrimination'.[29]

The history behind Australia's racial vilification law reflects sustained concern about racist violence. In response to a series of violent attacks against migrant communities during the late 1980s, then Race Discrimination Commissioner Irene Moss conducted the *National Inquiry into Racist Violence*. The final report in 1991 found that, 'Physical violence is not the only, or even in some cases the most important, form of racist violence. The physical effects of violence often cause less damage to the individual victim than the psychological effects.'[30] The *National Inquiry into Racist Violence* recommended that the RDA be amended to include civil remedies for racist harassment and incitement to racial hostility.[31]

Two other major reports in the late 1980s and early 1990s made similar recommendations. The Royal Commission into Aboriginal Deaths in Custody recommended the introduction of legislation to 'proscribe racial vilification and to provide a conciliation mechanism for dealing with complaints of racial vilification'.[32] The Royal Commission stressed that such legislation would recognise 'the important fact that language itself can be a form of violence'.[33] Similarly, the Australian Law Reform Commission's *Multiculturalism and the Law* report, tabled in 1992, supported making incitement to racist hatred unlawful, though it stopped short of recommending that it should be made a criminal offence. The Australian Law Reform Commission recommended that the law be amended to include a conciliation process for complaints about racial hatred, backed up by civil remedies when conciliation fails.[34]

The current federal racial vilification provisions were introduced to Parliament through the Racial Hatred Bill 1994. In his second reading speech, attorney-general Michael Lavarch highlighted the causal link between racial vilification and racist violence: racist violence begins with threats of violence and a milieu of hatred and intolerance.[35] It was in the public interest to counter this, while also being attentive to freedom of speech.

Part IIA of the RDA – the final result of the Racial Hatred Bill – includes sections 18C and 18D. Section 18C states that it is unlawful to commit a public act that is reasonably likely to 'offend, insult, humiliate or intimidate' someone on the grounds of race (language that was drawn from the sexual harassment provisions of the *Sex Discrimination Act 1984*). Section 18C is accompanied by section 18D, which ensures that artistic works, scientific debate, and fair comment on and fair reporting of a matter of public interest are exempt from being in breach of section 18C – provided that something has been done reasonably and in good faith. As it stands, Part IIA provides only a civil prohibition of racial vilification; it gives force to no criminal sanction against racial hatred.

Much like the rest of the RDA, these racial vilification provisions emphasise a conciliation process as the central mechanism for complaints about racial hatred. This educative and civil quality of Part IIA is frequently overlooked. For example, it is commonly assumed that breaching section 18C results in a 'prosecution' or criminal penalty. No one can be prosecuted or convicted for racial vilification under Commonwealth law. In most cases, litigation does not even occur: in 2013–14, for example, only six of the 116 complaints concerning racial hatred (5 per cent) ended up in court; in 2012–13, this was the case with only five of 192 complaints concerning racial hatred (3 per cent). In recent years, the Australian Human Rights Commission has successfully conciliated the majority of complaints concerning the RDA.

Some examples of conciliated cases illustrate the type of complaints commonly made under section 18C. In one case, an Aboriginal complainant claimed that his supervisor at work had made racially derogatory comments: for example, referring to him as 'a putrid Abo'. The respondent employer agreed to apologise to the complainant, in addition requiring the employee responsible to undertake Aboriginal cultural awareness training. Another case involved a complainant of Indian origin alleging that one of his managers at work said, 'Hey, you black man, clean my

Freedom of speech and its limits

shoes' – part of an alleged pattern of racial humiliation. The complaint was resolved with the employer providing an apology and $5000 compensation.

As to the case law around Part IIA, for almost 20 years, the courts have interpreted section 18C in a consistent manner. Contrary to what many of its critics say, the section does not make it unlawful merely to offend or insult someone. In the first place, any conduct that is potentially captured by the law must offend, insult, humiliate or intimidate someone *on the basis of race*. This means, among other things, that the law does not cover conduct that may offend people on the grounds of religion. Commentators who have claimed, for example, that *Charlie Hebdo*-style cartoons depicting the prophet Mohammed would be 'banned' because they may offend Muslims are simply wrong.[36] Moreover, section 18C does not involve a subjective test of hurt feelings. The courts have emphasised that the legislation states that an act is only unlawful if it is proven reasonably likely, in all the circumstances, to cause harm involving 'profound and serious effects'; 'mere slights' are not enough to be a breach of the law.[37] Any conduct must be assessed against an objective standard, judged from the perspective of a reasonable or ordinary person from the relevant racial group.[38]

The courts have also made clear that section 18C must be read alongside section 18D. The interpretation of the exemptions afforded by the latter has been very broad. Section 18D has overridden section 18C on numerous occasions. The courts have held it to exempt a comedic performance of someone pretending to be an Aboriginal person who swears and drinks as an 'artistic work'.[39] The contents of a book published by Pauline Hanson and her One Nation Party in 2000, which was highly critical of governments' supposedly favourable treatment of the Aboriginal community, were also regarded as having been 'done reasonably and in good faith for a genuine purpose in the public interest'.[40] The full Federal Court has held that a racially offensive cartoon published in the *West Australian* newspaper was artistic work and fair comment on a matter of public interest, which enjoyed the protection of section 18D.[41] This latter case, in particular, indicates that satirical cartoons such as those published by *Charlie Hebdo* would likely enjoy the section 18D exemption – even if they were to cause racial offence or insult to some groups.

The courts have not allowed section 18D to prevail in all cases involving social and political commentary. In the prominent case of *Eatock v Bolt*, columnist Andrew Bolt was found to have contravened section 18C and to have been unable to claim the defence of section 18D. According to the court, Bolt could not be considered to have acted reasonably and in good faith, as his articles concerning fair-skinned Aboriginal people involved inflammatory and provocative language, distortions of the truth and errors of fact.[42]

Freedom of speech and its limits

For some free speech advocates, this was a demonstration that the RDA goes too far. But the exemptions of section 18D remain of a wide character. In the case of *Eatock v Bolt*, the court crucially found that it was the *combination* of provocation, distortion and error, which meant the free speech exemption did not apply.

A RIGHT TO BIGOTRY?

Clearly, the RDA in its existing form recognises no general right to be a bigot. In providing for the means of making legal complaints about racial vilification, it makes public expressions of racial bigotry unlawful. While a right to free speech is recognised through section 18D, the right is by no means absolute or one that automatically trumps another person's right to be free from bigotry's effects.

In March 2014, Attorney-General George Brandis released an exposure draft of the Freedom of Speech (Repeal Section 18C) Bill which aimed to shift the RDA's treatment of vilification. According to Brandis, the proposed amendment would 'strengthen the Act's protections against racism, while at the same time removing provisions which unreasonably limit freedom of speech'.[43] In an apparent reference to the *Eatock v Bolt* case, he added, 'laws which are designed to prohibit racial vilification should not be used as a vehicle to attack legitimate freedoms of speech'.[44]

The main proposed changes in the exposure draft concerned the removal of sections 18C and 18D. In their place, a new provision would have made unlawful anything that was reasonably likely to 'vilify' or 'intimidate' on the grounds of race. Whether an act was reasonably likely to vilify or intimidate was 'to be determined by the standards of an ordinary reasonable member of the Australian community, not by the standards of any particular group within the Australian community'.[45] Effectively replacing section 18D was a new category of exception: anything that was communicated 'in the course of participating in the public discussion of any political, social, cultural, religious, artistic, academic or scientific matter' would be excepted from being considered unlawful vilification or intimidation.

As noted, these proposed amendments were later withdrawn in 2014, following concerted criticism and opposition. Multicultural and Aboriginal community organisations were united in condemning the government's move – sentiments reflected in broader public opinion. One Fairfax-Nielsen poll in April 2014 found that 88 per cent of respondents believed it should remain unlawful to offend, insult or humiliate someone on the grounds of race.[46] Another survey conducted by academics in mid-2014 at the University of Western Sydney and the University of

Freedom of speech and its limits

Technology, Sydney found that nearly 80 per cent of Australians supported existing legal protections against racial vilification.[47]

Even so, it remains important to understand what the proposed changes in the Freedom of Speech (Repeal Section 18C) Bill would have meant. The bill certainly represented a radical departure from the status quo.

We can begin with the replacement of section 18C's prohibition of any act that 'offends, insults, humiliates and intimidates' on racial grounds with provisions directed only at acts that 'vilify' or 'intimidate'. At first glance, this may appear only to have been a cosmetic change. Yet the implications would have been profound.

The bill's definition of 'vilify' would have limited prohibited conduct to a much smaller range of racially motivated behaviour. In using 'vilify' to refer only to the incitement of racial hatred, the bill would have made the law take no account of the harm that racist conduct inflicts on its target. Instead, the consideration would be the effect of the behaviour on a third party or public audience: namely, whether it could incite feelings of racial hatred. Such an incitement test has proven extremely difficult to satisfy in existing state racial vilification laws. More fundamentally, the replacement of section 18C would have meant the effects of racial abuse in degrading a target were irrelevant, no matter how serious or severe the

I'm not racist but ...

vilification. One could be abused by co-workers, customers or strangers in public as a 'filthy coon', 'stupid boong', 'slit-eyed gook', 'shifty Jew', 'sand-nigger' or 'Arab terrorist'. But unless such abuse was capable of *inciting a third party*, the proposed law would have left the target without an avenue for seeking redress.

The definition of 'intimidate', meanwhile, was confined to situations where the target feared physical harm. Forms of intimidation that did not involve fear of physical harm would not have been covered. This, again, would have failed to capture the harms that are caused by racial vilification. As highlighted above, there has been for some time now a considerable body of evidence about the damage that racism can cause to people's health.

The proposed introduction of a test based on an 'ordinary reasonable member of the Australian community' represented another significant departure from the status quo. As the courts have interpreted the current law, whether something is reasonably likely to offend, insult, humiliate or intimidate on the basis of race is to be judged according to the reasonable member *of the particular group of the community that has been maligned*. But under the proposed changes, the reaction of the target of racial vilification would not be considered. But who exactly is the ordinary reasonable person meant to be in the case of racial vilification? What kind of cultural background does this person have? Is this person someone who embraces cultural diversity, or someone who is sceptical of it? Does this person have prejudicial thoughts about some, or all, ethnic minority groups?

As law professor Simon Rice has described it, this proposed test would have been 'a double whammy to a victim of vilifying conduct', as it involved a 'blithe assertion of a dominant cultural perspective'. The law should be 'respectful of the lived reality of racial difference' – the fact that members of a racial minority will experience life every day, most likely conscious of their different heritage, colour, accent or appearance. According to Rice, 'no member of the Australian racial majority – politicians, policymakers, opinion writers – can understand what it is to have one's life defined by one's difference'.[48]

The most disturbing deficiency of the exposure draft, though, concerned its remarkably broad category of exemption. This exemption covered anything that is done in the course of participating in public discussion. But the draft changes would have removed the current requirements in section 18D for protected speech to be conducted with reasonableness and good faith. The mooted exemption was so wide it is hard to imagine what, if any, conduct the proposed law would have prohibited.

The effects of having such an exemption would have been profound. It would have allowed people to threaten physical harm, incite others to racial hatred, or racially abuse someone in any other way.

People may have done this dishonestly, unreasonably or in bad faith. So long as it could be justified as being done in the course of public discussion, it would have enjoyed a leave pass under the proposed law. For example, under the proposed bill, a case such as that involving Frederick Toben, who published on his website material denying that the Holocaust had occurred, along with anti-Semitic generalisations about Jewish people, could have seen Toben enjoy a 'public discussion' exemption. As the case was decided in 2003, the full Federal Court found that Toben could not enjoy an exemption given his lack of bona fides and deliberately inflammatory language. Under the terms of the proposed Bill, it would have been immaterial whether Toben could demonstrate that he acted reasonably or in good faith.

In other words, the dividing line between free speech and hate speech would be removed by the proposed amendment. Had it been passed by Parliament, there would no longer be a distinction between venting racial hostility and conducting legitimate public debate about ideas. The law would have endorsed the notion that expressions of racial bigotry somehow contribute to the end of public debate in a liberal democracy.

Freedom of speech and its limits

COUNTERING RACISM WITH 'GOOD SPEECH'

The abandonment of the move to repeal section 18C was a welcome decision. The danger in removing a provision that has been in place for almost two decades, of dismantling an important part of the Racial Discrimination Act that has enjoyed strong community support, is that it might license racial hatred. It might encourage people to think there is no harm in dealing out racial vilification. It might unleash a darker, even violent, side of our humanity, which revels in the humiliation of the vulnerable. It might, in short, encourage freedom without responsibility.

There were dubious grounds for having contemplated a legislative amendment in the first place. Part IIA of the RDA has worked as it was intended to work: to provide a civil and educative remedy for racial hatred. If there is to be a change to the existing law, there should be a compelling case for change. Proponents of section 18C's repeal were unable to answer some simple questions: What is it that you want to say that is not already protected by the legislation's free speech exemption? Why should a right to be a bigot outweigh a right to be free from bigotry's effects?

There are, of course, some who argue that racial vilification is best fought in the marketplace of ideas. Let good speech override bad speech – let there be an open contest and put our faith in the goodness of our fellow citizens. If someone is subjected to hate speech they should be free to exercise their own speech to counter it. According to writer Richard King, a state that seeks to protect its citizens against hate speech runs the risk of 'infantilising those citizens [and] undermining their dignity, by assuming that they can't stick up for themselves'.[49]

There is in such arguments a naive optimism. One is reminded of Dr Pangloss in Voltaire's satirical novel *Candide*, for whom all evil and misfortune have a purpose and necessity, even if we may be unable to discern them. As Pangloss put it to young Candide, 'all this is for the best ... it is impossible that things should not be as they are, for all is well'.[50] For our latter-day Panglossian free speech absolutists, it seems enough to say to those on the receiving end of racial abuse that this is how it will always be, and that there may be a virtue in copping abuse, even if you do not know why. As one perceptive scholar has observed, there is frequently an element of 'homeopathic machismo' in some liberal defences of absolutist free speech.[51] The idea is that we should imbibe the poison of racial hatred in small doses so that large draughts will not hurt; let us see racism firsthand so that can lift us to heights of tolerance and enlightenment.

Any debate on this matter should never be divorced from reality. Celebrating the ugly contest of speech may be fine as a speculative matter. Those who laud the ethos of homeopathic machismo may have a point if the only relevant perspective is that of the impartial spectator. For the stranger who is fortunate enough to remain insulated from racial vilification and to live in a social world free of violence – let us call him Barry – there may well be a benefit in coming across an ugly incident of racism. Barry may be shocked by what he sees. He may, for the first time, realise the confronting nature of racism. He may leave with a new appreciation of the harms it causes. Who knows, Barry may even leave with a newfound sense of indignation about racism and become an advocate for racial tolerance.

Yet from the perspective of someone who is the target of racial abuse – let us call them Minh or Mohammed – there is little that is edifying about the experience. It is not clear why Minh or Mohammed should be grateful to a bigot for giving them the opportunity to improve their soul. Sure, they may take heart from knowing that there are sympathetic Barrys out there. But there is no guarantee that an enlightened Barry will be there to stand in solidarity when Minh and Mohammed may need him. For all of Barry's learning in the face of bigotry, he may never have to walk in the same shoes as those who may be arbitrarily confronted with racism as they go about their lives. It seems perverse to say that we must all tolerate hate when not everyone has to bear the burden of tolerance in the same way.

There is a slightly different way of explaining this. The supposedly 'classical liberal' view of free speech may actually have a deeply reactionary logic. It appears to involve a particular aesthetic understanding of freedom, which elevates racism into a strangely sublime experience. The seminal conservative thinker Edmund Burke explained the sublime the following way:

> ... if pain is not carried to violence, and terror is not conversant about the present destruction of the person ... they are capable of producing delight; not pleasure, but a sort of delightful horror, a sort of tranquillity tinged with terror; which, as it belongs to self-preservation, is one of the strongest of all the passions.[52]

Is there not something in the 'classical liberal' mindset that reflects such thinking? This reactionary strand would explain why 'classical liberals' speak a lot about the freedom to unleash bigotry but not much at all about the freedom of those subjected to such delightful horror.

As for fighting bad speech with good speech, that can be an easy thing to prescribe for those who are articulate and well-educated professionals or those accustomed to enjoying the privilege of social power. But the marketplace of ideas is not an arena of perfect competition. We cannot realistically expect that the speech of the strong can be countered by the speech of the weak. It is telling that in the Australian Human Rights Commission's consultations about racism, mentioned above, respondents indicated that experiencing racism made them feel less free to speak. As one respondent said, '[r]acism makes me feel intimidated [and] curtails my freedom ...'.[53] Another said, 'I cannot exercise my basic human rights in freedom of speech, opinions and expressions'. If such testimony is any indication, racism can have a profound effect in silencing its targets, and in debilitating their ability to enjoy freedom of expression. It seems disingenuous to suggest that the victims of racism should be content with fighting bad speech with their own speech, when they may not be in a position to speak back with the same power.

Finally, the idea that any restriction of speech is demeaning, even to those it aims to protect, does not stand up to scrutiny. In recent debates about the RDA, numerous communities have spoken out against any change to existing legislation. Organisations such as the National Congress of Australia's First Peoples, the Executive Council of Australian Jewry, the Chinese Australian Forum, the Australian Hellenic Council, the Arab Australia Council and the Armenian National Committee of Australia have all made clear their view that, '[t]he Racial Discrimination Act is one of Australia's most iconic pieces of legislation', and that 'vilifying entire groups of people because of their race has nothing to do with free speech'.[54] To the views put forward by those who believe any restrictions on speech can demean and offend the dignity of those whom we desire to protect from harm, we may question what is more likely to amount to infantilising our fellow citizens. Is it to have protections against hate speech? Or is it to tell some communities that in spite of what they say, we may know better what is in their interests? To tell them that they do not know it is in their interests to be subject to abuse and to enjoy lesser protections under the law?

A PROPORTIONATE DEBATE

No freedom can be absolute. Nor can there be a hierarchy of freedoms. Freedom of expression, fundamental though it is to a liberal democracy, is not absolute. And a right to free speech does not always triumph over other competing rights. This is the messy, practical business of human rights: often there will need to be a balancing act between rights and interests.

Any debate about freedom of expression needs to be conducted with a level of proportion. One of the strange features of recent debate about free speech and race is that so much passionate attention was paid to a law that offers modest, but nonetheless important, protection for people against racial vilification. After all, we have many laws and other instruments that restrict the use of offensive language – in all sorts of social and political settings.[55]

Start with our parliaments. The House of Representatives' Standing Order 89 prohibits a member from using offensive words against another member or a member of the judiciary. The Senate's Standing Order 193 states that a senator shall not use offensive words against other parliamentarians and members of the judiciary. The parliaments of New South Wales, Victoria, Queensland, South Australia, Western Australia, Tasmania – and the assemblies of the Australian Capital Territory and the Northern Territory – each have standing orders addressed to the use of offensive words or language.[56] Where is the public clamour calling for the repeal of these standing orders that protect politicians and judges from mere offensive language? Why is it acceptable for parliamentarians to object to merely offensive language, but not for others to object to speech that offends, insults, humiliates or intimidates because of their race?

Where is the public outrage about all the offensive language provisions in the various criminal summary offences legislation that exist in New South Wales, Queensland, Victoria, South Australia, Tasmania and the Northern Territory? If there is to be such zealous interest in freedom of expression in Australia, surely attention would be properly devoted to summary offence laws that impose fines and possible sentences of community work or imprisonment on the use of merely offensive language. In one New South Wales case, a man pleaded guilty to an offence under the *Summary Offences Act 1988*, for yelling, 'Annissa Widders I love you. Annissa Widdes I f***in' love you'.[57] One man in Queensland was convicted under the public nuisance offence provision of the then *Vagrants, Gaming and Other Offences Act 1931* for calling a police officer, 'You f***ing c**t'.[58] In one South Australian case, a man was convicted under the *Summary Offences Act 1953* (SA) for telling a police officer, 'F***ing leave him alone' and 'F***ing crap'.[59]

And, if we were to identify areas of the law that may seriously impinge on our freedom of speech, why do the champions of absolutist free speech appear not to be troubled by the impact of the law of defamation? One recent defamation case resulted in $280 000 damages to a woman who was described as a 'grub' and 'you silly silly woman' on Sydney's 2GB radio station.[60] Another recent case involved $200 000 damages for each of the three plaintiffs – a total of $600 000 – in relation to a restaurant review in a newspaper, where the reviewer described a number of dishes as 'simply unpalatable' and the restaurant as 'a bleak spot on the culinary landscape'.[61]

If, as a society, we accept that our parliaments should refrain from offensive language, that our laws can result in criminal sanctions for trivially offensive language, that there can be six-figure damages for calling someone 'silly' or for saying that a restaurant was not especially good, why should we also not hold people accountable for racial vilification that causes profound harm to individuals and families? We are entitled to ask why it is, exactly, that laws concerning racial vilification have been singled out for such disproportionate attention.

In the spirit of proportion, we should also return to Sir Isaiah Berlin, whose real insight on the nature of freedom can sometimes be neglected. Berlin was a liberal, to be sure; many would even consider him an archetypical 'classical liberal'. But he was ultimately an advocate of pluralism. He believed that an approach that privileged one value or goal over all others was a dangerous thing. In his lecture 'The Pursuit of the Ideal', Berlin made clear the inevitability of clashes between values – and issued a warning about privileging liberty above all other values in a dogmatic manner:

> Both liberty and equality are among the primary goals pursued by human beings through many centuries; but total liberty for wolves is death to the lambs, total liberty of the powerful, the gifted, is not compatible with the rights to a decent existence of the weak and the less gifted … Equality may demand the restraint of the liberty of those who wish to dominate; liberty –

I'm not racist but ...

without some modicum of which there is no choice and therefore no possibility of remaining human as we understand the word – may have to be curtailed in order to make room for social welfare, to feed the hungry, to clothe the naked, to shelter the homeless, to leave room for the liberty of others, to allow justice or fairness to be exercised.[62]

We can only hope that those devoted classical liberal followers of Berlin have read him as closely as they would like to boast. The next time they invoke the wisdom of Sir Isaiah, let them heed his warning about the wolves devouring the lambs.

THE REASONABLE MAN
ALICE PUNG

According to the proposed amendments to the *Racial Discrimination Act 1975*, the standards of 'ordinary reasonable members of the Australian community' will determine whether or not something is 'reasonably likely to vilify' a particular race, colour, nationality or ethnicity. Let me introduce you to three 'ordinary reasonable members of the Australian community'.

It is just after midday in the back room of an electrical appliance store, and these men are having lunch. They are retail veterans, having done the same job for at least two decades: the guy from the warehouse who has hands like leather gloves and can dismantle a fridge box in a few minutes, the fast-talking guy from the shop floor who's planning his once-in-a-lifetime holiday to Europe, and the manager who likes to put heartfelt homages to Steve Irwin in his shop ads. But business isn't so good these days. The store is in one of the most archaic and faltering of commercial places, a shopping strip. Down the same street are a Mediterranean restaurant, an African hairdresser, a Vietnamese chemist. Around the corner there used to be an adult video store next door to a halal butcher and an optometrist.

The manager and the warehouse man lean over the salesman, who is holding an open newspaper. Reading this particular paper is a sign of cultural belonging and a protection against the hostile world outside. 'Look at this', the salesman says, referring to the sentiments expressed on their favourite columnist's page. 'The government says no to racism, but yes to free speech.'

The manager knows all about this freedom of speech. In his previous life some soldiers once caught him speaking his own language to another man. The two men were made to kneel down and stick out their tongues, while the soldiers – young boys, really – wielded sickles to inflict a medieval punishment. The men begged their way out, but the manager will never forget such terrorism. Luckily, that kind of thing doesn't happen in this country. They've all come here for safety.

In his younger days, the warehouse man once saw a truck that was loaded with starved bodies on their way to burial. 'Some of their limbs were still moving!' he said, shaking his head. They vote for the party that will give each man and his family a sense of security.

The proposed amendments to the Racial Discrimination Act say that whether something racially

The reasonable man

vilifies or intimidates will not be determined 'by the standards of any particular group within the Australian community'. This neighbourhood is a place where 'no particular group' resides, so maybe these lunchroom guys are the 'ordinary reasonable members of the Australian community' on whose views this judgment will be based. I certainly hope so, because one of them is my father.

The people in my father's shop have come from places like the former Yugoslavia, the south of Italy, Vietnam, Cambodia and India, and they have escaped communism, socialism, ethnic cleansing, anti-Semitism, war and hunger. They see themselves as real men, not wusses with easily 'hurt feelings'. They know that one day the talk will come back to them again. How they should not be in this country if they are ungrateful. How they should not be here if they continue to speak their own language, if they don't assimilate.

These guys may have to look up the word 'bigot' in a dictionary, yet they understand racism on a visceral level. In their sixth or seventh decade of life, they sigh and know nothing has changed about human nature or racism but at least laws in Australia protect them from getting killed or bashed.

'Australian newspapers are not like the ones back home', Dad tells me. 'They would never publish anything untrue.' These men know they'll never be in the paper unless they do something dodgy, and that's fine. Their hope is for their kids to be better educated and to have a voice.

My university studies and legal work taught me how to engage in reasoned debate. Yet I take no comfort in the fact that I may belong in this 'reasonable member' group that determines standards, because the problem with my voice is this: I have never known what it is like to be denied housing or jobs because of my race, to be dragged away by soldiers in the middle of the night, to be forcibly separated from loved ones or have my land pilfered. If someone yells abuse at Salesman Charlie, Warehouse Jack or my dad, if someone clenches their fist at one of these guys because of their skin or language or food, these men think there will be a knock on the door, their houses will be burnt down, their tongues cut off, bodies carted away in trucks, accented sons bashed up in the street.

The sort of fear that exists in their minds might lead a more 'reasonable' person to wonder: *Why are you carrying on like Armageddon will come? Why can't you form a decent coherent sentence? You can't even let go of past grievances and move on, you behave irrationally, and for crying out loud, speak English on a bus!*

Under the proposed amendments, these reactive, inarticulate, overly emotional 'feeling' types will suddenly not be reasonable persons by any stretch of the law. Fear is not an abstract thing debated by politicians. These folks see fear where no one else does: in public transport inspectors even though you bought a train ticket, in realising you have too many soccer mates walking down the street at the same time because you're all black, in always having a light on in the house even when you sleep.

If my dad and his mates stick up for one another when they feel vilified or intimidated, will they be regarded as 'sticking up for their own', considering that their neighbourhood is often written up in the media as an 'ethnic' enclave?

Imagine if you, reasonable reader, had been assigned the task of burying the bodies of your starved loved ones in a mass grave – as my dad had to do when Pol Pot's bigotry directly led to the deaths of half our extended family in Cambodia – and you might want to consider whether it is wise to give those with the loudest media voices the right and liberty to be 'bigots'.

It is 12.40 and lunch is ending. 'Of course we're reasonable', my father concludes, and the lunchroom supports him. These folk have more faith and trust in Australian democracy and the media than any flag-waving patriot. 'Of course they're going to judge it by the ordinary individual, and not the terrorist extremist or the sort that has their head stuck in books.'

***

A version of this essay was first published in *The Monthly*, May 2014.

4
CASUAL RACISM AND BIGOTRY
THE MANY FACES OF PREJUDICE AND DISCRIMINATION

People often ask how they should respond when confronted with a racist incident. Imagine being in a train carriage when a fellow passenger has started abusing another passenger because of their race. Or imagine being in a shop when a fellow customer has just been refused service because of their ethnicity. What should you do? Maybe more to the point, what would you do?

We all like to think that we would not tolerate such conduct, that we would readily intervene. There appears to be an encouraging trend of people taking a stand. For example, when Karen Bailey launched into her notorious racist, expletive-ridden rant on a crowded Sydney train in July 2014, other passengers were quick to express their disapproval. Only a few weeks later, when a café owner in Sydney's Darlinghurst declined to hire a Brazilian barista because he was black, the confrontation prompted customers present to walk out (the café would shortly after close its doors, in part because customers were not returning). While such responses indicate that racism can be met with public resistance, we cannot take this for granted. There exists a significant body of psychological research that illustrates the so-called bystander effect.[1] Faced with situations where strangers are put in harm's way, people may not always respond to help, particularly when others are present. In the case of racism, bystander behaviour may not be as forthcoming as we would hope.

Such a phenomenon can be understandable. People may be reluctant to become involved, especially in situations that could include physical danger. But should this kind of reluctance occur when there is no threat of imminent violence? How should we respond to 'low-level' incidents of casual racism and bigotry? And how should we understand the connection between casual prejudice and contemporary racism at large?

Recognising casual racism involves one of the generational challenges in combating discrimination today. Contemporary racism is not always based on earlier notions of racial superiority, nor is it always expressed through physical violence. Yet it is not divorced from such forms, either. Where low-level forms of racism are tolerated, or given tacit endorsement, they can quickly escalate to higher forms.

One of the obstacles in dealing with casual racism is the tendency to downplay or dismiss it: people can explain it away as playful humour, or to believe that an intervention may not be worth the price. Few would like to be regarded as politically correct killjoys. This highlights another difficulty, that of finding ways to question people's behaviour without foreclosing the possibility of changing their attitudes.

It is also important to put casual prejudice into context. We should not ignore the persistence of structural discrimination and unconscious bias. In addition, any understanding of contemporary racism requires a nuanced understanding of the relationship between race and religion. Religious differences can sometimes be conflated with racial ones. As demonstrated by forms of bigotry directed at Muslims, there can be ambiguity about the difference between race and religion. But whatever form racial prejudice and discrimination take, an educational response remains paramount.

CASUAL RACISM

The historian John Hirst has described Australia as a democracy of manners – we treat each other as social equals.[2] We are certainly informal and familiar in our manners. We sit in the front seat with a taxi driver; we like to call strangers by their first names. We also

Casual racism and bigotry

like to let rip with robust banter. Our raillery and our talent for levelling are expressions of our distinctive egalitarianism.

There are times when such tendencies can assume less exalted forms. Just as our egalitarianism is primarily a cultural trait, so racism is expressed primarily in cultural form. The phenomenon of racism is not about explicit rules of exclusion or discrimination (though institutional dimensions remain). For the most part, it resides in social encounters. As others have described it, when it comes to race in Australia, the problem may be that we have a high level of low-level intolerance – a significant level of casual racism.[3]

To say that something is casual can denote a number of things. We speak of people having a casual job. We speak of casual dress. We speak of a casual remark and of casual observers. These various meanings also apply to casual expressions of racism. You need not be someone who advocates violence or noxious doctrine to do something with racist implications. A racist remark or act can be made or done without thought or premeditation. It can happen by chance. The effects of racist speech or discrimination do not depend on someone being a dedicated full-time bigot.

In this sense, casual racism refers to conduct involving negative stereotypes or prejudices about people on the basis of colour, ethnicity or national origin. Often, it can involve jokes or comments that

I'm not racist but ...

rehearse racist tropes. Alan Joyce, the Irish-born chief executive of Qantas, has remarked on his annoyance with people who label him as an Irish 'leprechaun', lamenting that such 'racism seems to be in some way acceptable'.[4] Another foreign-born corporate leader, former Telstra chief executive Sol Trujillo, appeared to have experienced something similar. Few seemed to understand why he took umbrage at being caricatured in the press as a sombrero-wearing Mexican or being described as one of the 'three amigos' running his company. Many thought Trujillo had overreacted in 2009 when he described then prime minister Kevin Rudd's reaction to his resignation from Telstra as racist. (Rudd had offered a one-word response: 'Adios'.)[5]

Such incomprehension seems characteristic of casual racism. In 2009, for example, the now defunct television show *Hey Hey It's Saturday* aired a sketch in which five men impersonated the Jackson Five. The men appeared in golliwog wigs and in 'blackface' make-up. They were joined by another performer, with face painted white, pretending to be Michael Jackson. Members of the group were blithely unaware of their sketch's racist implications – namely, its homage to American minstrel shows that had typically lampooned black people during the 19th and early 20th centuries. When American singer Harry Connick Jr, a guest on the program, objected to the performance, members of the group stressed that

Casual racism and bigotry

they had 'not meant to be racist in any way at all' and that Connick Jr had been 'taking it the wrong way'. For Connick Jr, the matter was more grave: 'Man, if they turned up looking like that in the United States, it'd be hey hey there's no more show.'[6]

More recently, during a segment on breakfast radio in 2013, Collingwood Football Club president Eddie McGuire entangled himself in a controversy involving player Adam Goodes. Only a few days earlier, Goodes had been racially slurred as 'an ape' by a young Collingwood fan. Commenting on an inflatable gorilla that was being used to promote the musical production of 'King Kong' in Melbourne, McGuire suggested, 'Get Adam Goodes down for it, you reckon?' McGuire would later apologise, but he denied 'racially vilifying anybody', adding that any association with racism 'burns me to the core'. Observing the episode, the BBC's then Australian correspondent Nick Bryant wrote, 'it felt like a return to the bad old days of *The Bulletin* in the early 1960s when "Abo" jokes were a staple of the cartoon page'.[7]

The term casual racism enjoys considerable currency in light of such episodes, but its usage is also contested. On the one hand, some question whether it should be counted as 'really' racism at all. According to journalist Mark Sawyer, it is 'frankly crazy to label people racist on the basis of one or two remarks'. Instead, 'it may pay to look at the bigger picture'. Racism should be a term limited to describing the ideas of people who believe in the supremacy of their race. Those who engage in casual racism are only guilty of momentary lapses: 'people can say racist things because they are afflicted, temporarily or permanently, with stupidity, but that doesn't make them a racist'. After all, the argument runs, we live in an era when there are no bad people, only bad acts.[8]

On the other hand, some question whether the nomenclature of 'casual' goes far enough. It is said that referring to racist language or racist incidents as casual can trivialise the issue. There is nothing casual, it is argued, about racism – whether in importance or even in regularity. It would be better for us to refer to 'everyday' racism. Using 'everyday' instead of 'casual' better captures the forms of subtle prejudice and discrimination that people may regard as normal in daily interactions.[9]

No term will ever perfectly capture a social phenomenon. But it is important that we acknowledge casual racism as a distinct category. In the first place, it is simply erroneous to believe that racism only truly existed in the past, or is confined only to those intent on spreading hatred and perpetrating violence. Perhaps only someone who is insulated from discrimination or disadvantage would claim that racism no longer exists in any meaningful way.

Displacing the terminology of casual racism with everyday racism, meanwhile, runs the risk of confusing two aspects of prejudice. Everyday racism may be concerned with the sorts of interactions people have on a daily basis, but the description of 'casual' seems to refer to forms of racism that are defined by ignorance and insensitivity. Put another way, everyday racism appears to refer more to the *settings* in which racism can occur, while casual racism refers more to the *manner* in which discrimination is expressed. It is wrong to suggest that the two exist on the same plane. To use a sporting analogy, it is a bit like conflating the surface of tennis courts (grass or hardcourt) with a style of play in tennis (baseline or serve-volley).

That we are talking about two different aspects of contemporary racism becomes clearer with the facts. Consider the recent findings of the 2014 Scanlon Foundation survey on social cohesion in Australia. The survey found that 18 per cent of respondents reported they had experienced racial or religious discrimination during the past 12 months. Among other things, the survey identified the locations where people experienced racial or religious discrimination. The largest proportion (58 per cent) indicated they experienced this in their neighbourhood. Forty-two per cent said they had experienced discrimination in a shopping centre, with 39 per cent indicating they had experienced it at a place of work.[10]

This highlights one respect in which racism can be 'everyday' in nature. It can occur in those places where people go about their ordinary affairs as a member of society. Yet the findings of the Scanlon survey also point to reasons why everyday racism should not displace casual racism as a category. Because describing something as being of an everyday nature fundamentally implies an everyday frequency. To suggest that casual racism is better described as everyday racism, in this sense, would be fundamentally inaccurate.

There are, it must be noted, some groups that experience racism with alarming regularity – in particular, Aboriginal and Torres Strait Islander people. Research commissioned by the Lowitja Institute showed that among Aboriginal and Torres Strait Islander people surveyed, 97 per cent had experienced racism during the previous year. This included being called racist names (92 per cent), being physically assaulted because of their race (67 per cent) and having property vandalised because of their race (54 per cent). More than 70 per cent of those surveyed experienced eight or more instances of racism in the past twelve months.[11]

Such regular experience of racism is not the case for most. According to the Scanlon findings, of those who reported discrimination, the largest proportion, 47 per cent, indicated that it occurred infrequently, 'just once or twice in the last year'. Twenty-two per cent indicated they experienced it 'three to six times in the last year'. By contrast, 14 per cent indicated that discrimination occurred 'about once a month in the last year', while 15 per cent indicated that it occurred 'often – most weeks in the year'.[12] In other words, the majority of those who experience racism in Australia appear *not* to experience it with everyday frequency. Describing something as casual racism is accurate in conveying not just the demeanour of those who express it, but to a large extent the frequency with which it is experienced.

There is nothing inherent in this observation that diminishes racism's importance, or that trivialises the harms it causes. It may not rank as the most severe form of racial discrimination conceivable, but the harm of casual racism can be corrosive. Passing off bigotry as jokes can give permission for intolerance. It can make racial stereotypes more easily accepted. It can embolden bigots, while desensitising people to the degradation of others. Seemingly innocuous forms of racial prejudice can, over time, grow into voracious hate. As journalist Julia Baird has written, while reflecting on the 70th anniversary of the Holocaust and the recent rise of anti-Semitism across Europe and in Australia, 'we must not forget that the greatest of crimes begin with slurs, hatred and common prejudices that are not quashed'.[13]

Escalation is a particular problem with casual racism, which is often accompanied by levity. Toleration of casual racism allows people to justify bigotry on the basis that they are just having a laugh. We have all heard the refrains before: Why can't you just take a joke? Why are you making such a fuss? Isn't it part of the Aussie sensibility not to take yourself too seriously? But for those on the receiving end of casual racism, the feeling can be far from funny. And it is not just about hurt feelings. It is all about exclusion. The things we say and the things we do matter: they define who belongs and who does not. Intolerance and incivility sow seeds of unease and distrust, which we should never allow to take root.

STRUCTURAL RACISM AND MEDIA

Casual racism does not exhaust the entire field of contemporary racism. Racism resides not only in social interactions, but also in society's institutions. It may be there in the systems and rules, written and unwritten, which govern what is normal and what is deviant. As I explore in chapter 5, such systems and rules may have the effect of placing some groups at a disadvantage and others in a privileged position.[14]

Such structural forms of racism can be covert and go unrecognised. They can exist in the economy, in schools, in hospitals, in the justice system, in government. There is one setting, though, that warrants our particular attention: the media. The media occupies a special position in filtering our civic sentiments. It is through media, to a large extent, that a society projects its identity. If we wish to eliminate racial discrimination, our prospects would be improved if we could do that work through our media.

Casual racism and bigotry

Ordinarily, we might expect that the task is already half-accomplished. In so many other respects Australian multiculturalism has been an exemplar. Where social cohesion or economic participation are concerned, Australia does remarkably well. Our national life is not blighted by the periodic racial rioting and ethnic disturbances that characterise life in some other countries. The children of migrants outperform those of native-born Australians in education and employment.[15]

Yet when it comes to our media – especially our television screens – such multicultural success is not replicated. In some cases, it might even be said that racism, at least of the casual variety, appears to thrive. Channel Nine's AFL *The Footy Show* is one regular offender, particularly in the form of its long-time presenter Sam Newman. In one show in 2009, Newman hosted a segment in which he commented on the wedding of a 107-year-old woman in Malaysia: 'What sort of monkey would be marrying that woman?' Reflecting on the groom and brandishing a picture of him, Newman added, 'That man is not long out of the forest.' The NRL version of *The Footy Show* also has had its moments. For many years, it featured a sketch character called 'Mahatma Cote', a Punjabi Sikh commentator for the fictional 'National Naan News'. Former Test cricketer Greg Ritchie was the real man behind Cote: to play the part, he wore brown make-up, donned a blue turban, and spoke with a pronounced Indian accent.

These are arguably minor infractions compared to some of commercial television's news and current affairs programs. For example, Channel Nine's *A Current Affair* earned a formal rebuke from the Australian Communications and Media Authority for breaching its code when, in 2012, it aired its notorious 'Asian Mall' story. Labelling a shopping centre in Sydney's Castle Hill, 'the Great Mall of China', the program had inaccurately claimed that Asian businesses were displacing 'Australian' shop owners. The report featured concerned citizens speaking about an 'Asian invasion'. The program's former Channel Seven rival, *Today Tonight*, was similarly notorious for frequently raising fears about unassimilable Asians and threatening yellow hordes from Asia. In 2012, the program even sent Pauline Hanson on a mission to Southeast Asia to expose a black market in duplicating Australian passports that was purported to be putting Australian border security in danger.[16]

Any structural racism in the media goes beyond a relaxed tolerance for casual racism and ethnic stereotyping in sport and tabloid current affairs. It is reflected as well in the lack of cultural diversity on screen. On this count, Australia fares somewhat poorly when compared to similar English-speaking societies. In Britain, for example, journalists from ethnic minority backgrounds have fronted the major news bulletins for decades: figures such as Trevor

McDonald, George Alagiah and Krishna Gurumuthy have been senior newsreaders on ITV, BBC and Channel Four. Here, such equivalent prominence or seniority for journalists of non-Anglo background has arguably been rare. In one interview in 2013, Stan Grant, one of the few Indigenous journalists on commercial television, lamented how during the past 20 years the ABC has not succeeded in sending one Indigenous journalist overseas as a foreign correspondent.[17] The same criticism could be levelled with respect to non-Anglo journalists more generally. We see few Australians of non-European background reading the news, particularly on commercial channels.

This has been the case in other forms of programming, too. While there are admittedly some non-European faces on television, they seem largely to be confined to being exotic adornments – whether as presenters of programs about the delightful sophistication of modern Australian fusion cuisine, or as plucky contestants in cooking shows such as *MasterChef*. Few non-Anglo faces intrude upon spheres such as sport, that definitive domain of mainstream Australia: think of those commentators of the cricket, AFL, rugby league, rugby union, tennis, or swimming. (Soccer seems to be the notable exception.)

The realm of dramatic entertainment is especially egregious. Actors from minority backgrounds periodically emerge with scathing criticisms about a 'White

Australia' policy in Australian television.[18] Where minority actors are cast to play roles on television dramas they are often consigned to play stereotypical roles as drug dealers, criminals or otherwise shady characters. The numbers tell the story. The popular Channel Ten drama *Wonderland*, for example, features a cast of nine main characters – all white (although one is played by an actress who is part-Chinese). Other popular dramas are similar in composition. Perennial soapie *Home and Away* currently has a cast list of 27, which includes only three with non-English surnames (Nicodemou, Giovinazzo, Hara). *Neighbours* is even more conspicuous in having as its sole cast member of non-Anglo background Indigenous actor Meyne Wyatt.

It was only in 2012, of course, that *Neighbours* attracted plaudits for the arrival of the Kapoor family to Ramsay Street. Local lawyer Ajay, his school principal wife Priya and their daughter Rani were to become permanent fixtures marking fictional Erinsborough's entry into 21st-century multicultural Australia. But the Indian-Australian family lasted only a year, before being written out of the show (writers sent the family back to India, despite the family members being born, educated and raised in Australia). The fate of the Kapoors was similar to the two 'ethnic' Chinese and Italian families who were but transient lodgers on Ramsay Street. For whatever reason, neither the Lims nor the Cammenitis –

or indeed, the Kapoors – enjoyed the same staying power as the Robinsons and the Kennedys.

Such patterns are sometimes explained away as merely an expression of the television viewing market. It is said that Australian audiences may turn off from diversity, that they are not ready to see more colour on their television screens. This is a difficult view to sustain, given how accepting Australian society is with the reality of multiculturalism. Some recent studies in the United States have shown that television viewers are more likely to watch shows that have racially diverse casts and writers.[19] If we can accept cultural diversity in just about every aspect of our life, why not also in television?

In all this, there is an element of what has been described as colourblind dominance. This is a form of structural racism, in which there are proclamations of robust anti-racism accompanied by failures to improve the status quo.[20] Thus, in response to criticisms about a lack of non-white faces on Australian television, one producer quoted in a media report maintained that there was no agenda to exclude people of certain backgrounds. 'I respect the opinion of people who say we should reflect a wide ethnic cast but we can't go out and search for specific people', according to this producer. As he further explained, 'we are accused of racism but to do it another way would be equally racist'.[21]

One thing should be made clear about structural

racism. To say that racism exists within certain institutions is not to say that all those who work in such institutions are consciously seeking to discriminate against people. The point is not about apportioning individual blame. It is about recognising that race cannot be understood without acknowledging power, and that a conscious effort to boost diversity may be required. Here, it is worth reflecting on some of the initiatives being undertaken in Britain in improving ethnic and racial diversity on television. The director-general of the British Broadcasting Corporation Tony Hall has pledged that one in seven presenters and actors are to be black, Asian or minority ethnic within the next three years.[22] BBC's news boss, James Harding, has also commented on the need to increase ethnic minorities on-screen as a result of biases that, he feels, manifest in a tendency to recruit in our own image.[23] It is hard to say with confidence that we are having such conversations in Australia.

LEADERSHIP AND UNCONSCIOUS BIAS

Barriers to equal opportunity may also exist with respect to leadership positions, in the form of a 'cultural ceiling'. Not everyone accepts that such barriers exist. It is said that we live in an egalitarian, meritocratic society. Some will respond by highlighting examples of Australians from minority cultural back-

Casual racism and bigotry

grounds who have succeeded as leaders in public life or business: the fact that such individuals have made it to the top should be ready proof that racism does not exist, at least not in a way that cripples opportunity. Other responses are more dismissive: if people of certain backgrounds are not represented in leadership positions, it is because they may not aspire to them; they may be more comfortable avoiding the pressures and prominence that come with being a leader.

However one explains things away, the facts are unambiguous. Nearly 50 per cent of our population was either born overseas or has a parent who was born overseas. About 20 per cent speaks a language other than English at home. While it is difficult to offer a precise total figure of Australians who have non-European ancestry, the number is significant. It is estimated, for example, that close to 10 per cent of the Australian population has Asian cultural origins or ancestry.[24] But such diversity is far from proportionately represented when it comes to positions of leadership in both the public and private sectors.

Consider the current 44th Federal Parliament, where there are fewer than 10 MPs and senators who appear to have non-European cultural origin or ancestry, out of a total of 226 combined members of the Senate and House of Representatives (about 4 per cent). This is mirrored in the composition of leaders in the Australian public service. Of the

I'm not racist but ...

17 heads of federal government departments, there is only one who is of non-European cultural origin. It is interesting to study the names of current departmental secretaries: Moraitis, Glyde, Clarke, Richardson, Paul, Leon, Halton, Varghese, Bowles, Campbell, Pezzullo, Beauchamp, Mrdak, Pratt, de Brouwer, Thawley, Lewis, Fraser. An audit of Australia's business leaders in the ASX 200 companies, conducted by Diversity Council Australia in 2013, found among other things a very low representation of leaders with non-European background: only 1.9 per cent of executive managers and 5 per cent of directors has a non-European cultural origin.[25]

There is evidence to suggest racial discrimination could be a contributing factor. In 2010, economists at the Australian National University found substantial racial discrimination in hiring by Australian employers.[26] The researchers sent more than 4000 fake job applications for entry-level jobs. The applications contained the same qualifications but with different names, distinguished by their ethnic origin. The researchers found that in order to get as many interviews as an applicant with an Anglo-Saxon name, someone with a Chinese name needed to submit 68 per cent more applications. Those with a Middle Eastern name would need 64 per cent more. By comparison, those with an Italian name needed to put in 12 per cent more applications.

While such discrimination concerns entry into

employment rather than professional advancement, its presence does raise important questions about the under-representation of diversity in leadership positions. Could it be that unconscious bias may contribute in some way to the pattern of representation for Australians of non-European backgrounds in the ranks of leadership? Such forms of bias refer to those associations that are activated without us being aware. As social psychologists have demonstrated, we all make implicit assumptions – including about ethnic or racial groups – even if we consciously think that we reject a group stereotype.[27]

It may be the case, for instance, that unconscious bias shapes perceptions of Australians of Asian background, particularly their suitability for positions of leadership (an example worth considering, given that Asian-Australians are generally regarded as examples of successful migrant integration in employment). To draw upon one encounter I had recently, someone newly introduced to me asked what I did for work. When I responded that I worked at the Australian Human Rights Commission, my new friend then asked: 'So, do you work in the Finance section or IT section at the Commission?' It was an innocent question, to which I responded by explaining my responsibility for matters concerning racial discrimination. But the question, asked with every good intention, was one that revealed some of the assumptions my new acquaintance had about what someone who looked like me was likely to have as an occupation.

There remains the dominant 'model minority' stereotype of Asians: the law-abiding, hard-working family with studious and obedient children. So far as stereotypes go, this appears benign enough. Yet the model minority stereotype may also belie a more negative stereotype, especially when it applies to a context of leadership. What one perspective may regard as the laudable qualities of being inoffensive, diligent and productive can, from another perspective, sound a lot like passivity, acquiescence and subservience. Western culture has long entertained the trope of the invisible, inoffensive and submissive Asian – whether it is the obsequious Charlie Chan, the unassuming Mister Miyagi, or, more recently, the meek-mannered Jackie Chan. As these examples in Western culture illustrate, even when the Asian may defy the expectations of his counterparts who underestimate his abilities, he never seeks to challenge the status quo.[28]

In the realm of professional employment, such cultural images or associations may contribute to certain biases and assumptions. Based on their recent research study on 'Asian talent' in the corporate world, Diversity Council Australia found that only 18 per cent of Asian background workers surveyed felt their workplaces were free of biases and stereotypes about culture. About 61 per cent reported feeling pressure to conform to 'Anglo' styles of leadership, emphasising

Casual racism and bigotry

self-promotion.[29] This is corroborated by one corporate leader, Ken Woo, a partner at accounting firm PricewaterhouseCoopers (PwC), who has observed a paralysing cycle of bias and behaviour. In his experience, Woo has observed that Asian members of his team have exhibited patterns of behaviour including a healthy respect for elders, a directness in performing tasks and a commitment to working harder than others.[30]

On the face of it, these would appear to be commendable traits. But when placed in the context of unconscious bias and cultural stereotypes, they may actually prompt others to make unfavourable observations and assessments. A respect for elders may appear to others like unwillingness on the part of an employee to challenge authority, and an assessment that the employee lacks leadership potential. Being direct in one's manner may lead others to observe abruptness or rudeness, and conclude there is a lack of social awareness. Resolving to work harder in the face of adversity may lead others to observe an employee who is buried in the detail and who may lack a certain perspective.[31]

How then are we to respond to unconscious bias? Clearly, bias can undermine an ideal of merit. Our understandable instinct may be to reaffirm merit as the sole criterion for reward and advancement in the workplace. The very notion of merit, though, is complex. Sometimes invoking it can even get in the way of a constructive conversation about unconscious bias. For instance, some argue that introducing targets or quotas to ensure better representation of minorities may have the counter-productive effect of weakening meritocracy. Yet the conditions of a truly level playing field are rarely ever met. Judgments about potential and performance, and decisions about hiring and promotion, are invariably coloured by cultural perceptions of merit. Such ideas can influence decision-making in favour of some groups over others, without people being aware.[32]

Australians of minority cultural backgrounds, in one sense, appear to have been the great beneficiaries of egalitarian meritocracy. But we should be vigilant of some potential dangers. We must avoid a situation where unconscious bias is mindlessly reproduced. What we must avoid is a situation where we end up creating, without intending to do so, a class of professional multicultural coolies in the 21st century. It would be neither just nor good to have a country where people may comfortably believe that a class of well-educated Australians of non-European background are perfectly content to remain in the background, perennially invisible and permanently locked out from the ranks of their society's leadership.

RELIGIOUS BIGOTRY

There is another dimension to contemporary prejudice and discrimination in Australia: that concerning religious bigotry. It is true that a distinction can be made between race and religion. Race refers to immutable qualities of a person or group, while religion concerns doctrinal beliefs that govern how a person, or group, lead their lives. To be sure, such a distinction has its limits: many would dispute the implication that their religion is 'chosen' and would say that it is integral to their identity. But the distinction between race and religion is one that is effectively applied in federal law. The Racial Discrimination Act is concerned only with race. As the RDA currently operates, any complaint about discrimination or vilification on the grounds of religion falls outside the scope of the law. Racial discrimination laws may come into play only when conduct relates to race, ethnicity or national origin.

There are occasions when race and religion appear to merge. This is most obvious in the case of 'ethno-religious' groups, those whose identity involves both ethnic and religious components. For example, anti-Semitism has generally been regarded as racist for this reason: Jews can be considered as both an ethnic group and a religious group. In his historical survey of race, the American scholar George M Frederickson in fact argues that the prototypical forms of modern racism can be found in the discriminatory treatment and persecution of *conversos*, Jewish converts to Christianity in 15th and 16th century Spain.[33] In the case of other religious groups, by contrast, it makes little sense to suggest that religious bigotry may also contain traces of racism. We may frown upon bigotry against Christians or Buddhists, but it would be inaccurate to describe it as racist, given that members of those faiths come from different racial backgrounds and do not share a common ancestry.

There is one category of religious bigotry, however, that warrants closer attention: namely, the anti-Muslim sentiment that has recently intensified amid community anxiety about the threat of terrorism. Since the raising of Australia's official terror alert to 'high' in August 2014, there have been reports of mosques being defaced and of Muslim Australians being abused or threatened in public places. In September 2014, the presiding officers of Parliament took the dramatic step of confining those wearing the burqa or niqab to a sealed section in the public galleries of the House of Representatives and the Senate (a ruling later reversed, but widely criticised for treating Muslim Australians as second-class citizens in their own Parliament).[34] Other forms of anti-Muslim sentiment have recently emerged, such as that focused on halal certification of food. Anti-halal campaigners have targeted food businesses that comply with Islamic dietary standards, suggesting that fees paid

Casual racism and bigotry

for halal certification are used to fund Islamist terrorism.[35]

Such forms of anti-Muslim sentiment should have no place in our society. As a basic proposition, every person should be free to live their lives, without being harassed, intimidated or discriminated against because of their religion. The overwhelming majority of Muslim Australians are law-abiding and loyal Australian citizens who should not be tarred by the brush of prejudice. We can all condemn acts of terrorism – as in the case of Man Haron Monis and his murderous siege in Sydney in December 2014 – but we should not be judging entire communities on the basis of a small minority of fanatical extremists. Muslim community leaders have consistently condemned extremism and assisted authorities in countering domestic radicalism (some privately express disappointment that the media do not report their regular condemnations of extremism and radicalism).[36] As citizens and residents, Muslims should also enjoy a right to practise their religion freely within the limits of the law. In the case of the short-lived burqa-niqab ban in Parliament, there was no compelling reason given for such a prohibition. There was no formal basis for concluding that the wearing of a burqa or niqab represented an additional security risk that could not be dealt with by existing screening protocols.

As for ongoing campaigns against halal, they illustrate that some sections of the community are seeking to stimulate fear and division through anti-Islamic bullying. Any suggestion that halal certification fees are proceeds to terrorism is, to date, unfounded. Australia has laws that forbid people and organisations from funding illegal activity such as terrorism – halal certification organisations are in no way immune. Halal labelling is itself primarily focused on hygiene and ingredients: on ensuring, for instance, that ingredients are free from pork and that machinery involved in making food has not been cleaned with alcohol.[37] Most halal slaughter in Australia is also consistent with standards of animal welfare. According to the RSPCA, the vast majority of halal slaughter in Australia complies with the national standard requiring that all animals be stunned unconscious prior to slaughter.[38] Those who are alarmed by some of the claims made by anti-halal campaigners should be reassured by the facts.

Returning to the bigger picture, it is not only the rise of anti-Muslim sentiment that is concerning, but also the manner in which it is framed. Many of those airing anti-Muslim bigotry justify their views by saying that Islam is a religion, and not a race or ethnicity. They argue that any charge of racism is misplaced. And yet there can sometimes be a racial undertone to anti-Muslim feeling. Verbal and other attacks against Muslim Australians often involve racialised sentiments. When it concerns Muslims and Islam, the negative stereotypes are directed

Casual racism and bigotry

particularly at people who come from the Middle East. This stereotype emphasises a supposed incompatibility of Muslim practices with an Australian way of life – but frequently it also takes on a racial tinge.

Take some of the recent commentary about the suburb of Lakemba, which is home to some of Sydney's Muslim communities. One newspaper in August 2014 featured a two-page spread about the suburb titled, 'Inside Sydney's Muslim Land'. The article led with the statement that the correspondent had spent 24 hours in a place 'where a pervasive monoculture has erased the traditional Aussie way of life'. In the piece itself, the correspondent would observe that the suburb had an ethnic mix 'similar to what you'd find in any Arabic city'.[39] In the space of a few sentences, then, we see 'Muslim' being defined as 'Arab'. We see religion quickly expanding into something more cultural, ethnic, and arguably racial.

It is in this sense that anti-Muslim sentiment can involve racialised cultural hostility. Anyone who may look like a Muslim will be presumed to be a bearer of a certain culture that is incompatible with Australian culture. But what determines whether someone looks like they are Muslim will necessarily draw upon race and ethnicity. Not everyone will be necessarily aware of, say, the difference between a Lebanese-Australian Muslim or an Egyptian-Australian Coptic. To those who may rehearse negative stereotypes about Muslims, such distinctions may not be obvious.

CIVILITY AND TOLERANCE

In the many conversations I have about race, there is a familiar note on which people conclude: 'We need more education; if only we had more education.' On matters of human rights and social justice, so much rests on education and the changing of attitudes. Writing in 1979 as Community Relations Commissioner, Al Grassby described it as 'the supreme challenge in combating racial discrimination'. Since the school was 'the only place where all Australians come together at some time in their lives', it would be 'in the classrooms of the nation that the battle for tolerance will ultimately be won'.[40]

There is an undoubtedly fundamental role for schools to play in educating children about racial discrimination. This can be done through subjects such as history and civics, as well as through subjects such as physical education (since racism has implications for personal health). But any education must involve more than just knowledge. It should not be confined to the classroom and should extend to adults as well as schoolchildren; it must also go beyond formal instruction and involve equipping its beneficiaries for action. As noted earlier, one of the obstacles in combating racism is that of bystander complacency. This is one reason why the Australian Human Rights Commission's 'Racism. It Stops with Me' awareness campaign has emphasised the importance of people doing something whenever they witness a racist incident: if not making a direct intervention, then reporting an incident or providing support to a target of racism. When bystanders speak out against racism, it can have profound effects, since those who racially abuse others tend to believe that their attitudes are shared by those around them. Bystander action prevents the person committing an act of abuse from thinking that the community accepts their behaviour.[41]

Underpinning such preparedness to act are certain qualities. Obviously, the good citizen is one who is prepared to fulfil their duties and show solidarity with others. More than this, they are capable of making sound judgments. They are able to think for themselves, have the confidence to hold their ground, and possess the moral imagination required to put themselves in the position of others.

These qualities in turn point to certain virtues that an ideal citizen should possess. A mind open to inquiry points to a civic virtue of tolerance. The tolerant citizen is someone who can regard other citizens – specifically those with different social values, cultural identities, religious commitments or philosophical beliefs – as reasonable people who are worthy of respect and equal treatment. At the same time, tolerance need not mean total indifference or moral relativism. Leaving open the possibility of empathy towards those people with whom we disagree does

I'm not racist but ...

not mean that someone should renounce their own values. What tolerance implies is a particular way of reconciling moral disagreement: we should seek to educate others and persuade them of our position, rather than coerce them to accept it.

Some have reservations about tolerance. On many occasions, community representatives have stressed to me that they are uncomfortable with the idea that their cultural identities are merely 'tolerated' by the rest of Australian society. Such misgivings have a point. The word tolerance has its roots in the Latin *tolerare* – which means to have endured. To tolerate something plainly means to put up with it, such as when we put up with something that is wrong or that we do not especially like. We tolerate annoying behaviour from strangers on buses and trains; we tolerate the bad habits of our family and friends. But if used in the sense of racial tolerance, it may fairly be asked whether this implies a standard that is not demanding enough. Tolerance can, after all, imply that a person's race or culture is somehow wrong or distasteful, but must be endured. Even so, it makes little sense to demand that we *must* offer wholehearted acceptance and endorsement of diversity. This is something that not everyone can genuinely grant to others. Being asked to tolerate diversity may be entirely appropriate, at least as a minimum.

There is, in any case, a distinction between tolerance and *toleration*. Historically speaking, toleration emerged in the 17th century as a response to religious conflict between Protestants and Catholics. In practice, it was defined by permission and co-existence. Toleration was about an authority or a majority group giving permission to a minority to live according to their beliefs, conditional on them accepting an authority or a majority's position of dominance. In other cases, toleration was pursued as a means of avoiding conflict between groups that were roughly equal in power – that is, toleration was pursued for the sake of peace.[42]

Tolerance is different as it is about respect and recognition. Where tolerance prevails, different parties – with different identities, cultural practices and ethical beliefs – recognise each other as moral and political equals. Such tolerance may also imply that the parties have a kind of esteem for each others' identities and beliefs: they recognise that these are held with good reasons, even if they differ from one's own.[43]

Implied in such a form of tolerance are a number of other virtues: fairness and civility. Where people take others as equals, they will abide by a standard of fairness, expressed in the rules that govern society and in the decorum that citizens adopt towards one another. That is to say, relations between citizens should be civil. Citizens can disagree with respect, and debate matters in good faith. Some matters may never find resolution, but parties should be prepared

I'm not racist but ...

to find common ground. In a multicultural setting, tolerance and civility call for a certain discipline. Not least, they demand that people refrain from discriminating on the grounds of race and that people desist from racial abuse and denigration.

While most of us would find such demands to be entirely reasonable, a small minority may argue that standards of tolerance and civility are just another way of smuggling so-called political correctness into our public life. Much is said about political correctness. Some regard the term as pejorative – as an attitude where one is inordinately concerned with not causing others offence to the point of being 'convulsed into censoriousness'.[44] But if political correctness does stifle debate, it does so in both directions. Those who make the charge that someone is being politically correct are doing just as much to foreclose debate as any alleged member of the 'PC police'. The mere suggestion that something is politically correct is often enough to silence people into acquiescence.

But why exactly must tolerance and civility be considered as censorship? To borrow the words of the British writer AA Gill, surely they stand for the proposition that, 'while respect is something that individuals have to earn, it's also something that groups and sections of society have a reasonable right to expect'. As Gill elaborates, these demands should be regarded as wholly uncontroversial:

Casual racism and bigotry

> How could you possibly find fault with wanting to put people at ease – being polite and not offering unintended offence? … It costs nothing more than the thought to change a word here and there, and the result is equally small but important. A term of address, an added politeness, doesn't get anyone a job or a better house or an education or a free lunch, but it does indicate that the user is aware of those other things and that you want them to be better. That you want those whom you address and talk about to be part of a pluralistic, accommodating, comfortable society.[45]

Tolerance and civility may, for some, involve stifling expressions of political correctness. For most of us, they add up to a modest price to pay for an Australian society that is relaxed and comfortable.

CALLING OUT CASUAL RACISM
MAXINE BENEBA CLARKE

I

When I'm handed my class participation mark for the second year law subject I'm dismayed, shocked by the 12 marks out of 20 my law lecturer has awarded me. The participation mark is worth 20 per cent of the entire course mark, based on class attendance and contribution to discussion. I've missed only one lecture and have been an active participant in discussions.

Less than a week later the only other black student in the class, a friend of mine, who's been ill and barely attended tutorials, mentions she was given 18.5 out of 20 for her class participation mark. We both agree on what's happened. All instinct – and extensive previous experience – tells me not to rock the boat.

Try as I might, the outrage refuses to dissipate. After the next class I wait for the professor outside the lecture hall. 'Hi, I'm wondering if you have a minute or so to chat.'

Calling out casual racism

'Yeah sure, no worries.'

'I'm Maxine. I'm in your Tuesday tutorial, and I'm wanting to speak to you about my class participation mark.'

'Oh?'

'Yes, well, umm, I was given a 12 out of 20, and I haven't really missed any classes, and I always participate in discussions ...'

'I mark the students off. In every class.' She looks at me as if I'm trying to pull a fast one.

'I know you do.'

She shuffles the papers she's carrying.

'Well. It's just that, um, another, um, student, who's, uhh ... been away quite a lot ... told me she got quite a high participation mark.' I mention the other student's name. 'I was wondering if maybe ...' I don't want to say it out loud, wanting her to suggest the error herself.

The lecturer stops adjusting her papers and looks up at me. I can see it slowly dawning on her what's happened, can tell that she's just realised she's been marking me off as the other student for the entire semester. I smile reassuringly, to try and show it's not a big deal, that I'd just like to get my real mark back and that's all I'm here for. Her face closes over in panic, shuts down like stone.

'I don't know what you're getting at,' she says, 'but if you wanted a better participation mark, you should have come to class more often, and participated more often.'

Before I can open my mouth, she's already started walking away.

II

Shortly after finishing my law degree, I undertook an internship with the New South Wales Anti-Discrimination Board, as one of two work placements to fulfil the requirements for my undergraduate law degree. In addition to drafting a set of plain English guidelines for the racial discrimination provisions of the New South Wales *Anti-Discrimination Act 1977*, I spent considerable time sitting in on face-to-face mediations, and with the team fielding initial phone inquiries.

This experience laid bare the brain of white middle-class Australia: jam-packed with prejudice, writhing with racism, steeped in denial.

I heard shocking reports of discrimination within the workplace and in other areas of public life. But in addition to these reports, there were many phone calls that evidenced just how misunderstood the general public was about what racism and discrimination actually entailed.

There was the Anglo-Australian man who phoned up to complain that his call-centre boss kept 'hiring Asians'.

'I'm ringing up to find out if there's anything you can do about it,' he said hopefully. An Anglo-

Australian father, concerned about his teenage daughter's Tongan boyfriend, phoned for advice on how he might officially intervene in the union.

'She was a good girl,' he kept saying. 'She's never given me any trouble. She has a university degree and everything. She was such a good girl.' You could hear his voice wavering as he shook his head in despair.

In face-to-face mediations, a vilified Indian school teacher of colour sat down to a 'good faith' mediation with a pair of highly experienced Education Department lawyers, and a sacked factory manager similarly sat down to talk with his ex-employer's expert legal counsel about the alleged discrimination he'd encountered. In both cases, the distressed complainants, on recounting their experiences, were met with denial and a barrage of intimidating legal jargon. On no occasion did I witness the alleged individual perpetrators of racist discrimination brought to direct account for racist behaviour, or asked to address their alleged actions in front of their complainants.

The internship was a largely defeating experience for an impending graduate majoring in Anti-Discrimination Law, but highly illuminative in understanding the behaviour I'd experienced frequently in my then 24 years of growing up in white, middle-class Australia, and the privileged, institutionalised power systems that continued – and continue – to underpin those behaviours.

I understood, more clearly, the defensiveness of

my law lecturer. I understood the baffled look on the face of my grade five teacher when I complained about another kid in the class consistently calling me Blackie.

'Well, that's what you are. You can call him Whitey if you like.' Her matter-of-fact reply suddenly made more sense.

The lack of understanding around the very concept of racism and discrimination amongst the general public that I encountered in my time at the Anti-Discrimination Board validated my ongoing reluctance to call out behaviour that was clearly racist. And it validated my attempts to avoid the further trauma of additional racism, continued denials or even genuine confusion, by completely disengaging with the perpetrator, at least in circumstances where it was possible to do so.

III

It's my first job-agency interview since finishing my law degree. I nervously approach the front desk. The interviewer is buzzed down to reception. When she arrives, looks me up and down quizzically.

'Oh. You're ... Maxine? I'm uhhh ... I'm really sorry I kept you waiting. I thought you must be here for someone else. I uhhh ... didn't think ... you didn't. You don't look like you sounded in the phone interview.' She laughs nervously, staring at my coffee-coloured complexion, short afro, smart black dress-suit and crisp white shirt as if she can't quite believe her eyes.

'Well, come on through and let's get started.' She motions for me to follow her.

Beyond the doorway of the legal recruitment firm is a smartly decorated open-plan office, circled by several plush interview rooms. The five or so staff working in the open area stare over at us as the woman ushers me into one of the interview offices.

'Take a seat.' She gestures to the armchair facing the window, taking the chair closest to the door. 'Did you bring your resume? I'm really sorry ... I mean, you get a certain image of someone in your mind when you interview them on the phone. It's silly, I know. Your English is just so ... so *good*.'

IV

In order to have a full and open discourse about racism in Australia we need to recognise racism and bigotry in all of its guises: beyond just the redneck ute driver hurling violent abuse as he screeches past; beyond the angry foul-mouthed woman on the tram whose antics have been uploaded as a YouTube spectacle.

We need to see it in the factory worker who does not want Chinese colleagues; in the father whose only criticism of his daughter's boyfriend is his ethnicity; in the academic who does not bother to tell the difference between students of similar ethnic backgrounds; and the interviewer stunned that a person of colour could speak English better than her. We need to dissect our preconceived assumptions about the class, ability, background, life experience, trustworthiness and capacity of people around us; to lay bare our deep-seated fears, and our shameful reservations.

Racism may be a fearful thing to tackle, but our silence is what allows that fearful thing to propagate.

5
EMPATHY AND PRIVILEGE
PUTTING YOURSELF IN ANOTHER'S SHOES

Walking together is one of our universal acts of affirmation. Whether it is a parade, march or rally, walking with others is a powerful demonstration of unity and commitment. In recent years, across the country, Australian anti-racism activists have organised annual walks for cultural diversity and harmony. The idea is based on a simple proposition: that people, from all backgrounds, can walk in solidarity. But before we can truly walk *with* someone we may first need to walk in their shoes. It is easy to do this when people share a lot in common. When we have little in common with someone, stepping into their shoes involves less of a step and more of a leap – an imaginative leap.

During the 1980s and 90s, one television show took on this premise in its most literal sense. The science fiction drama *Quantum Leap* enjoyed considerable

I'm not racist but ...

popularity; it remains a cult favourite. Episodes centred on the trials of the main protagonist Sam Beckett (played by actor Scott Bakula). Each week, Sam, a physicist who had been conducting a time-travel experiment, would fantastically *leap* into the past and into the body of another person. Sam would then have to right some wrong concerning that person, before leaping again: out of one body and into a new one.

Quantum Leap was more than just science fiction. The program regularly ventured into social commentary. Not surprisingly, the program included numerous plot lines centred on race. In one episode, Sam takes the place of Jesse, an elderly black man in the American deep South during the segregationist 1950s. In another, Sam becomes Clyde, a new inductee of the Ku Klux Klan during the 1960s. Viewers watched Sam grapple with occupying another person's form. As a white man in a black man's body, how does Sam deal with experiencing discrimination first-hand? How does Sam respond when he leaps into the body of a committed white supremacist?

In reality, the task of stepping into the shoes of others cannot be as neat as an episode of *Quantum Leap*. It is beyond us to put ourselves magically into another person's body. Yet empathy is vital to our preparedness to walk in solidarity with our fellow citizens. Prejudice and discrimination thrive on ignorance and incomprehension. The best antidote is to cultivate better understanding of racial differences.

Doing so, though, requires people to exercise a certain moral imagination, among other things, to grasp the influence of social power and privilege. Genuine racial empathy may be as much about understanding one's own position in society as it is about understanding the position of another.

EMPATHY

The word empathy is derived from the Greek *empatheia*: *em* meaning 'into', *pathos* meaning 'feeling'. The psychologist Edward Titchener introduced the term into the English language in 1909, in an attempt to translate the German word *einfuhlung*. As it was originally used, empathy meant being able to relate to the experience of another person by mirroring it in one's mind.

Empathy might be a relatively new word, but most moral codes regard it – or something approximating it – as a fundamental and timeless concept. It is written into the golden rule shared by all religions and systems of ethical thought: you should treat others as you would like others to treat you. This maxim is, at face value, one about reciprocity. Yet to reciprocate implies empathising. Mutual respect would be impossible unless people were able to place themselves in the position of others and to imagine another person as themselves.

I'm not racist but ...

Within the English-speaking tradition, we can trace notions of empathy to the Scottish Enlightenment of the 18th century. According to the philosopher David Hume, 'reason is and ought only to be the slave of the passions', with sympathy comprising 'the foundation of morals'.[1] As it was invoked by Hume and his contemporaries, sympathy was equivalent to our contemporary understanding of empathy. Adam Smith explained that sympathy involves observing someone and considering 'what we ourselves should feel in the like situation'. For example, 'when we see a stroke aimed and just ready to fall upon the leg or arm of another person, we naturally shrink and draw back our own leg or our own arm'.[2]

Although it clearly has its place in our ethical and philosophical traditions, empathy is frequently resisted in our contemporary debates. Some commentators openly mock empathy as an emotion expressed only by those who wish to flaunt their compassion for those in suffering. This was one response to the SBS program *Go Back To Where You Came From*. In the program's first season in 2011, a number of people were taken on a journey to recreate the experiences of refugees who came to Australia. In one episode, participants were placed on a leaky boat at sea. Conditions were simulated to replicate a sinking ship, which would be rescued by the Australian navy. Not long after the participants were rescued, one of them protested that the exercise was

Empathy and privilege

illegitimate. It was fraudulent, he said, because it had elicited his empathy without consent. The complaint was echoed by newspaper columnist Paul Sheehan, who slammed the program for involving 'an empathy forced march'. According to Sheehan, *Go Back To Where You Came From* distorted public understanding of asylum seeker issues. The debate '[was] not about empathy', but 'about principle: control the borders'.[3]

The withholding of empathy also occurs in situations involving overt bigotry and racism. Consider the controversy in August 2014 concerning a *Sydney Morning Herald* cartoon about Gaza, which many regarded as anti-Semitic. The cartoon showed an elderly Jewish man, with a large nose and wearing a kippah, watching the bombing of Gaza from an armchair that had stamped on its back the Star of David. The *Sydney Morning Herald* subsequently apologised for the cartoon (an apology that I, and many others, welcomed at the time). It was striking, though, that the newspaper initially declined to apologise: it denied that the cartoon was anti-Semitic and noted that the cartoonist in question normally drew old people with pronounced features, including big noses.[4] There was an initial refusal by the newspaper to put itself in the position of a Jewish person and to consider the history of anti-Semitic representations being replicated in the now infamous cartoon.

Consider, as well, ongoing debates about community harmony. Amid rising public anxiety over terrorist threats in 2014, members of Muslim communities publicly expressed their concerns about safety and security. There were media reports of Muslim women being physically attacked, and of mosques being defaced with anti-Islamic slogans. Yet among some commentators there was an apparent denial that some of this had been happening. Some even appeared to suggest that certain minority groups were engaging in a form of imagined victimhood for speaking out about hate attacks.[5] Such denial has a double effect. When those who are targets of anti-Muslim threats or assaults report an incident they are derided for playing the victim card. But were these people not to report an incident, suggestions about anti-Muslim sentiment would become more easily dismissed as the unsubstantiated allegations of self-identified victims.

THE CONDITIONS OF EMPATHY

In Harper Lee's novel *To Kill a Mockingbird*, the hero Atticus Finch teaches his daughter Scout a lesson: 'You never really understand a person until you consider things from his point of view [...] until you climb into his skin and walk around in it'.[6] As the novel progresses, Scout gets to put her father's lesson into practice. She is there at the trial in which her lawyer father defends Tom Robinson, a black man

Empathy and privilege

accused of raping a white woman, watching from the gallery reserved for 'coloured' people. At the conclusion of the novel, after having her life saved by the mysterious Boo Radley – a figure of malign gossip and speculation among townsfolk – Scout pauses to imagine what life would be like if she were the marginalised and isolated Boo.

Clearly, Scout is a child with a certain character. She is smart, headstrong and courageous. She gets into fights while defending her father's honour. She shows no fear in approaching a mob that sets out to lynch Tom Robinson. A creature of fiction though she is, Scout's personality highlights some perennial questions. Do compassion and a sense of justice come from nature or nurture? Is empathy something that has more to do with our intrinsic qualities or with our personal experiences? Is it possible for us to educate people to empathise?

A medical school is one place that teaches and examines empathy. Medical students are routinely assessed for their bedside manner. In a recent collection of essays, *The Empathy Exams*, the American writer Leslie Jamison describes the process. A medical school finds actors, who they pay to play sick, and whose imaginary illnesses the medical students must guess. The actors are given scripts outlining what is wrong with them, what hurts and how to express their pain. They also give details of the actor's fictive lives: how many children they have, the names of their husbands' work, what sport or television shows they like, and so on.

When they play their part, the actors participate in a simulated 15-minute encounter. They then complete an evaluation of the students, including of how empathetic they are during the encounter. The actors are instructed that it is not enough for the medical students to have a sympathetic manner: they must also display 'voiced empathy' for the patient's situation. They have to 'say the right words to get credit for compassion'. As Jamison explains, such a checklist can go only so far. The true test of empathy is not whether someone merely says the right thing. It is about 'acknowledging a horizon of context that extends perpetually beyond what you can see'.[7] Thus understood:

> Empathy isn't just something that happens to us – a meteor shower of synapses firing across the brain – it's also a choice we make: to pay attention, to extend ourselves. It's made of exertion, that dowdier cousin of impulse. Sometimes we care for another because we know we should, or because it's asked for, but this doesn't make our caring hollow. The act of choosing simply means we've committed ourselves to a set of behaviours greater than the sum of our individual inclinations …[8]

Empathy and privilege

To the extent that empathy does come naturally, psychologists have found that some of us are better at feeling it than others. Empathy correlates with personality traits such as sensitivity, nonconformity, even-temperedness and social self-confidence. Some scholars even suggest there may be an ideological quality to the conditions of empathy – namely, that left-wing liberals are more inclined than right-wing conservatives to be sensitive to need and suffering, and to value caring for those who are vulnerable.[9]

There are also people who are literally prepared to go much further than most to step into another's skin. Perhaps the most extreme example involved the journalist John Howard Griffin. In 1959, Griffin, a white American, posed himself a question: 'What is it like to experience discrimination based on skin colour, something over which one has no control?' With the help of a dermatologist, a course of drugs and ultraviolet treatments, Griffin managed to turn his skin from fair to dark. For six weeks, he travelled as a black man through the deep South – in Louisiana, Mississippi, Alabama, South Carolina and Georgia. He caught Greyhound buses; occasionally, he hitchhiked. He closely observed his treatment by his fellow Americans, particularly those who were white. His experiences would eventually be published as the book, *Black Like Me* (1961). In it, Griffin grieves at how 'my own people could give the hate stare, could shrivel men's souls, could deprive humans of rights they unhesitatingly accord their livestock'.[10] Griffin had seen his society from the eyes of another.

In 2009, a filmmaker in Germany conducted a similar, though less radical, exercise in racial impersonation. For more than a year, Gunter Wallraff painted his white skin dark brown and donned an afro wig in the persona of 'Kwami Ogonno', an African immigrant who spoke in broken German. Equipped with a secret camera, Wallraff travelled across Germany to find out how he would be treated by his compatriots. His film, *Black on White*, documented his experiences with casual racism and racism of a more full-blooded variety. In one encounter as he sought accommodation, he is told by a landlady that she could not possibly rent out a flat of hers to a black person. In eastern Germany, he was confronted by neo-Nazi hooligans after a football match, and barely escaped being beaten up. According to Walldraff, 'it was crucial that I take on these dangers myself', in order to understand his country's attitudes on race. In his film, he reflects on being defined exclusively based on the colour of his now black skin: 'When you're black, people don't focus on or even recognise what really makes you a person.'[11]

Of course, very few of us would have the commitment to undertake the kind of transformation chosen by Griffin in the American South and, in more qualified form, Wallraff in Germany. In any case, it is open to ask whether it is in fact necessary to resort to

Empathy and privilege

such extremes. Empathy does not need to mean total impersonation. As the critics of Wallraff in Germany said, he may have been motivated by good intentions, but he could have experienced empathy simply by filming the experiences of real black people in Germany – by speaking with black people rather than speaking paternalistically for them.[12] At the end of each day, Walldraff could wash off the black make-up on his skin. This was one option unavailable to the actual black people with whom he was seeking to empathise.

EXPERIENCE, THINKING AND IMAGINATION

There *have* been experiments in educating for empathy. Arguably the best known remains that conducted by Jane Elliott. A schoolteacher in Iowa, Elliott first tested her 'Blue Eyes–Brown Eyes' exercise in 1968 on a group of her third-grade students. Believing that her students would not understand what it felt like to be discriminated against unless they had been in that position themselves, Elliott decided to segregate her students. She divided her students, all of whom were from a white, Anglo-Saxon background, according to an attribute over which the children had no influence or control: eye colour.

Splitting the students into two groups, brown eyes and blue eyes, Elliott informed her students that the blue-eyed children were superior. She sat the blue-eyed children in the front of the classroom, and placed the brown-eyed ones at the back. She gave the blue-eyed children extra privileges, and went out of her way to praise them whenever she could. She made a special effort to dwell on the mistakes of brown-eyed children, and to belittle them at every opportunity. The following day Elliott reversed the exercise: she treated the brown-eyed students as the superior ones and the blue-eyed ones as inferior.

Elliott's experiment was a confronting one and continues to divide opinion. Yet it was a democratic experiment in the pragmatic tradition of the educational philosopher John Dewey. According to Dewey, knowledge is not passively transmitted but is actively created through experience. You can teach a child about fire by asking them to read about it, or you can teach a child by getting them to stick a finger into a flame. We should not confuse experience, in this sense, with mere activity. Rather, we learn from experience because of the consequences that come from acting upon something. Being burned involves a mere physical change, but the experience lies in knowing that sticking a finger into flame means being burned.[13]

Experience, then, must involve an element of thought or reflection. People must be able to understand the relationship between the things they do and their consequences. For the experience to have

Empathy and privilege

been a success, the child who has gone through the Blue Eyes–Brown Eyes exercise must understand not only that notions of superiority and the effects of discrimination are connected, but also *how* they are connected.

In addition to experience and thought, empathy also involves affect. We may experience something and appreciate it through thoughtful reflection, but empathy is incomplete unless we can feel something. In the case of Elliott's students, the child in her exercise must be able to feel the pain of prejudice and the discomfort of discrimination. Then there is the component of imagination. This is important because we may need to empathise with people with whom we have no direct contact. The historian Benedict Anderson, in his work on nationalism, famously referred to the modern nation-state as an imagined community.[14] In our globalised world, with our ubiquitous digital technology, we live not merely in imagined communities but increasingly in virtual communities as well.

When we think of empathy, we are often thinking of what has been called moral imagination: the power 'that compels us to grant the highest possible reality and the largest conceivable claim to a thought, action or person that is not our own, and not close to us in any obvious way'.[15] The first writer to invoke moral imagination was the conservative thinker Edmund Burke. Writing in his *Reflections on the*

I'm not racist but ...

Revolution in France, Burke lamented what he saw as the passing of an age of chivalry and the emergence of a more demotic temper. This new condition of democracy would dissolve all the pleasing and benevolent illusions of the ancient regime:

> All the decent drapery of life is to be rudely torn off. All the superadded ideas, furnished from the wardrobe of a moral imagination, which the heart owns, and the understanding ratifies, as necessary to cover the defects of our naked shivering nature, and to raise it to a dignity in our own estimation, are to be exploded as a ridiculous, absurd, and antiquated fashion.[16]

For Burke, moral imagination was all about concealing our defects and decorating our manners. It was about honour and duty; it was about noblesse oblige. But it was always conventional. The wardrobe of a moral imagination may furnish the decent drapery of life, but the ideas are habitual ones, ones that sit on the rack, ready to be worn. As one scholar has recently explained, 'there is nothing original or individual about moral imagination on this view ... the moral imagination simply offers wisdom without reflection'.[17]

Burke's notion of moral imagination stands some distance from the kind implied in the concept of empathy. If there is anything to which empathy is directed, it appears to be wisdom *with* reflection. Empathy is about experience rather than convention, about emotional authenticity rather than courtly decorum. Here, we may contrast Burke with Dewey, who regarded routine behaviour as the antithesis of thoughtful action. In Dewey's view, the routine 'accepts what has been customary as a full measure of possibility and omits to take into account the connections of the particular things done'. It says, in effect, 'let things continue just as I have found them in the past'.[18] Conventional routine can be as much an obstacle to responsibility as an enabler of fellow feeling – certainly on matters of race.

POWER AND EMPATHY'S LIMITS

There are limits to our empathy, in a number of respects. First, we cannot feel empathy all the time, or for everyone. When we are provoked into feeling empathy, it is more likely that we do so with those with whom we have some connection. Even then, empathy can never amount to the intensity of feeling we have about our personal welfare. In a much-cited passage in *The Theory of Moral Sentiments*, Adam Smith considered the example of a European responding to an earthquake in China. While the European may express his sorrow for the misfortune of those caught in the disaster, he would nevertheless go about his business as if nothing had happened:

> The most frivolous disaster which could befall himself would occasion a more real disturbance. If he was to lose his little finger to-morrow, he would not sleep to-night; but, provided he never saw them, he will snore with the most profound security over the ruin of a hundred millions of his brethren, and the destruction of that immense multitude seems plainly an object less interesting to him, than this paltry misfortune of his own.[19]

Second, empathy does not mean partisanship. We do not empathise in order to take sides, although sometimes our compassion may lead us to do so. The challenge of stepping into the shoes of another is one of understanding; it is not one of endorsement. To say that we must be capable of empathy does not mean that we are compelled to assume that another's world view is correct.

This is one error made by some critics of multiculturalism. Such critics believe that any celebration of diversity must collapse into cultural relativism. It is suggested that multiculturalism permits people to use their culture as an excuse for not complying with general rules or standards. In its most general sense, multiculturalism does make a demand of recognition.

Empathy and privilege

It demands that we should not be blind to difference or assume that equal treatment must always mean identical treatment.[20] Multiculturalism says that we must be open to empathetic dialogue: that, whether we endorse them or not, we are at the very least prepared to listen to claims made in the name of cultural identity.

This involves no cultural relativism. Indeed, Australian multiculturalism has been based on the principles of liberal citizenship. As a public policy, it says that everyone should be comfortable in their own skin and that everyone can be Australian in their own way. But multiculturalism is not without its limits. Our multicultural policy has never, for instance, said that it is acceptable to let Christian canon law or Jewish halacha law or Islamic sharia law prevail over Australian secular law if they should be inconsistent. Any right we have to express our cultural identity is accompanied by responsibilities – namely, to commit to parliamentary democracy, the rule of law, the equality of sexes, freedom of religion and freedom of speech.[21]

There are also limits to empathy, in a third sense: namely, we may be *limited* in our ability to empathise. We may not always succeed in understanding the perspective of another.

In 2009, Jane Elliott took her Blue Eyes–Brown Eyes exercise to the United Kingdom. She recreated it with a group of British adults that included a mix of white, Afro-Caribbean and Asian backgrounds. The aim remained the same: to allow participants to experience what it feels like to be on the receiving end of discrimination. But on this occasion, the exercise was a failure. A number of participants were asked to leave or chose to excuse themselves part-way through. In short, some of the participants refused to go along with the premise. One participant objected that the exercise was unfair because it labelled all white people as racist. Another participant, a young white man, objected that it was 'an exercise that removes choice, freedom and autonomy' and that he was exercising his choice not to become an 'aggressor'. Others dismissed the value of the experiment by saying that it was wrong to make the issue all about racism felt by the brown-eyed people in the group. One such participant complained that she had:

> ... been in a situation many times where I have had people comment about my person, that I am white, blonde, older, whatever. I have come across just as much discrimination in my life as possibly many black people have.[22]

A similar thing happened on SBS TV's *Living with the Enemy* (2014). The program had brought together people with diametrically opposed views by making them live together in each other's homes for a week.

Empathy and privilege

One episode featured a young Muslim couple, Ahmed and Lydia, and Ben, who staunchly believed that Islam is a fanatical and violent religion. Ben got along well with the Muslim couple, but then abruptly decided after a few days to withdraw from the experiment – ostensibly because Ahmed and Lydia were too moderate and failed to match his expectations. Ben refused to agree that Ahmed and Lydia were real Muslims (since he believed that all Muslims were extremists or fundamentalists).

We see from these two examples illustrations of the obstacles to empathy. The example of *Living with the Enemy* reveals the moral challenge that comes with experiencing empathy. Taking the view of another may mean questioning your own views and values. It can involve suspending, if only momentarily, one's own beliefs, leaving them open to challenge. For some of us, particularly those who crave certainty or feel threatened by change, this can be too much to demand. Not everyone can cope when confronted with the stress of dissonance, the reality that one may have drawn the wrong conclusion or acted too hastily. It is not at all surprising that psychologists have found, as mentioned earlier, a correlation between empathy and social self-confidence. Fortitude may be a prerequisite of empathy.

In the case of Blue Eyes–Brown Eyes, we see that empathy can be resisted because of power and arrogance. The experiment failed because some white volunteers refused to accept there was anything they could learn from participating. Here, we see one aspect of enjoying the position of social power: you can feel that you are always in the right, you can feel absolutely certain that you already know all that needs to be known. But to feel empathy requires something else. It demands a dose of humility.

PRIVILEGE

The example of Elliott's failed British experiment can also be understood in terms of *privilege*. The concept of privilege refers to how some may enjoy unearned or unacknowledged advantages over others. The concept emerged in the 1980s through the work of feminist scholar Peggy McIntosh. In a celebrated essay, McIntosh wrote that, 'as a white person', she had been taught not to see how social privilege placed her at a certain advantage. Privilege was like an 'invisible package of unearned assets', a 'weightless backpack of special provisions, maps, passports, codebooks, visas, clothes, tools and blank cheques'.[23]

McIntosh listed more than 40 ways in which she could cash in on such privilege each day. Some of these examples related to the mundane details of everyday life. Thus, if McIntosh wanted to do so, she could be pretty sure of moving into an area and be assured that her neighbours would be neutral or pleasant to her. She could turn on the television or open the front page of the newspaper and see people of her race widely represented. Then there were the ways in which privilege could shape others' perception of McIntosh. She could swear or dress in second-hand clothes or not answer letters, without having people attribute those choices to the bad morals, poverty or illiteracy of her race. She could speak in public without putting her race on trial; and if she did so well, she would never be called a credit to her race. She would never be asked to speak for all the people of her racial group.

The beneficiaries of social privilege may not be aware of their privileged position. Part of this is because conversations about discrimination tend to focus on those who are disadvantaged by prejudice. We do not always consider the other side of the coin: what it says about those who do *not* experience discrimination.

In 2013 economists at the University of Queensland conducted a study on Brisbane buses, where four groups of students boarded a bus with a faulty ticket and asked drivers if they could travel for free. The four groups were defined along racial lines. One group was defined as black; one was defined as Indians; one was defined as fair-skinned Asians; and one group defined as fair-skinned Caucasians. The study found that in 72 per cent of the encounters white Caucasian passengers were given a free ride and in

73 per cent of the encounters the Asians were given a free ride. This compared to 51 per cent of encounters for the Indians and 36 per cent for the blacks.

There are two ways of making sense of these findings. One would be to say that there are particular groups that appear more susceptible to experiencing racial discrimination: blacks and Indians. The other interpretation is to say that we see those of a majority racial background or with fairer skin ostensibly enjoying a form of social privilege.

Raising questions of privilege is not easy, and not only because those who enjoy privileged positions may be reluctant to acknowledge it.[24] The manifestations of such social power can be subtle and structural. According to Charles W Mills, an American scholar of race relations, the source of privilege may lie in the very assumptions of our liberal society. In his view, the Western social contract is in fact underpinned by a racial contract – a contract that serves to entrench a hierarchy with respect to racial groups. This begins with the so-called state of nature, the imagined position of people's 'natural' state prior to their transformation into 'political' society. Race, it is argued, intervenes in this hypothetical process. In white settler states, the state of nature was a device used to demarcate the pre-political state of non-white people and the arrival of civilised white Europeans:

Empathy and privilege

The establishment of society thus implies the denial that a society already existed; the creation of society *requires* the intervention of white men, who are thereby positioned as *already* socio-political beings. White men who are (definitionally) already part of society encounter non-whites who are not, who are "savage" residents of a state of nature characterised in terms of wilderness, jungle, wasteland. These the white men bring partially into society as subordinate citizens or exclude on reservations or deny the existence of or exterminate.[25]

As Mills explains, the end result of this racial contract is singular: duties, rights and liberties are assigned on a racially differentiated basis.[26] In historical terms, such discrimination was frequently done in an explicit manner. For much of the 20th century, as we have seen, the Australian polity was emphatically a racial polity, defined by the supreme ideal of White Australia.

Structural notions of race continue to shape contemporary society. In the approach to Australia Day in 2014, for instance, there was extended public debate about so-called patriotic T-shirts that were being sold by the Big W chain of shops. The shirts were emblazoned with an Australian flag and the text, 'Australia: Est. 1788'. Many were quick to criticise the T-shirts as offensive and racist, while others rushed to defend them as legitimate expressions of national pride. In one sense, the shirts were not racist: they did not explicitly articulate support for propositions of racial superiority or racial hatred. Yet, in another sense, you could plausibly interpret the shirts as evidence of precisely the kind of racial contract that, according to Mills, underpins a modern social contract. Here, after all, was a statement that appeared to endorse Australia as a racial polity. It seemed to say that we could ignore all civilisations that existed in this land before 1788 because they did not live up to certain white European standards.

The point of talking about privilege is not to point the finger at anyone. In an interview with *The New Yorker*, Peggy McIntosh reflected on how talking about privilege should lead to positive changes, not divisive arguments or bitter confrontations. It should ideally be about understanding: 'it has to do with looking around yourself the way sociologists do and seeing the big patterns in the rest of society, while keeping a balance and respecting your experience'.[27] It was a way not only of seeing the oppression of others, but also seeing how systems oppress oneself.

This is easier said than done. Our human frailty is eternal. There will inevitably be times when attempts at such individual or collective self-understanding will fail. They can fail because people want to protect their social power, because their social power makes them arrogant, or because some people may not have

Empathy and privilege

enough power in the first place. This is a reminder for all of us that empathy – that basic moral task of stepping into the shoes of another – is in fact something that is political. Little wonder that it is so frequently resisted and so difficult to realise.

THICK SKIN
BINDI COLE CHOCKA

My identity is made up of many things. Some of those things are fluid, like political alignment, world view and taste. Others are unchangeable like race, skin colour, geographical origins and gender. I'm a mixed race, fair-skinned, Melbourne-born woman. I have Jewish, English and Aboriginal heritage. It's quite an odd mix. Most people think I look Irish. It's the curls and the occasional foray as a faux redhead.

I didn't begin identifying as Aboriginal during my adult life – I have always done so. Some of my earliest memories are of sitting on the floor playing with toys, hearing my Mum telling her friends that I was Aboriginal. It was the only part of my racial heritage that was ever actively acknowledged and celebrated. I grew up being told I was Aboriginal and my father's family have always identified as such. It's in my DNA, whether I look like it or not. I'm proud of my Western Victorian Wadawurrung heritage. It's an important and cherished part of who I am.

Over the years, other parts of my identity have

altered. I no longer vote Labor after a lifetime of doing so, perhaps because my deepest, fundamental moral values shifted six years ago when I became a passionate follower of Jesus. No one is more surprised than me by this change. I'm also now a blonde after years of being a brunette and occasional redhead. This might change again. But one thing that will never change, no matter how much I might like it to or how much easier it could make my life, is my racial heritage.

I clearly remember the first derogatory blog post I read about myself: how my heart squeezed tight with anxiety, the sick feeling in my stomach and the disorienting sensation of wanting to flee. It was the beginning of an onslaught of hatred, vilification and racism directed at me in the press and online across Australia. I was accused of being opportunistic, calculating and manipulative by 'constructing' my Aboriginal identity to benefit me politically and elevate my career. I was told that I had no right to identify as such because I didn't look stereotypically Aboriginal. For years, I spent much time in tears. I didn't want to leave the house; I felt a dark cloud of shame hanging over me. Through the national exposure I was subjected to I lost friends, acquaintances, community standing and professional opportunities. The worst part was that the discrimination always came from people who had never met me and knew absolutely nothing about me.

I'm not racist but ...

Everyone has the right to his or her own opinion. I've got heaps of them. Yet, in this country, the freedom to express those opinions has its limits. Our laws strike a beautiful balance between preserving freedom of opinion and expression while protecting people from unfair discrimination and treatment. There are ways of expressing opinions without including hateful, shaming, denigrating, humiliating and intimidating speech. Yet some seem to want hate speech to be our highest priority. It's just not on and I'm not sure how we arrived at a destination where some believe this behaviour is acceptable or an absolute right.

Often, when someone is granted his or her rights, someone else has to lose theirs. This proves true when we address the Racial Discrimination Act (RDA). The RDA protects people and groups against abuse and it is their right to be protected. On the flipside, it has the effect of limiting, within others, a right to voice their bigotry. Surely this is a good thing in a society where bullying and suicide are everyday occurrences and a huge problem? In Australia, the suicide rate of young Aboriginal people has been rising over the last 20 years and is now claimed to be the highest in the world. Not everyone has a thick skin, nor should they need to. If we make the right to free speech our highest priority, enshrining in law the right to deeply hurt others, what is that really saying about us as a whole?

This doesn't mean there is no place in our community to discuss our controversial or offensive opinions. It's just that we need to thoughtfully consider how we go about it. Many people talk, write, publish, share, perform, make art and debate on subjects that are difficult and uncomfortable everyday. But they do it in a way that doesn't shame, defame, humiliate or intimidate others. In fact, if you read beyond Section 18C of the RDA you find that, in 18D, there is provision for free speech on matters of race – as long as it is done 'reasonably and in good faith' in practically any public situation, and as long as it is a 'fair and accurate report of any event or matter of public interest'. To go beyond this and contravene the RDA, you must do much more than just publicly present or discuss something racially offensive or controversial.

It is imperative that those on the receiving end of discrimination have a way to protect themselves and potentially achieve some sort of vindication through conciliation or the courts. This is a system that provides a protected and safe avenue for those who cannot speak for themselves and ensures justice for those being affected. The RDA is not about censorship but about giving everyone in this country a fair go, levelling out the playing field and providing a guarantee of fairness and equality. This is significant when we live in a society where power is not equally distributed. The RDA gives the powerless the right to hold those with more power, privilege and platform to account.

The provisions of the RDA are about more than just protecting people from hurt feelings. If you tried to take someone to court over hurt feelings I doubt you would get very far. From my personal experience these court cases take years, require rigorous investigation and need to be more than just a public discussion or presentation of something offensive. In fact, when read as a whole, the RDA does not restrict the airing of unpopular or unsavory opinions but encourages them, while protecting the community and in particular the vulnerable from people taking these opinions to the extreme.

Free speech should come with responsibility. There is the responsibility we all share as decent human beings not to savagely hurt others or incite hatred within the community. We have the right to express offensive opinions but care needs to be taken that they are not misinformed, exaggerated and vicious. Freedom of speech is not an excuse to openly denigrate and harm others. As a community we need to care for and take responsibility for each other – and not just ourselves and our loved ones. When we meet or refer to each other, the least we can do is always show respect, whether or not our beliefs are in alignment. That way we can grow, learn and expand our understanding, coming away better, fuller and happier people. There is no one in this world, whatever

Thick skin

their beliefs, we cannot learn something from. Even someone like me: a Melbourne-born, right-leaning with some leftist ideals, blonde, Jewish, English, Jesus-loving, sensitive, female, white Aborigine.

6

FRIENDSHIP
THE CIVIC BONDS OF PATRIOTISM

The ideal of mateship runs deep in the Australian psyche. It is a defining cultural myth. More than just a local version of the universal value of friendship, mateship is inseparable from our image of the national character.[1] While the essential quality of mateship is notoriously elusive, most would associate it with a certain egalitarian spirit. As described by historian Russel Ward in his classic work *The Australian Legend*, the 'typical Australian' is someone who is practical, rough and ready in their manners, and is always willing 'to have a go'. They believe that Jack is not only as good as his master but probably a good deal better. But, above all, this typical Australian 'will stick to his mates through thick and thin, even if he thinks they may be in the wrong'.[2]

Ward was under no illusions that the mateship legend was 'mystique', though he insisted it had some basis in historical fact.[3] Writing in the late 1950s, he recognised the need to renovate the legend to ensure it would remain 'valid in modern conditions'. In light of the changes brought about by postwar immigration, Ward concluded it was necessary to modify our national traditions. He was optimistic about the prospect, believing that nothing could be more thoroughly Australian than to 'give it a go'.[4] For others, the influx of so-called New Australians from Europe required affirmation of the national myth rather than reflection. In his bestselling 1957 book *They're a Weird Mob* (penned under the pseudonym Nino Culotta), author John O'Grady called for the immigrant to do no more than assimilate into the Australian way:

> There is no better way of life in the world than that of the Australian. I firmly believe this. The grumbling, growling, cursing, profane, laughing, beer drinking, abusive, loyal-to-his-mates Australian is one of the few free men left on this earth. He fears no one, crawls to no one, bludges on no one, and acknowledges no master. Learn his way. Learn his language. Get yourself accepted as one of him; and you will enter a world that you never dreamed existed. And once you have entered it, you will never leave it.[5]

Intervening decades have seen Australia develop into a successful society of immigration. The vision of assimilation gave way to one of multiculturalism.

Instead of being expected to conform to Anglo-Australian culture, everyone would be free to express their cultural heritage. But the aspiration of ensuring newcomers would enter the national family has remained. For the most part, Australia has proven to be an open and accepting country, which has welcomed new arrivals in the spirit of civic friendship. Those who have come here as immigrants – whether from Europe, Asia, Africa or the Americas – have gone from being foreigners to being fellow citizens. As the experience of some European countries has demonstrated, not all liberal democratic states have extended such membership to immigrants. Some have preferred to treat immigrants as guest workers or permanent aliens graciously accorded rights by the state. Australia has chosen an alternative path – that of nation-building.

Such an ethos should inform any response to racism. Admittedly, this task can sometimes be thought of only in terms of fighting prejudice or confronting bigotry. But it should be accompanied by the positive aspiration of extending the rights and status of citizenship to all who live permanently in a society. Eliminating racism should go hand in hand with cultivating civic friendship. In today's Australia, this should mean a multicultural patriotism. We should have a sense of national belonging that is not only open to all, but which regards racial and cultural diversity as part of the national identity. Endorsing this, I will argue, should also be accompanied by a 'civic architecture' – comprising our laws and our Constitution – that reflects a commitment to racial equality and liberal democratic citizenship.

CLASSICAL IDEALS OF FRIENDSHIP

Friendship can mean different things to different people. As with all words of significance, 'friend' and 'friendship' can be stretched to the point of losing their true meaning. Yet, in essence, friendship refers to the particular character of a relationship we have with another person. It is the bond that transcends the other reasons we entered into an association with someone in the first place. Some friendships may begin from relationships that are not chosen, as with family relations, classmates, or workmates. Others may be elective: we may meet someone and then take a liking to them. In all instances, the defining qualities remain the same. With a friend, you enjoy their company, share their joys and comfort their sorrows. Friends are part of the fabric of each other's worlds, and develop a mutual sense of trust and obligation. 'Friendship', as philosopher AC Grayling has recently explained, is arguably 'the highest and finest of all human relationships'. It is 'only the supremest moments of the intimacy of love that can compare in value to friendship – and even then we hope that, in the ideal, the former will be prelude to the latter for the rest of our days'.[6]

Understanding friendship requires us to delve into the concept's history. Within the Western tradition, the idea of friendship has its philosophical roots in Aristotelian ideas of virtue and the good life. For Aristotle, friendship is necessary for a good life: 'without friends, no one would choose to live, even if he possessed all other goods'.[7] Friendship was, if anything, most necessary for those who possessed wealth or who had acquired office or power. The more prosperity or power one has, he argued, the more precarious one's moral position.

There was also a political requirement of friendship. Aristotle believed that friendship was something that 'holds cities together'. Any city required like-mindedness among its people. By like-mindedness, Aristotle did not mean to suggest there must be unanimity of opinion. Rather, 'cities are like-minded whenever people are of the same judgment concerning what is advantageous, choose the same things, and do what has been resolved in common'. Where there was no such common sentiment, Aristotle believed there were civic dangers. For a city may then be populated with people who merely wish to take more from others, but who are unwilling to give more of themselves. When people fail to keep watch over the commons, it is destroyed. And the result is that 'they fall into civil faction, compelling one another by force

Friendship

and not wishing to do what is just themselves'. A just city, in other words, needs more than justice; it also needs friendship.[8]

What was most memorable about Aristotle's formulation was his distinction between three kinds of friendship. And here Aristotle referred not to civic friendship – a sense of general like-mindedness – but to friendships among individuals.

The first was friendship based on pleasure. This, he said, was the friendship of the young, for the young live 'according to passion and most of all pursue what is pleasant to them and at hand'. Two individuals may share a passion for some particular activity, or enjoy each other's wit and humour. Aristotle also categorised erotic love as part of this category of friendship, 'for the greater part of erotic love is bound up with passion and is based on pleasure'. This was why, in his view, the young 'love and swiftly cease loving, often changing in the course of the same day'.[9]

The second kind of friendship was based on utility. These are friendships in which friends associate with each other because it is advantageous. Such 'friends' may not necessarily like each other or even be pleasant to each other. They are friends because they wish to obtain something from the relationship. You scratch my back, I'll scratch yours.

In Aristotle's view, these two sorts of friendships were inferior to a third kind. This was because a friendship based on either pleasure or utility is easily dissolved. If a friend is no longer pleasant or useful, the reason for the relationship's existence no longer exists. The third kind of friendship avoids this problem. This is friendship based on virtue: a complete or perfect friendship in which friends are morally good and alike. In such a relationship, friends have reciprocal love and concern. They wish for good things to happen to their friends not because it will bring personal pleasure or advantage, but because they wish the best for their friends.

Such friends are not susceptible to the kind of envy that Gore Vidal described when he said, 'Every time a friend succeeds, I die a little'. This is because a friend of virtue regards a friend as himself or herself: 'to perceive a friend […] is necessarily in a manner to perceive oneself, and to know a friend is in a manner to know oneself'.[10] The friend, in other words, is a reflection of one's self.

This was a demanding view, as Aristotle recognised. It is impossible to be a friend to many when it comes to complete friendship. The classical view upheld this stringent conception. The Roman statesman Cicero echoed Aristotle in taking up the idea of friendship as virtue. Friendship was something so intense that its bonds of affection could unite 'at most two or just a few'. This was because 'friendship is nothing other than agreement about divine and human affairs, accompanied by good will and affection'. It was something that 'arises from nature rather than from need' and 'from the inclination of the soul accompanied by love, rather than from calculation of a relationship's potential usefulness'.[11]

The classical perspective drew a clear ethical line with friendship. It was something that existed only among good, virtuous individuals. 'Seek only good from friends, do only good for the sake of friends', Cicero wrote. Good friends, moreover, should be attentive and ready to give advice freely and cheerfully, though never harshly. Good friends should also accept advice patiently, and not reluctantly. Giving and taking criticism: this was 'the mark of a true friendship'.[12]

MODERN CONCEPTIONS OF FRIENDSHIP

The classical ideal of friendship was clearly one imbued with a spiritual quality and bound up with values of the good and the noble. This seems far removed from modern thinking. The demands of friendship appear different in a commercial-industrial society. As sociologists would explain, modern times reflect a historic shift from *Gemeinschaft* to *Gesellschaft*, from community to society.[13] Whereas there may once have been solidarity with others in a community in which everyone knew everyone else, the bonds of society are more 'thin' in character. A more transactional logic defines our relationships. The things we do for another tend to be done with a contractual expectation that they will be returned in kind.

According to the philosophers of early market society, this was not a pernicious development; far from it. The thinkers of the Scottish Enlightenment in fact argued that the rise of market relations led to the development of new forms of benevolence and social trust. After all, the social relations that preceded the growth of commercial society were typically cold and unfriendly. One thinks here of the kind of life that lurks in the background of Montaigne's *Essays* – a life where disease, war and conflict were never far away.[14] The historian Lawrence Stone has written that our modern minds cannot comprehend how, at all levels of society, men and women from the 15th to the 17th centuries were 'extremely short-tempered' and prone to frequent violence.[15] This was a time when the philosopher Thomas Hobbes would describe the state of nature as one marked by 'continual fear and danger of violent death', one in which the life of man was 'solitary, poor, nasty, brutish and short'.[16]

For Scottish Enlightenment thinkers like Adam Smith, David Hume and Adam Ferguson, the market had a revolutionary effect. The rules of commercial society were giving room for a new form of friendship to flourish, one based on 'natural sympathy'. Friendships were no longer just relationships that one cultivated in order to deflect enemies. At the same time, commercial society meant that you

Friendship

did not have to treat friends as though they might turn out to be your enemies. This meant two things. First, a clear distinction could be made between those relationships based on interest and those relationships based on sympathy and affection. Second, commercial society brought into being a system of co-operation based on the independence of ordinary people. Friendships were now relationships born of free choice and autonomy.

If such freedom were a prerequisite of modern friendship, it would also, in time, become its justification. Consider Ralph Waldo Emerson's view of friendship: 'We walk alone in the world. Friends, such as we desire, are dreams and fables'. Emerson, a 'transcendentalist' romantic and prophet of radical individualism, wrote, 'I do then with my friends as I do with my books. I would have them where I can find them, but I seldom use them'. Friends no longer existed as a mirror to oneself, as they did for Aristotle and Cicero. Nor did they exist as objects of natural sympathy and affection, as they might have for Smith and Hume. Friendship now existed as an instrument for self-improvement. It was employed in the service of a transcendent individual will. As Emerson explained, 'The soul environs itself with friends, that it may enter into a grander self-eloquence or solitude'.[17] We have friends in order to remind us that the highest form of life is to live not with them, but without them.

A less radical conception of friendship can be found in the writings of CS Lewis. According to Lewis, friendship was one of 'the four loves', along with affection, eros and charity. There was in this view much of Lewis's sympathy with a muscular Christianity, as demonstrated by his concern that St John's precept of 'God is love' was being transformed into the subversive idea that 'love is God'.[18] Whether you subscribe to his Christian view or not, Lewis says a good deal worth revisiting. Not least, he captures what is at the heart of modern friendship. As he put it, friendship arises from companionship:

> when two or more of the companions discover that they have in common some insight or interest or even taste which the others do not share and which, till that moment, each believed to be his own unique treasure (or burden). The typical expression of opening Friendship would be something like, 'What? You too? I thought I was the only one'.[19]

The shared activity, Lewis said, could be a common religion, common profession, or common recreation. But while all who share that thing in common will be our companions, only one or two or three will be our friends. It is when people share their common vision that friendship is born. It is then that 'instantly they stand together in an immense solitude'.[20] In contrast

Friendship

to the Emersonian understanding of solitude, this is a solitude that exists *among* friends, rather than *from* friends.

It is nonetheless a distinctively modern view of friendship. There is, for example, no straightforward celebration of friendship as virtue. As Lewis noted, while friendship can be a school of virtue, it can also be a school of vice. There is also the affirmation of friendship as a product of choice. It is the least natural of loves, in that it is 'the least instinctive, organic, biological, gregarious and necessary'.[21] In the context of a modern commercial, late-industrial society, friendship was an exercise of individual expression:

> Friendship ... repeats on a more individual and less socially necessary level the character of the Companionship which was its matrix. The Companionship was between people who were doing something together – hunting, studying, painting or what you will. The Friends will still be doing something together, but something more inward, less widely shared and less easily defined ... still travelling companions, but on a different kind of journey. Hence we picture lovers face to face but Friends side by side; their eyes look ahead.[22]

I'm not racist but ...

FRIENDSHIP TODAY

In the five or so decades since Lewis wrote *The Four Loves*, the social matrix of friendship has changed. While we may look at literary or intellectual sources, there is perhaps a source of more representative insight into what friendship today must mean. Let us take three representations of friendship in contemporary Western popular culture, all of which involve television programs that have had significant cultural impact.

First, consider *Seinfeld*, the sit-com that aired from 1989 to 1998. Its characters: Jerry Seinfeld, a stand-up comedian with a penchant for beautiful girlfriends, Superman and cereal; Elaine Bennis, a former love interest of Seinfeld's who works in the publishing industry; George Costanza, a neurotic and pathological liar who moves from job to job; and Cosmo Kramer, a big-haired eccentric buffoon who lives opposite Seinfeld in his Manhattan apartment building.

Second, consider *Friends*, another sit-com from the 1990s and 2000s. The program featured as its main protagonists Ross Geller, a paleontologist at a New York university; Monica Geller, a chef and Ross's sister; Rachel Green, Ross's on-and-off love interest and a waitress; Chandler Bing, a wise-cracking statistical analysis executive; Joey Tribbiani, a minor soap opera actor with comically low

Friendship

intelligence; and Phoebe Buffay, a hippy musician naive in the ways of the world.

And then consider *Sex and the City*. A show that ran from 1998 to 2004, it was regarded as capturing the friendship zeitgeist when it came to single professional women in New York during those millennial years. The show documented the adventures of Carrie Bradshaw, a sex columnist with a newspaper, and her three friends. There was Samantha Jones, a sexually confident public relations businesswoman; Charlotte York, a romantic optimist who worked at an art gallery and constantly dreamed about her perfect wedding day; and Miranda Hobbes, a cynical career-minded corporate lawyer.

For a so-called show about nothing, *Seinfeld* epitomised the possibility that friendship may morph from a relationship into just about nothing. There were few interests or values that Seinfeld and his friends shared except for a certain amorality or opportunism – demonstrated in their regular deception or manipulation of others so as to get their desired ends. While not as extreme as *Seinfeld*, it also seemed that the characters of *Friends* had very little to share among themselves except for some vague sense of a shared journey during youthful adulthood. These were not friends who necessarily shared the kind of interest that CS Lewis would have found to be central to friendship: there was not that much in common between the characters to make them friends rather than merely companions. They certainly did not share what Cicero referred to as a shared understanding of divine and human affairs (though this may be an unfair standard against which *Friends* should be judged).

Part of the *Friends* dynamic was replicated in *Sex and the City*. Admittedly, the program explored the boundaries of friendship with some subtlety and insight. There was a sophistication in the sketching of its characters. As television critic Emily Nussbaum has described it, Carrie, Miranda, Samantha and Charlotte were 'jagged, aggressive, and sometimes frightening figures … simultaneously real and abstract, emotionally complex and philosophically stylized'.[23] As Nussbaum continues, 'the four friends operated as near-allegorical figures, pegged to contemporary debates about women's lives', mapping along emotional, ideological and indeed sexual terms: the romantics versus the cynics; egalitarian second-wave feminists versus third-wave feminists focused on the power of femininity; and the prudes versus the libertines. One thing the program could not be accused of was being blind to questions about eros, attraction and friendship.

Taken together, *Seinfeld*, *Friends* and *Sex and the City* arguably provide a representative late-western cultural picture of friendship. We are seeing friendship move increasingly into the realm of mere companionship. Friends these days are really just

Friendship

fellow travellers in our meandering journey of self-discovery. Whereas in CS Lewis's time companionship was a necessary but not sufficient condition of friendship, today it may actually be sufficient. In another sense, we are seeing something of an apotheosis of the Emersonian creed of self-cultivation. We are glimpsing what friendship must look like in a society defined by a therapeutic culture of self-regard and performance.[24] As late moderns – some would say post-moderns – we crave the approval of those around us. We construct our lives and identities in dialogue with others; we need constant recognition of our worth. The idea of friendship has clearly evolved through time, as the American literary critic William Deresiewicz has outlined.[25] For the ancients, for the likes of Aristotle and Cicero, friendship represented the highest calling in life. Friends would declare their love for each other even if they did not share beds. Where one called another a friend, one had to be prepared to put one's life on the line for them. Honour demanded such duty and devotion.

This classical view of friendship as a moral bond, dedicated to the pursuit of goodness and excellence, is completely detached from the moral worlds of *Seinfeld*, *Friends* and *Sex and the City*. Good friends these days are those prepared to take our side: to listen and provide comfort, to massage our egos and validate our self-worth. And now, as Deresiewicz has written, friendship has taken another turn. With the advent of online social networking, 'the friendship circle has expanded to engulf the whole of the social world, and in so doing, destroyed both its own nature and that of the individual friendship itself'. Friendship has not so much evolved as it has devolved 'from a relationship to a feeling'.[26] There is the risk that our new electronic lifestyle degrades friendship even further. Embracing social networking can mean we value a friendship only in terms of connection. In the world of Facebook and Twitter, friends become passive observers, an audience for our online performances.

CIVIC FRIENDSHIP AND PATRIOTISM

So where does all this leave us? There is much that remains appealing about the Aristotelian or classical view of friendship. A good society needs not only justice but also some sense of fellow-feeling or civic friendship. A good society cannot be built on good laws alone; it requires good citizens who are prepared to make sacrifices for the common good. At the same time, when friendship is transported from private life and into the public sphere, the results are not always attractive. There are many instances when friendship is transformed into clientelism or corruption, when public power is used to defend one's friends and to persecute one's enemies. To cite some recent examples, in 2013 the NSW Independent Commission

Friendship

Against Corruption (ICAC) found that former state Labor mining minister Ian Macdonald had corruptly awarded a coal exploration licence to a company chaired by his 'mate' John Maitland.[27] In another case in 2014, ICAC found that NSW State Emergency Services commissioner Murray Kear had engaged in corrupt conduct in failing to investigate allegations of wrongdoing against his deputy (who happened to be a 'good mate').[28]

Even if there should be a positive relationship between friendship and the common good, we should be careful not to overstate it. Modern political theorists of a communitarian bent have certainly been inspired by Aristotle's treatment of friendship, calling for a revival of a fraternal spirit of co-operation among citizens.[29] And yet, it would seem that Aristotle himself would never have gone so far as to define civic friendship in such terms. He was clear that any civic friendship must fall short of that virtuous friendship which he celebrated as the most superior. This was because Aristotle understood friendship among citizens to involve friendship based on shared advantage. Rather than an elevated moral ideal, this friendship was a mundane feature of political life.[30]

Still, there is value in focusing our moral attention on that category of virtuous friendship that Aristotle so famously celebrated. The kinds of complete friendships, which we can only enjoy in our private lives, may have public implications. If excellence does reside in practice, if good character is cultivated only through habit, then friendships remain that most precious of realms: a nursery for the kind of mutual concern and generosity that are the hallmarks of virtuous citizens. But in a modern society, what exactly does such virtue involve?

Modern civic friendship can best be understood in terms of patriotism. This may not be obvious to everyone at first. If patriotism means loving one's country, that on its own says very little. We can, after all, love many different things about our country. Australian patriots may love a lifestyle they associate with an easygoing land of sun and surf, beaches and barbecues. They may claim a deep affection for our landscape – for our sunburnt country and wide brown land. They may also profess a love for a certain national culture and character. In the words of the critic Peter Conrad, Australians have always maintained a collective identity by raillery and larrikin laughter. 'A joke', as Conrad puts it, 'deprives us of our unearned advantages, reduces us to parity with everyone else'.[31]

If we can love many things about a country, we can also love it in different ways. Some who describe themselves as patriotic believe their country is not only the best in the world but must be protected jealously from any criticism. It is in this manner that patriotism can morph into jingoism. Loving your country may mutate into a belief in your country's

Friendship

superiority, and into a sentiment directed at minorities and outsiders. Consider the case of those controversial Australia Day T-shirts, mentioned in chapter 5. In response to criticisms that the shirts' printed message of 'Australia. Est. 1788', were insensitive and racist many people were outraged that their national pride was being censured. As one reader on the Nine MSN website commented:

> You know what is racist? Being told that we can't wear an Aussie shirt in Australia. Wow, I am disgusted that we as a nation are not permitted to proudly wear a T-shirt pronouncing our nationality. Australians one and all should buy a T-shirt and wear them with pride. Those minority groups that complain and whinge, yet take money from our welfare system, should take a leaky boat back to where they came from![32]

We may understandably be sceptical about patriotism. There is no doubt that patriotic feeling can be dangerous when expressed as dogmatic conviction. But patriotism is to countries what self-respect is to individuals: you need it as a condition of collective self-improvement.[33] Not all forms of patriotism need to involve an aggressive imposition of pride.

Patriotism and pride can – and should – be tied to civic membership. What holds Australians together is not race or ethnicity, but our political culture and

I'm not racist but ...

our historical tradition. We should all share a commitment to certain democratic values and aspirations: a deep sense of equality, a fervent belief in a fair go, a willingness to help our mates. This is the kind of commitment given by newly naturalised Australians who pledge their national loyalty at citizenship ceremonies: 'From this time forward, I pledge my loyalty to Australia and its people, whose democratic beliefs I share, whose rights and liberties I respect, and whose laws I will uphold and obey.'

Patriotism need not mean blind loyalty or ethnic chauvinism, either. An acceptable patriotism must accept a multicultural Australia as reality. We live in a country where nearly half of us are first-generation or second-generation Australians; where there are people from more than 200 ancestries, where one in five of us speaks a language other than English at home.[34] Today, surnames such as Nguyen or Rossi or Wang are almost as commonplace as Newman or Ross or White.[35] Most Australians regard such cultural diversity as something that adds to our national identity rather than as something that detracts from it.[36] Our multiculturalism has, in this respect, a distinctive character: it represents an exercise in nation-building. It stands for the proposition that you can be an Australian without having to give up your cultural heritage; that you can be part of Australia and its story, no matter where you were born or who your parents may be. A patriotism that is based

Friendship

on citizenship is entirely compatible with this multiculturalism. Both are based on ideals of civic friendship. Both have a common aspiration – of ensuring that one's country can be at its best.[37]

THE CONSTITUTION AND THE ARCHITECTURE OF CIVIC FRIENDSHIP

There remains the question of how we cultivate a condition of civic friendship, of how we promote a sense of common good in a multicultural society. There is no simple or singular answer, though at the most basic level there must be 'an education of the sentiments'. This is a task that goes beyond legislative action against racial discrimination, and beyond encouraging people to take a stand against prejudice in their lives. Whereas the anti-racist imperative is concerned with people's tolerance of racial and cultural differences, the ambition of civic friendship demands something more.

The demand, as I have suggested, is one of multicultural patriotism. This is concerned with more than just an acceptance of multicultural realities. Rather, it must also involve a certain historical sensibility. To be a patriot is, essentially, about being loyal to a national tradition. One loves one's country not just because it is one's own, but because it has certain merits or achievements. In the Australian context, the past

65 years or so have seen few greater national achievements than the successful integration of waves of immigrants. This has been done without the kind of social fragmentation that has occurred elsewhere. Multicultural Australia is a historical achievement – a testament not only to the spirit of those who have come here to start anew, but to the decency of Australians to give new arrivals a fair go.

Any patriotism is also about improving one's country. A genuine love of country is a matter of responsibility and not merely one of pride: when your country falls short of its best, it may be your obligation to make sure it does better.[38] For all of the successful incorporation of immigrants into Australian society – the triumph of multicultural nation-building – there has been one lingering racial shortcoming. Australian nationhood has always, as the anthropologist WEH Stanner argued, been defined by a great silence, 'a cult of forgetfulness practised on a national scale'. According to Stanner, 'we have been able for so long to disremember the Aborigines that we are now hard put to keep them in mind even when we most want to do so'.[39] This forgetfulness may appear less powerful today than it was in the past. But it still persists. We see it in the limited contact and familiarity that non-Indigenous people – both native-born and immigrant Australians – have with Indigenous peoples and cultures. As yet, we still lack the civic architecture we need if forgetting

Friendship

Indigenous Australians is *not* to be the default.

There is one obvious opportunity for us to do better. It appears likely that there will be a referendum on the recognition of Aboriginal and Torres Strait Islander peoples in the Constitution. Such recognition would redress one of the moral deficiencies of the Constitution, which in its current form says nothing about Indigenous people as the first Australians. It is hard to overstate the importance of Constitutional recognition. We are talking about something fundamental to a liberal political society. The Constitution is the document that captures, however imperfectly reflecting our history, something of the spirit of how we conduct our lives together. As a statement of our collective political morality about decency and justice, it holds profound power in shaping our civic sentiments.[40]

What then is required for the recognition of Aboriginal and Torres Strait Islander peoples in the Constitution? According to the report of the Expert Panel appointed by former prime minister Julia Gillard to investigate options for Constitutional amendment, it is not enough to have recognition in the preamble to the Constitution. There may need to be more. Namely, any recognition would be incomplete unless there were also changes to the body of the Constitution itself. There are two current provisions of the Constitution, which, apart from offending any notion of Australia's first peoples, also discriminate on the ground of race. Section 25 entertains the possibility that persons of particular races can be disqualified from voting at state elections. Then there is Section 51 (xxvi), the so-called race power, which confers on the Commonwealth Parliament the power to make laws with respect to 'the people of any race, for whom it is deemed necessary to make special laws'.

The race power, as courts and scholars have agreed, can be used both for and against the benefit of people of any race. Its origins are to be found in the Constitutional debates leading up to Federation. There was consensus among the 'founding fathers' of Federation that an Australian Government should have 'the power to regulate the affairs of the people of coloured or inferior races who are in the Commonwealth'.[41] The purpose of the race power was clear. It was about enabling the Commonwealth Parliament to control the settlement of people of coloured races, to confine them to certain occupations, and potentially to return them to their countries of origin.[42] The inclusion of the race power in the Constitution was a precursor to that defining legislation of those early years of Federation – the Immigration Restriction Act, which gave effect to the White Australia policy. Speaking in support of the bill, Edmund Barton, Australia's first prime minister, would state:

> I do not think either that the doctrine of the equality of man was really ever intended to

Friendship

include racial equality. There is no racial equality. There is basic inequality. These races are, in comparison with white races – I think no one wants convincing of this fact – unequal and inferior. The doctrine of the equality of man was never intended to apply to the equality of the Englishman and the Chinaman.[43]

That the race power remains latent, still there in the letter of the law of the land, is remarkable for all the wrong reasons. If, as Australians we celebrate our liberal and democratic traditions, we should not tolerate the persistence of racially discriminatory provisions in our Constitution.

The Expert Panel did propose a number of amendments, which have underpinned the 'Recognise' campaign. In addition to the removal of section 25 and deletion of section 51 (xxvi), it also advocated the insertion of a new section 51A to recognise Aboriginal and Torres Strait Islander peoples and to preserve the Australian government's ability to pass laws for their benefit, and the adoption of a new section 116A to prohibit governments passing laws that discriminate on the basis of race.[44] The first two amendments – concerning sections 25 and 51 (xxvi) – have been accepted by most without controversy. The other two proposals have been met with more resistance.

Such opposition has been disheartening. There is no compelling reason to reject a constitutional guarantee of racial non-discrimination for all Australians. While the Racial Discrimination Act provides an important protection, it is not immune from being overridden by the Commonwealth parliament. The states and territories might have their powers limited by the RDA (as discussed in chapter 2), but the Commonwealth parliament has the power to repeal, amend or suspend the legislation. Indeed, the parliament has suspended the operation of the RDA on a number of occasions, most recently with regard to the first Northern Territory Intervention in 2007. As law professors Megan Davis and George Williams explain, the introduction of a prohibition on racial discrimination would 'incorporate a new, significant protection into the Constitution'. It would promote greater deliberation and scrutiny of laws that may have racially discriminatory effects, acting as 'a significant check upon the rushing of legislation through Parliament'.[45] The absence of any constitutional protection was telling when the Parliament suspended the RDA in 2007. Both houses passed the five legislative bills that enabled the Northern Territory Intervention barely a week after they were first introduced, with very limited parliamentary debate.

Even so, a non-discrimination clause may go too far for some 'constitutional conservatives', who fear it would create a 'one-clause bill of rights' that would subvert a principle of parliamentary sovereignty and create uncertainty by enabling the High Court to interpret human rights into the Constitution.[46] Lawyers Julian Leeser and Damien Freeman, for example, have argued in favour of a symbolic declaration about equality and Indigenous recognition, which would exist as a separate statement to the Constitution.[47] Responding to conservative concerns, in a 2014 essay Indigenous advocate Noel Pearson has proposed some alternative provisions – namely, to create a new consultative body or mechanism to guarantee that Indigenous voices have 'a fair say' about any laws and policies that may affect them.[48] West Australian Liberal MP Ken Wyatt, chair of the Joint Select Committee on Constitutional Recognition of Aboriginal and Torres Strait Islander People, also expressed doubt in March 2015 about the prospect of a new section 116A being included in a referendum question. In light of opposition to a racial non-discrimination clause, Wyatt argued the next best alternative might be to strengthen the RDA instead: specifically, by requiring an absolute majority of both houses of parliament to set aside or remove any part of the Act.[49]

Yet are such concessions on the proposed section 116A warranted? It seems strange to suggest that a single clause prohibiting racial discrimination would turn into a 'bill of rights' by stealth, when it would be confined only to protections from discrimination on the grounds of race, and not on other grounds such as sex or age.[50] It is also worth noting the experiences of countries with similar histories on constitutional matters and the common law. The constitutions of Canada, South Africa and India each prohibit racial discrimination; a similar prohibition is contained in the Bill of Rights Act 1990 in New Zealand. The Australian Constitution remains anomalous in not having anything equivalent.

The proposal for a new legislative power in the form of section 51A admittedly raises more complex questions. Some argue that such an insertion is required if the race power of section 51 (xxvi) were deleted – among other things, to ensure that existing legislation relating to Aboriginal and Torres Strait Islander peoples would remain constitutionally valid.[51] One concern, though, is that explicit references to Aboriginal and Torres Strait Islander peoples would perpetuate race-based distinctions and thus run counter to any correction of existing racial discrimination within the Constitution. Accordingly, some commentators suggest that the Commonwealth may simply rely on its external affairs power in section 51 (xxix) of the Constitution to enact laws relevant to Indigenous peoples and affairs, insofar as they implement Australia's international legal obligations. Others argue that a new legislative power could be framed in a manner 'based not on race but on the special place of those peoples in the history of the nation'.[52] We should, on this view, understand any mention of Aboriginal people in the Constitution as an entirely appropriate recognition of them

Friendship

'as the original inhabitants and peoples of Australia', and of their 'historical and cultural connection to the land upon which the nation has been founded'. A glance at international experience may help to put us at some ease. The constitutions of Canada, Norway and Finland, for example, recognise the unique status of their Indigenous peoples while also rejecting the concept of racial discrimination.[53] It does appear possible to do both.

At the time of writing, it remains unclear when Australians will consider proposals for Constitutional recognition of Aboriginal and Torres Strait Islander peoples at referendum. Prime Minister Tony Abbott has hinted that his preference is for it to occur in May 2017, on the 50th anniversary of the landmark 1967 referendum, though there has yet to be any formal announcement of a date. It also remains unclear exactly what any proposal put to referendum may look like. One thing, though, is clear. We have an important opportunity to acknowledge the histories and cultures of Australia's first peoples. It is time that we make a statement about racial equality. It is time that our Constitution is purged of ideas about racial superiority and the natural order of imperial power. Our Constitutional document should be truer to the spirit of our liberal democratic morality. Without a change, it seems difficult to see how our society could be serious about equal citizenship and the rejection of racial discrimination.

IT'S EASY TO MAKE FRIENDS WITH WHITE PEOPLE
BENJAMIN LAW

For a while there, my friends forgot I was Asian. Just plain forgot. I'm not exactly sure how this happened, but I guess it was one of those seemingly obvious things that nevertheless slip someone's mind, like a toddler in the back seat or a shopping list for medication.

This was in the mid-1990s. We were at high school in coastal Queensland and the student population was blindingly white: a sea of Caucasian skin, with a few Asian and black kids flecking each year level like bits of exotic fruit in an otherwise beige porridge. As a result, me and my friend Vanessa (whose dad is Chinese) were the only Asian kids – or ethnic minorities, period – in our circle of friends.

Over lunch, my friends and I would sometimes discuss politics. I know: a bunch of snot-nosed teenagers discussing politics sounds annoying at best, pretentious at worst, but you have to remember, Queensland is prone to gifting Australia some of its most memorably absurd politicians: a belligerent state Premier who came from a peanut farm; a Titanic-sized gazillionaire who showcases robot dinosaurs on golfing ranges. You can't *not* talk about them. The big news at the time was a recently minted MP from Ipswich: a flame-haired fish-and-chip shop owner who spoke with a voice that sounded like she was furious over the fact she was being slowly strangled. Pauline Hanson was getting so famous, Australian TV journalists would travel to Asian countries and snap-poll strangers there, showing them photos of Hanson and asking them who they thought she was. Most knew Hanson was racist; many thought she was our prime minister.

Hanson's One Nation headquarters were in Ipswich, but her other political stronghold was on the Sunshine Coast, where we lived. It was like JRR Tolkien's *The Two Towers*, where there are two main power bases of evil. If Ipswich was Pauline Hanson's Bara-dur (the tower of flame-eyed Sauron), then the Sunshine Coast was Orthanc, Saruman's tower at Isengard. Her popularity in our region was so widespread some school students were dropped off in cars and vans emblazoned with Hanson's party logo. Their parents weren't just One Nation supporters; they were One Nation *candidates*.

As a result, a lot of my friends saw merit in the types of things Hanson was advocating. To improve the economy, why *shouldn't* we just print more money?

I'm not racist but ...

If you're going to live in Australia, why *shouldn't* you just learn the language? And plus – not to be racist – but wasn't the volume of Asian immigration getting a bit, you know, out of control? As these conversations went on, I couldn't help but think of my grandmother – my dad's mum – who arrived here in the 1970s. She still doesn't speak a word of English besides 'Hello', 'Goodbye', 'Pretty girl' and 'Handsome boy', like an adorable elderly Chinese parrot. Still, she's an Australian citizen contributing to the economy and paying taxes like everyone else. Who *cared* whether she speaks English proficiently or not?

When I started to protest what they were saying, furiously jabbing at my face with my fingers – *HELLO? WHAT DO YOU MEAN, THERE ARE TOO MANY ASIANS?* – my friends looked at me, blinking, then laughed. 'Don't be stupid, Ben', one of them said. 'We don't see you as Asian.' At the time, it felt weirdly like a compliment. It was only later – years and years later, really – that I realised how bizarre that comment was. If my friends didn't see me as Asian, what *did* they see me as? Latino? African? White?

I knew what they were trying to say of course. Even now, I hear well-meaning adults insist that they 'don't see race'. It's a well-meaning sentiment – 'I'm so advanced and worldly, I don't judge people by anything but the content of their character, blah-blah-blah' – but it really is one of the dumbest expressions around. Honestly, you don't see race? What happened? Did you develop a terrible ocular disease? Did you put your head in an oven? Did magpies attack your face and eat your corneas? Smugly insisting you're colour-blind just allows you to ignore how – or why – 19 per cent of Australians experienced bigotry due to their skin colour, ethnic origin or religious beliefs in 2014, an increase from 2012. And being colour-blind gives you the ability to evade the fact there are few non-white faces on Australian prime-time and breakfast television. This whole idea of being colour-blind doesn't help you face up to the reality there's a significant average life expectancy gap if you're an Indigenous Australian. Plus, I *like* being Chinese. I don't *want* to be seen as some neutral-coloured, race-emptied, human-shaped blob, or however you weird so-called colour-blind people see me. Just because we should treat each other with equal respect doesn't mean everyone's the same. Why should we have to be?

It would take me years – leaving home, going to university, making friends in other cities – before I'd make friends who got what I was trying to say. Which is to say (and this is a strange and sad realisation), it wasn't until I left home that I made any non-white friends at all. If you grew up in a big Australian city – which are all so successfully multicultural you can happily take diversity for granted – this might seem vaguely shocking. But keep in mind, we also live in a country where two-fifths of surveyed Australians have had no contact with Aboriginal or Torres Strait Islander people whatsoever. In a world where everything from professional opportunities to community cohesion starts with friendship, this strikes me as a problem.

Nowadays, when I go back to my home town in Queensland, it's a lot more diverse. Asians are everywhere. (I guess Hanson was right about that.) I saw my first hijab recently, as well as a black family shopping for groceries. I was pleasantly taken aback. Self-identified 'colour-blind' people might baulk at the fact that I'm identifying these people by race at all, but I don't think they'd mind. After all, I don't mind being identified as Chinese – it's accurate, for starters – as long as you see me as more than that. Especially once we're friends.

AFTERWORD

I am asked often about my cultural identity. My answer is that I am a first-generation Australian of Chinese and Lao heritage. It is a bit of a mouthful, but it is the most accurate description I can think of. For most of my generation, there is nothing too complicated about having an identity with more than one layer. We have reached a point where most agree there is no single authoritative way that you can be Australian. It is one of the strengths of our society that people can be comfortable in their own skin. For the most part, people are not made to feel ashamed of their origins.

If there is such broad public acceptance of our multicultural society, it is because we live amid such diversity every day. In early 2015, the Australian Bureau of Statistics confirmed that the proportion of Australians who were born overseas hit its highest point in 120 years. Twenty-eight per cent of the population – or 6.6 million people – arrived here as immigrants; a further 20 per cent have a parent who was an immigrant. Moreover, immigration has during the past decade contributed more than half

I'm not racist but ...

of the population growth in Australia, with arrivals from Asian countries representing an increasing share. China and India now trail the United Kingdom and New Zealand as the most common birthplaces for Australians born overseas.[1]

The first forty years of the Racial Discrimination Act's existence have been defined by significant changes in the complexion of Australian society. While no one can predict the future, few would dispute that the next forty years will be characterised by further change. No society ever stands still; no national identity is ever frozen in time. Consider how, in the space of half a century, this country has gone from one dedicated to a White Australia to one that triumphantly celebrates our multicultural character.

The next destination in the national journey remains unclear. Some forecast we will become a 'post-racial' society, one no longer afflicted by racial discrimination. With ethnic and racial mixing, it is argued, notions of racial difference will no longer hold any significance. This prediction is made periodically in Australia and some other Western liberal democracies. Observers in the United Kingdom and the United States, to name but a few places, have also suggested that race – and racism – will fade into obsolescence with the inevitable march of social progress.

Yet experience has demonstrated that any Whiggish optimism should be tempered. Racism seems

Afterword

far from defeated in the United Kingdom, where the xenophobic UK Independence Party (UKIP) has defied expectations to become a potentially enduring presence in the British political system. In the United States, the post-racial confidence that accompanied the start of Barack Obama's presidency has all but dissipated – America's old racial wounds have been reopened by the unrest and ructions in Ferguson, Missouri, and elsewhere.

Here, it is easy to find reminders of just how far we have to go before we can even entertain the vision of a 'post-racial' Australia. Despite almost ten years of formal efforts to 'close the gap', there remain significant inequalities experienced by Aboriginal and Torres Strait Islander people when it comes to health, education and employment.[2] As my colleague the Aboriginal and Torres Strait Islander Social Justice Commissioner Mick Gooda has noted, the dramatic rise in incarceration rates among Indigenous people represents a catastrophe that is one of the most urgent human rights issues facing Australia today.[3] We are also faced today with many potent sources of social friction and cultural division. Community anxieties about the threat of terrorism and Islamist extremism have fed a rise in the harassment of Muslim and Arab Australians. At the same time, there has been a marked increase in reports of anti-Semitism across the country, activity that has been fuelled by hate preaching conducted in the name of Islamist

I'm not racist but ...

ideology.[4] Organised racist extremism, having been in retreat for some time, appears to be revitalised. Not unrelated to this, cyber-racism has emerged as a new challenge in combating racism. The internet has made it easy for any fringe dweller to spread messages of hatred, and to find a willing audience lurking somewhere online, with the benefit of anonymity.

Faced with all this, the Racial Discrimination Act has only gained in importance. Its history, as should be clear, remains an evolving one. But it is worth recalling the original context in which it appeared. In 1995, speaking at a ceremony marking the 20th anniversary of the Act, then prime minister Paul Keating observed, 'this was a very brave piece of legislation', which 'came at a time of great change in Australia – at a time when a lot of the old attitudes were beginning to show signs of crumbling away, and some inevitably were resisting fiercely'.[5] The Act's introduction in 1975 came only less than a decade following the referendum that put Aboriginal people on the census, and only a few years following the ending of state practices of taking Aboriginal children from their families.

Some twenty years on, in February 2015, the Governor-General Sir Peter Cosgrove would also reflect on the Act's historical significance. Speaking at a conference I convened in the Australian Human Rights Commission's Sydney office, Sir Peter spoke of the legislation as a 'crucial enabler'. It was not only

Afterword

an instrument for remedying acts of racial discrimination, but also 'the official voice on racism in the Australian community, a voice that speaks in tones of empowerment, not reprimand, one that seeks to educate and unite'. If they were stirring words, they were also accompanied by a note of caution. The Governor-General acknowledged it was a difficult brief to change attitudes about racism. Quoting Martin Luther King Jr, he noted the limits of the law: 'It may be true that morality cannot be legislated but behaviour can be regulated. The law may not change the heart, but it can restrain the heartless.'[6]

The law can only ever do so much, unless there is also an honest recognition from society about racism. There remains, most notably, the inexplicable blights within the Australian Constitution: numerous sections still empower governments to enact laws that may discriminate on the grounds of race. These must be expunged from our public life. The prohibitions on racial discrimination established by the Racial Discrimination Act continue to remain incomplete and fragile – as demonstrated by recent attempts to dilute the legislation – and will remain so unless they are also backed by constitutional guarantees of racial non-discrimination. Finally, any official statement about racial discrimination must be supported by the education of attitudes in civil society. Here, one hopes that there will continue to be a generational change in public thinking, particularly concerning

I'm not racist but ...

casual racism and bigotry. Slowly, people are coming to understand that low-level racism has its own peculiar psychological cruelty.

But we can only start from where we stand. Over four decades, decades of social change, the Racial Discrimination Act has stood firm against prejudice and bigotry. It stands to remind people that their country will protect them from discrimination and vilification – that their country will guarantee that freedom is not a privilege of the powerful, but something to be enjoyed by all. While no one law can ever eradicate the social evil of racism – no one law can ever banish hatred, ignorance and arrogance – an instrument such as the Racial Discrimination Act does make us stronger and more united. It means that every Australian can be free to pursue their happiness with the assurance of dignity and equality.

RACIAL DISCRIMINATION ACT 1975
(EXCERPTS FROM THE ACT)

Part II – Prohibition of Racial Discrimination

SECTION 8 EXCEPTIONS

(1) This Part does not apply to, or in relation to the application of, special measures to which paragraph 4 of Article 1 of the Convention applies except measures in relation to which subsection 10(1) applies by virtue of subsection 10(3).

SECTION 9 RACIAL DISCRIMINATION TO BE UNLAWFUL

(1) It is unlawful for a person to do any act involving a distinction, exclusion, restriction or preference based on race, colour, descent or national or ethnic origin which has the purpose or effect of nullifying or impairing the recognition, enjoyment or exercise, on an equal footing, of any human right or fundamental freedom in the political, economic, social, cultural or any other field of public life.

(1A) Where:

    (a) a person requires another person to comply with

a term, condition or requirement which is not reasonable having regard to the circumstances of the case; and

(b) the other person does not or cannot comply with the term, condition or requirement; and

(c) the requirement to comply has the purpose or effect of nullifying or impairing the recognition, enjoyment or exercise, on an equal footing, by persons of the same race, colour, descent or national or ethnic origin as the other person, of any human right or fundamental freedom in the political, economic, social, cultural or any other field of public life;

the act of requiring such compliance is to be treated, for the purposes of this Part, as an act involving a distinction based on, or an act done by reason of, the other person's race, colour, descent or national or ethnic origin.

(2) A reference in this section to a human right or fundamental freedom in the political, economic, social, cultural or any other field of public life includes any right of a kind referred to in Article 5 of the Convention.

(3) This section does not apply in respect of the employment, or an application for the employment, of a person on a ship or aircraft (not being an Australian ship or aircraft) if that person was engaged, or applied, for that employment outside Australia.

(4) The succeeding provisions of this Part do not limit the generality of this section.

Appendix

SECTION 10 RIGHTS TO EQUALITY BEFORE THE LAW

(1) If, by reason of, or of a provision of, a law of the Commonwealth or of a State or Territory, persons of a particular race, colour or national or ethnic origin do not enjoy a right that is enjoyed by persons of another race, colour or national or ethnic origin, or enjoy a right to a more limited extent than persons of another race, colour or national or ethnic origin, then, notwithstanding anything in that law, persons of the firstmentioned race, colour or national or ethnic origin shall, by force of this section, enjoy that right to the same extent as persons of that other race, colour or national or ethnic origin.

(2) A reference in subsection (1) to a right includes a reference to a right of a kind referred to in Article 5 of the Convention.

(3) Where a law contains a provision that:

    (a) authorizes property owned by an Aboriginal or a Torres Strait Islander to be managed by another person without the consent of the Aboriginal or Torres Strait Islander; or

    (b) prevents or restricts an Aboriginal or a Torres Strait Islander from terminating the management by another person of property owned by the Aboriginal or Torres Strait Islander;

not being a provision that applies to persons generally without regard to their race, colour or national or ethnic origin, that provision shall be deemed to be a provision in relation to which subsection (1) applies and a reference in that subsection to a right includes a reference to a right of a person to manage property owned by the person.

I'm not racist but ...

SECTION 11 ACCESS TO PLACES AND FACILITIES
It is unlawful for a person:
    (a)   to refuse to allow another person access to or use of any place or vehicle that members of the public are, or a section of the public is, entitled or allowed to enter or use, or to refuse to allow another person access to or use of any such place or vehicle except on less favourable terms or conditions than those upon or subject to which he or she would otherwise allow access to or use of that place or vehicle;
    (b)   to refuse to allow another person use of any facilities in any such place or vehicle that are available to members of the public or to a section of the public, or to refuse to allow another person use of any such facilities except on less favourable terms or conditions than those upon or subject to which he or she would otherwise allow use of those facilities; or
    (c)   to require another person to leave or cease to use any such place or vehicle or any such facilities;

by reason of the race, colour or national or ethnic origin of that other person or of any relative or associate of that other person.

SECTION 12 LAND, HOUSING AND OTHER ACCOMMODATION
(1)   It is unlawful for a person, whether as a principal or agent:
    (a)   to refuse or fail to dispose of any estate or interest in land, or any residential or business accommodation, to a second person;

Appendix

(b) to dispose of such an estate or interest or such accommodation to a second person on less favourable terms and conditions than those which are or would otherwise be offered;

(c) to treat a second person who is seeking to acquire or has acquired such an estate or interest or such accommodation less favourably than other persons in the same circumstances;

(d) to refuse to permit a second person to occupy any land or any residential or business accommodation; or

(e) to terminate any estate or interest in land of a second person or the right of a second person to occupy any land or any residential or business accommodation;

by reason of the race, colour or national or ethnic origin of that second person or of any relative or associate of that second person.

(2) It is unlawful for a person, whether as a principal or agent, to impose or seek to impose on another person any term or condition that limits, by reference to race, colour or national or ethnic origin, the persons or class of persons who may be the licensees or invitees of the occupier of any land or residential or business accommodation.

(3) Nothing in this section renders unlawful an act in relation to accommodation in a dwellinghouse or flat, being accommodation shared or to be shared, in whole or in part, with the person who did the act or a person on whose

behalf the act was done or with a relative of either of those persons.

SECTION 13 PROVISION OF GOODS AND SERVICES

It is unlawful for a person who supplies goods or services to the public or to any section of the public:

(a) to refuse or fail on demand to supply those goods or services to another person; or

(b) to refuse or fail on demand to supply those goods or services to another person except on less favourable terms or conditions than those upon or subject to which he or she would otherwise supply those goods or services;

by reason of the race, colour or national or ethnic origin of that other person or of any relative or associate of that other person.

SECTION 14 RIGHT TO JOIN TRADE UNIONS

(1) Any provision of the rules or other document constituting, or governing the activities of, a trade union that prevents or hinders a person from joining that trade union by reason of the race, colour or national or ethnic origin of that person is invalid.

(2) It is unlawful for a person to prevent or hinder another person from joining a trade union by reason of the race, colour or national or ethnic origin of that other person.

Appendix

SECTION 15 EMPLOYMENT

(1) It is unlawful for an employer or a person acting or purporting to act on behalf of an employer:

    (a) to refuse or fail to employ a second person on work of any description which is available and for which that second person is qualified;

    (b) to refuse or fail to offer or afford a second person the same terms of employment, conditions of work and opportunities for training and promotion as are made available for other persons having the same qualifications and employed in the same circumstances on work of the same description; or

    (c) to dismiss a second person from his or her employment;

by reason of the race, colour or national or ethnic origin of that second person or of any relative or associate of that second person.

(2) It is unlawful for a person concerned with procuring employment for other persons or procuring employees for any employer to treat any person seeking employment less favourably than other persons in the same circumstances by reason of the race, colour or national or ethnic origin of the person so seeking employment or of any relative or associate of that person.

(3) It is unlawful for an organization of employers or employees, or a person acting or purporting to act on behalf of such an organization, to prevent, or to seek to prevent, another person from offering for employment or from continuing

in employment by reason of the race, colour or national or ethnic origin of that other person or of any relative or associate of that other person.

(4) This section does not apply in respect of the employment, or an application for the employment, of a person on a ship or aircraft (not being an Australian ship or aircraft) if that person was engaged, or applied, for that employment outside Australia.

(5) Nothing in this section renders unlawful an act in relation to employment, or an application for employment, in a dwellinghouse or flat occupied by the person who did the act or a person on whose behalf the act was done or by a relative of either of those persons.

SECTION 16 ADVERTISEMENTS

It is unlawful for a person to publish or display, or cause or permit to be published or displayed, an advertisement or notice that indicates, or could reasonably be understood as indicating, an intention to do an act that is unlawful by reason of a provision of this Part or an act that would, but for subsection 12(3) or 15(5), be unlawful by reason of section 12 or 15, as the case may be.

Appendix

Part IIA – Prohibition of offensive behaviour based on racial hatred

SECTION 18C OFFENSIVE BEHAVIOUR BECAUSE OF RACE, COLOUR OR NATIONAL OR ETHNIC ORIGIN

(1) It is unlawful for a person to do an act, otherwise than in private, if:

    (a) the act is reasonably likely, in all the circumstances, to offend, insult, humiliate or intimidate another person or a group of people; and

    (b) the act is done because of the race, colour or national or ethnic origin of the other person or of some or all of the people in the group.

    Note: Subsection (1) makes certain acts unlawful. Section 46P of the *Australian Human Rights Commission Act 1986* allows people to make complaints to the Australian Human Rights Commission about unlawful acts. However, an unlawful act is not necessarily a criminal offence. Section 26 says that this Act does not make it an offence to do an act that is unlawful because of this Part, unless Part IV expressly says that the act is an offence.

(2) For the purposes of subsection (1), an act is taken not to be done in private if it:

    (a) causes words, sounds, images or writing to be communicated to the public; or

    (b) is done in a public place; or

    (c) is done in the sight or hearing of people who are in a public place.

(3) In this section:

public place includes any place to which the public have access as of right or by invitation, whether express or implied and whether or not a charge is made for admission to the place.

SECTION 18D EXEMPTIONS

Section 18C does not render unlawful anything said or done reasonably and in good faith:

(a) in the performance, exhibition or distribution of an artistic work; or

(b) in the course of any statement, publication, discussion or debate made or held for any genuine academic, artistic or scientific purpose or any other genuine purpose in the public interest; or

(c) in making or publishing:
- (i) a fair and accurate report of any event or matter of public interest; or
- (ii) a fair comment on any event or matter of public interest if the comment is an expression of a genuine belief held by the person making the comment.

Appendix

Part III – Race Discrimination Commissioner and functions of Commission

SECTION 19 RACE DISCRIMINATION COMMISSIONER
For the purposes of this Act there shall be a Race Discrimination Commissioner.

SECTION 20 FUNCTIONS OF COMMISSION
The following functions are hereby conferred on the Commission:

- (b) to promote an understanding and acceptance of, and compliance with, this Act;
- (c) to develop, conduct and foster research and educational programs and other programs for the purpose of:
  - (i) combating racial discrimination and prejudices that lead to racial discrimination;
  - (ii) promoting understanding, tolerance and friendship among racial and ethnic groups; and
  - (iii) propagating the purposes and principles of the Convention;
- (d) to prepare, and to publish in such manner as the Commission considers appropriate, guidelines for the avoidance of infringements of Part II or Part IIA;
- (e) where the Commission considers it appropriate to do so, with the leave of the court hearing the proceedings and subject to any conditions imposed

by the court, to intervene in proceedings that involve racial discrimination issues;
(f) to inquire into, and make determinations on, matters referred to it by the Minister or the Commissioner.

NOTES

INTRODUCTION
1   K Dunn, J Forrest, R Pe-Pua, M Hynes & K Maeder-Han, 'The spheres of racism and anti-racism in contemporary Australian cities', *Cosmopolitan Civil Societies Journal*, vol. 1, no. 1, 2009, p. 5.

1   RACE IN AUSTRALIA
1   N Bryant, *The Rise and Fall of Australia: How a Great Nation Lost its Way*, Random House Australia, Sydney, 2014, p. 150.
2   Bryant, *The Rise and Fall of Australia*, p.167.
3   S Lane, 'Trujillo's tirade: Australia has racist views and business is "a step back in time"', ABC Radio (AM), 26 May 2009, <www.abc.net.au/am/content/2009/s2580674.htm>.
4   N Pearson, The start of serious national reportage on original Australians and our affairs, *The Australian*, 16 July 2014, <www.theaustralian.com.au/50th-birthday-news/the-start-of-serious-national-reportage-on-original-australians-and-our-affairs/story-fnmx97ei-1226990205399>.
5   G Freudenberg, *Churchill and Australia*, Pan Macmillan Australia, Sydney, 2009, p. 3.
6   AWF Edwards, 'Human genetic diversity: Lewontin's fallacy', (2003) *BioEssays* 25, p. 798.
7   C Kenneally, *The Invisible History of the Human Race: How DNA and History Shape our Identities and Our Future*, Black Inc, Melbourne, 2014, p. 239.
8   CD Montesquieu, *The Spirit of the Laws*, Hafner Press, New York, 1949, p. 264.
9   C Mills, *The Racial Contract*, Cornell University Press, Ithaca, 1997, p. 20.
10 *Mabo v Queensland (No 2)* (1992) 175 CLR 1 para. 63 (Brennan J).
11 J Hirst, *Sense and Nonsense in Australian History*, Black Inc Agenda, Melbourne, 2006, p. 65.

Notes to pages 18–27

12 Mills, *The Racial Contract*, p. 29.
13 For an authoritative treatment of this history, see M Lake and H Reynolds, *Drawing the Global Colour Line: White Men's Countries and the International Challenge of Racial Equality*, Cambridge University Press, Melbourne, 2008.
14 See S Macintyre & A Clark, *The History Wars*, Melbourne University Press, Melbourne, 2004, 2nd ed.
15 N Pearson, 'A Rightful Place: Race, Recognition and a More Complete Commonwealth', *Quarterly Essay*, vol. 55, 2014, p. 24.
16 Pearson, 'A Rightful Place', pp. 20–21.
17 A de Gobineau, *The Inequality of Human Races*, William Heinemann, London, 1915.
18 A Curthoys, 'Liberalism and Exclusionism: A Prehistory of the White Australia Policy', in L Jayasuriya, D Walker & J Gothard (eds), *Legacies of White Australia*, University of Western Australia Press, Perth, 2003, p. 13.
19 Curthoys, 'Liberalism and Exclusionism', in *Legacies of White Australia*, p. 13.
20 Curthoys, 'Liberalism and Exclusionism', in *Legacies of White Australia*, p. 21.
21 H McQueen, 'Racists', in R Manne and C Feik, *The Words That Made Australia: How a Nation Came to Know Itself*, Black Inc Agenda, Melbourne, 2012, p. 140.
22 McQueen, 'Racists', in *The Words That Made Australia*, p. 140.
23 Curthoys, 'Liberalism and Exclusionism' in *Legacies of White Australia*, p. 29.
24 B Hoban, 'Restrictive immigration Acts', <www.sbs.com.au/gold/story.php?storyid=58>.
25 J Pitts, *A Turn to Empire: The Rise of Imperial Liberalism in Britain and France*, Princeton University Press, Princeton, 2005, p. 144.
26 D Walker, 'Race building and the disciplining of White Australia', in L Jayasuriya, D Walker & J Gothard (eds), *Legacies of White Australia*, p. 34.
27 M Lake, 'The white man under siege: New histories of race in the nineteenth century and the advent of white Australia', *History Workshop Journal*, vol. 58, no. 1, 2004, p. 41.
28 Walker, 'Race building and the disciplining of White Australia', in *Legacies of White Australia*, p. 42.
29 C Pearson, *National Life and Character: A Forecast*, Macmillan and Co, London, 1913, p. 83.
30 See Lake, 'The white man under siege'.
31 Pearson, *National Life and Character*, p. 83.

Notes to pages 27–39

32 Walker, 'Race building and the disciplining of White Australia', in *Legacies of White Australia*, p. 44.
33 J Hirst, *The Australians: Insiders and Outsiders on the National Character since 1770*, Black Inc Agenda, Melbourne, 2007, p. 13.
34 A Deakin, 'Second reading speech: Immigration Restriction Bill', House of Representatives, *Debates*, 12 September 1901, p. 4804.
35 Deakin, 'Second reading speech: Immigration Restriction Bill', p. 4804.
36 A Curthoys (ed.), *Connected Worlds: History in Transnational Perspective*, Australian National University E Press, Canberra, 2005, p. 225.
37 N Dyrenfurth and F Bongiorno, *A Little History of the Australian Labor Party*, UNSW Press, Sydney, 2011, p. 43.
38 Deakin, 'Second reading speech: Immigration Restriction Bill', p. 4806.
39 See J Jupp, *The Australian People: An Encyclopaedia of the Nation, Its People and Their Origins*, Cambridge University Press, Cambridge, 2001.
40 Jupp, *The Australian People*, p. 48.
41 See Department of Immigration, 'Fact Sheet 8 – Abolition of the "White Australia" Policy', 2009, <www.immi.gov.au/media/fact-sheets/08abolition.htm>.
42 R Manne (ed.), *The Howard Years*, Black Inc Agenda, Melbourne, 2004, p. 128.
43 G Tavan, *The Long, Slow Death of White Australia*, Scribe, Melbourne, 2005.
44 A Markus, 'Of Continuities and Discontinuities: Reflections on a Century of Australian Immigration Control', in L Jayasuriya, D Walker & J Gothard (eds), *Legacies of White Australia*, University of Western Australia Press, Perth, 2003, p. 185.
45 M Langton, 'The gripes of wrath', *Sydney Morning Herald*, 2 October 2011, <www.smh.com.au/federal-politics/political-opinion/the-gripes-of-wrath-20111001-1l2z5.html>.
46 M Dodson, 'Indigenous Australians' in Manne (ed.), *The Howard Years*, p. 141.
47 R Manne, 'The Road to *Tampa*', in L Jayasuriya, D Walker & J Gothard (eds), *Legacies of White Australia*, University of Western Australia Press, Perth, 2003, p. 163.
48 S Perera, *Australia and the Insular Imagination: Beaches, Borders, Boats, and Bodies*, Palgrave Macmillan, 2009, p. 98.
49 R Manne, *Making Trouble: Essays Against the New Australian Complacency*, Black Inc Agenda, Melbourne, 2011, p. 125.

50 Manne, 'The Road to *Tampa*', in *Legacies of White Australia*, p. 163; see also Manne, *Making Trouble*.
51 G Hage, *White Nation: Fantasies of White supremacy in a multicultural society*, Routledge, New York, 2000, p. 56.
52 As I have made clear on previous occasions, there are good reasons to have citizenship tests for immigrants who wish to naturalise as Australians. But the focus of such tests should be on civic content, concerning a knowledge of our political system and values. See T Soutphommasane, *Reclaiming Patriotism: Nation-Building for Australian Progressives*, Cambridge University Press, Melbourne, 2009; *The Virtuous Citizen: Patriotism in a Multicultural Society*, Cambridge University Press, Cambridge, 2012.
53 See Tariq Modood, *Multiculturalism: A Civic Idea*, Polity Press, Cambridge, 2007.
54 N Cater, *The Lucky Culture and the Rise of an Australian Ruling Class*, HarperCollins Publishers, Sydney, 2013, p. 251.
55 See Soutphommasane, *Reclaiming Patriotism*, ch 1.
56 J Sammut, '18C makes us all tongue-tied', *The Australian*, 20 January 2015 <www.theaustralian.com.au/opinion/c-makes-us-all-tongue-tied/story-e6frg6zo-1227189986845>.
57 WR Louis & MJ Hornsey, 'Psychological dimensions of racial vilification and harassment', Paper presented at the 'RDA@40' Conference on 40 Years of the Racial Discrimination Act, Australian Human Rights Commission, Sydney, 19 February 2015.

2 THE RACIAL DISCRIMINATION ACT

1 See Australian Human Rights Commission, 'Conciliation register', <www.humanrights.gov.au/complaints/conciliation-register> .
2 J Spigelman, 'The Common Law Bill of Rights' (University of Queensland, Brisbane, 10 March 2008) p. 25, <www.supremecourt.justice.nsw.gov.au/agdbasev7wr/supremecourt/documents/pdf/spigelman_speeches_2008.pdf> .
3 The RDA also provides an exception for 'special measures' under section 8 – that is, positive action designed to assist or protect disadvantaged racial groups. This reflects the legislation's protection of both formal and substantive equality in matters of race. See A Cowan, 'UNDRIP and the Intervention: Indigenous Self-Determination, Participation, and Racial Discrimination in the Northern Territory of Australia', *Pacific Rim Law and Policy Journal*, vol. 22, no. 2 (2013); A Vivian and B Schokman, 'The Northern Territory Intervention and the Fabrication of "Special Measures"', *Australian Indigenous Law Review*, vol. 13, no. 1 (2009); A Vivian,

'The NTER Redesign Consultation Process: Not Very Special', *Australian Indigenous Law Review*, vol. 14, no. 1 (2010); Australian Human Rights Commission, *Guidelines to understanding 'Special measures' in the Racial Discrimination Act 1975* (Cth), 2011, <www.humanrights.gov.au/sites/default/files/content/pdf/race_discrim/special_measures2011.pdf>.

4   N Pearson, 'The Reward for Public Life is Public Progress: An Appreciation of the Public Life of the Hon E.G. Whitlam AC QC Prime Minister 1972–1975' (2013 Whitlam Oration, Whitlam Institute, University of Western Sydney, 13 November 2013) p. 4.
5   A Fanfani, President of the United Nations General Assembly, 21 December 1965.
6   G Frederickson, *Racism: A Short History*, Princeton University Press, Princeton, 2002, p. 100.
7   Frederickson, *Racism*, p. 151–52.
8   *Official Record of the Debates of the Australasian Federal Convention*, Melbourne, Legal Books, Sydney, 1986, vol. 4, p. 667.
9   J Quick and R Garran, *The Annotated Constitution of the Australian Commonwealth*, Angus and Robertson, Melbourne, 1901, p. 622.
10 M Rosen, *Dignity: Its History and Meaning*, Harvard University Press, Cambridge, 2012, pp. 1–2.
11 UN General Assembly, *Universal Declaration of Human Rights*, 10 December 1948, 217 A (III), <www.refworld.org/docid/3ae6b3712c.html>.
12 UN General Assembly, *International Covenant on Civil and Political Rights*, 16 December 1966, United Nations, Treaty Series, vol. 999, p. 171, <www.refworld.org/docid/3ae6b3aa0.html>.
13 UN General Assembly, *International Convention on the Elimination of All Forms of Racial Discrimination*, 21 December 1965, United Nations, Treaty Series, vol. 660, p. 195, <www.refworld.org/docid/3ae6b3940.html>.
14 M Flanaghan, 'A History Consigned to Dust', *The Age*, 26 August 2006, <www.theage.com.au/news/in-depth/a-history-consigned-to-dust/2006/08/25/1156012738197.html>.
15 J Waldron, *Dignity, Rank, and Rights*, Oxford University Press, New York, 2012, p. 21.
16 See Rosen, *Dignity: Its History and Meaning*, ch.1.
17 Waldron, *Dignity, Rank, and Rights*, p. 33.
18 Rosen, *Dignity: Its History and Meaning*, p. 95.
19 Rosen, *Dignity: Its History and Meaning*, p. 97.
20 D Herzog, 'Aristocratic Dignity?' in Waldron, *Dignity, Rank, and Rights*, p. 106.

Notes to pages 60–71

21 Waldron, *Dignity, Rank, and Rights*, p. 50.
22 C Taylor, 'The Politics of Recognition' in A Gutmann (ed.), *Multiculturalism: Examining the Politics of Recognition*, Princeton University Press, Princeton, 1994, p. 25.
23 L Murphy, 'Second reading speech: Racial Discrimination Bill 1973', Speech, The Senate, 21 November 1973, p. 1.
24 K Enderby, 'Second reading speech: Racial Discrimination Bill 1975', Speech, House of Representatives, 13 February 1975, p. 1.
25 Enderby, 'Second reading speech: Racial Discrimination Bill 1975', p. 1.
26 G Sheil, 'Second reading speech: Racial Discrimination Bill 1975', Speech, The Senate, 15 May 1975, p. 1.
27 I Wood, 'Second reading speech: Racial Discrimination Bill 1975', Speech, The Senate, 22 May 1975, p. 1.
28 N Bonner, 'Second reading speech: Racial Discrimination Bill 1975', Speech, The Senate, 27 May 1975, p. 2.
29 J Howard, 'Racial Discrimination Bill 1975', Speech, House of Representatives, 3 June 1975, p. 1.
30 J Howard, 'Second reading speech: Racial Discrimination Bill 1975', House of Representatives, 8 April 1975.
31 F Chaney, 'Second reading speech: Racial Discrimination Bill 1975', Speech, The Senate, 22 May 1975.
32 I Greenwood, 'Second reading speech: Racial Discrimination Bill 1975', Speech, The Senate, 15 May 1975, pp. 1, 5.
33 Greenwood, 'Second reading speech: Racial Discrimination Bill 1975', p. 4.
34 K Enderby, 'Third reading speech: Racial Discrimination Bill 1975', Speech, House of Representatives, 9 April 1975, p. 1.
35 G Whitlam, 'Proclamation of the Racial Discrimination Act', Speech, 31 October 1975, p. 2.
36 A Markus, 'Mapping Social Cohesion: The Scanlon Foundation surveys 2014' (2014) pp. 1, 4.
37 B Gaze, 'The *Racial Discrimination Act* after 40 years: Advancing equality or sliding into obsolescence?', Paper to 'RDA@40' Conference on 40 Years of the Racial Discrimination Act, Australian Human Rights Commission, Sydney, 20 February 2015. These reported decisions include decisions between 1975 and January 2015 in the Human Rights and Equal Opportunity Commission, the Federal Circuit Court/Federal Magistrate's Court, the Federal Court of Australia, the Full Court of the Federal Court of Australia and the High Court of Australia.
38 Z Antonios *The Racial Discrimination Act: A Review*, 1995, p. 38.

Notes to pages 72–77

39. Howard, 'Racial Discrimination Bill 1975', p. 1.
40. These examples are drawn from the Australian Human Rights Commission's Conciliation Register, <www.humanrights.gov.au/complaints/conciliation-register>.
41. *Bull v Kuch* (1993) EOC 92–518.
42. *Carr v Boree Aboriginal Corp* [2003] FMCA 408. For further examples of successful cases argued under the RDA from 2000–2014, see *Gama v Qantas Airways Ptd Ltd (No 2)* [2006] FMCA 1767; *Qantas Airways Limited v Gama* (2008) 167 FCR 537; *Baird v Queensland* (2006) 156 FCR 451; *House v Queanbeyan Community Radio Station* [2008] FMCA 897; *Caves v Lewi Chan (No 2)* [2010] FMCA 817; *Trapman v Sydney Water Corporation* [2011] FMCA 398. These cases are mentioned in Gaze, 'The *Racial Discrimination Act* after 40 years'.
43. See *Australian Human Rights Commission Act 1986* (Cth) s 46PO(4).
44. S Rice, 'Why free speech comes at a price: Reflections on race, civility and the law' (Inaugural Research Seminar, Deakin University School of Law in association with Sladen Legal, 31 July 2014) p. 5.
45. B Gaze, 'Has the Racial Discrimination Act Contributed to Eliminating Racial Discrimination? Analysing the Litigation Track Record 2000–2004' (2005) 11(1) *Australian Journal of Human Rights*, 6.
46. See M Thornton, *The Liberal Promise: Anti-Discrimination Legislation in Australia*, Oxford University Press, Melbourne, 1990.
47. Thornton, *The Liberal Promise*, p. 84.
48. Gaze, 'Has the Racial Discrimination Act Contributed to Eliminating Racial Discrimination?'; Markus, 'Mapping Social Cohesion 2014'.
49. Enderby, 'Second reading speech: Racial Discrimination Bill 1975', p. 2.
50. Whitlam, 'Proclamation of the Racial Discrimination Act', p. 1.
51. P Keating, 'Speech by the Prime Minister, the Hon. PJ Keating, Anniversary of the Racial Discrimination Act, Melbourne, 9 June 1995, <www.pmtranscripts.dpmc.gov.au/browse.php?did=9625>.
52. *Koowarta v Bjelke-Petersen* (1982) 153 CLR 168.
53. *Commonwealth v Tasmania* (1983) 158 CLR 1.
54. Sir Harry Gibbs, 'The Constitutional Protection of Human Rights' (1982) 9 *Monash University Law Review* 1.
55. 'Section 109 of the Constitution provides: "When a law of a State is inconsistent with a law of the Commonwealth, the latter shall

prevail, and the former shall, to the extent of the inconsistency, be invalid.'"

56 G Williams & D Reynolds, 'The *Racial Discrimination Act* and Inconsistency with State and Federal Laws', Paper presented to the 'RDA@40' Conference on 40 Years of the Racial Discrimination Act, Australian Human Rights Commission, Sydney, 19 February 2015.
57 R French, 'The Practising of Law in a Global Neighbourhood', University of Newcastle, Ninian Stephen Lecture, 8 August 2014.
58 *Mabo v Queensland (No. 1)* (1989) 166 CLR 186.
59 *Mabo v Queensland (No. 2)* (1992) 175 CLR 1.
60 M Kirby, 'Koowarta – A Vital Turning Point for Aboriginal Rights', The University of Melbourne Law School, 29 May 2012, p. 4, <www.michaelkirby.com.au/images/stories/speeches/2000s/2012/2595.%20SPEECH%20-%20THE%20UNI%20MELB.%20TURNING%20POINTS%20SYMPOSIUM.pdf>.
61 See, e.g., Williams & Reynolds, 'The *Racial Discrimination Act* and Inconsistency with State and Federal Laws'; Megan Davis and George Williams, *Everything you Need to Know About the Referendum to Recognise Indigenous Australians*, NewSouth Publishing, 2015.
62 Gaze, 'Has the Racial Discrimination Act Contributed to Eliminating Racial Discrimination?'
63 *Racial Discrimination Act 1975* (Cth) s 20.
64 For more information about the National Anti-Racism Strategy, including the 'Racism. It Stops with Me' campaign, see <http://itstopswithme.humanrights.gov.au>.
65 Cited in F Chaney, 'Second reading speech: Racial Discrimination Bill 1975', Speech, The Senate, 22 May 1975, p. 3.
66 Rice, 'Why free speech comes at a price: Reflections on race, civility and the law', p. 8.
67 K Gelber & L McNamara, 'What are the effects of civil hate speech laws? Lessons from Australia' (forthcoming).
68 S Rice, 'Basic instinct, and the heroic project of anti-discrimination law', Roma Mitchell Oration 2013, Adelaide Festival of Ideas, 19 October 2013, p.10.
69 Rice, 'Basic instinct, and the heroic project of anti-discrimination law', p. 10.

3 FREEDOM OF SPEECH AND ITS LIMITS

1. See E Griffiths, 'George Brandis defends "right to be a bigot" amid Government plan to amend Racial Discrimination Act', *ABC*, 24 March 2014, <www.abc.net.au/news/2014-03-24/brandis-defends-right-to-be-a-bigot/5341552>.
2. T Abbott, 'Joint Press Conference' (Parliament House, 5 August 2014) <www.pm.gov.au/media/2014-08-05/joint-press-conference-canberra-0>.
3. L Bourke, 'Charlie Hebdo attack prompts renewed calls for race-hate law changes in Australia', *Sydney Morning Herald*, 12 January 2015, <www.smh.com.au/federal-politics/political-news/charlie-hebdo-attack-prompts-renewed-calls-for-racehate-law-changes-in-australia-20150112-12m7d6.html>; S Medhora, 'Racial Discrimination Act would outlaw Charlie Hebdo cartoons, say critics', *The Guardian Australia*, 13 January 2015, <www.theguardian.com/media/2015/jan/13/racial-discrimination-act-would-outlaw-charlie-hebdo-cartoons-say-critics>.
4. T Abbott, 'Interview with Nick McCallum, Radio 3AW', 14 January 2015, <www.pm.gov.au/media/2015-01-14/interview-nick-mccallum-radio-3aw-0>.
5. I Berlin, 'Two Concepts of Liberty' in H Hardy and R Hausheer, *The Proper Study of Mankind: An Anthology of Essays*, Farrar, Straus and Giroux, New York, 1998, pp. 194–206.
6. Berlin, 'Two Concepts of Liberty' in *The Proper Study of Mankind*, pp. 205–206.
7. See for example, C Taylor 'What's Wrong with Negative Liberty' in C Taylor, *Philosophy and the Human Sciences: Philosophical Papers 2* (1999) pp. 211–29.
8. *Beauharnais v Illinois* 343 US 250 (1952).
9. *Abrams v United States* 250 US 616 (1919) p. 630.
10. *Schenck v United States* 249 US 47 (1919) p. 52.
11. L Brandeis, *Other People's Money and How the Bankers Use It*, Frederick A. Stokes, New York, 1914, p. 92.
12. See *Whitney v. California*, 274 US 357 (1927).
13. JS Mill, *On Liberty and other writings*, Cambridge University Press, New York, 1859, p. 20.
14. JD Peters, *Courting the Abyss: Free Speech and the Liberal Tradition*, University of Chicago Press, Chicago, 2005, p. 150.
15. Mill, *On Liberty and other writings*, p. 45.
16. M Matsuda, 'Public Response to Racist Speech: Considering the Victim's Story' (1989) *Michigan Law Review* vol. 87, no. 8, p. 2336.

17 C Taylor, 'The Politics of Recognition' in A Gutmann (ed.), *Multiculturalism: Examining the Politics of Recognition*, Princeton University Press, Princeton, 1994, p. 25.
18 O Cox, *Caste, Class and Race: A Study in Social Dynamics*, Monthly Review Press, New York, 1948, p. 383, cited in R Delgado, 'Words that Wound: A Tort Action for Racial Insults, Epithets, and Name-Calling' (1982) *Harvard Civil Rights-Civil Liberties Law Review*, vol. 17, p. 136.
19 VicHealth, *Review of audit and assessment tools, programs and resources in workplace settings to prevent race-based discrimination and support diversity* (2010) pp. 14–15. Studies also highlight the negative consequences of racial discrimination such as difficulties accessing housing and health care and significantly lower life expectancy than non-Indigenous Australians: see Y Neto and A Pedersen, 'No Time Like the Present: Determinants of Intentions To Engage In Bystander Anti-Racism On Behalf Of Indigenous Australians' (2013) *Journal of Pacific Rim Psychology* 7 (1) p. 36.
20 Matsuda, 'Public Response to Racist Speech: Considering the Victim's Story', p. 2340.
21 Research shows that bystanders hearing racial hatred can become more prejudiced, and similarly, bystanders become less prejudiced when they hear non-prejudiced comments. And it has also been said that their lingering regret may be associated with negative health consequences through rumination: see J Goodman, J Schell, M Alexander, and S Eidelman, 'The Impact of a Derogatory Remark on Prejudice Towards a Gay Male Leader' (2008) *Journal of Applied Social Psychology* 38 (2) pp. 543–44; J Nelson, K Dunn and Y Paradies, 'Bystander Anti-Racism: A Review of the Literature' (2011) *Analyses of Social Issues and Public Policy* 11(1) p. 268.
22 S Warren & L Brandeis, 'The Right to Privacy' (1890) *Harvard Law Review* IV (5) p. 194.
23 Australian Human Rights Commission, 'National Anti-Racism Strategy: Consultation Report', 2012, p. 3.
24 Survey responses from the Australian Human Rights Commission's consultations as part of the National Anti-Racism Strategy in 2012 (unpublished).
25 Survey responses from the Australian Human Rights Commission's consultations as part of the National Anti-Racism Strategy in 2012 (unpublished).
26 J Waldron, *The Harm of Hate Speech*, Harvard University Press, Cambridge MA, 2012, p. 60.
27 S Joseph & M Castan, *The International Covenant on Civil and*

Political Rights: Cases, Materials and Commentary, Oxford University Press, 3rd ed., Oxford, 2013, p. 764.

28 See *Hobart Hebrew Congregation v Scully* (Unreported, Human Rights and Equal Opportunity Commission, Commissioner Cavanough QC, 21 September 2000; *Jones v Scully* (2002) 120 FCR 243; *Eatock v Bolt* [2011] FCA 1103.

29 *Toben v Jones* [2003] FCAFC 137, para 20 (Carr J).

30 Human Rights and Equal Opportunity Commission, *Report of National Inquiry into Racist Violence in Australia* (1991), p. 168, <www.humanrights.gov.au/publications/racist-violence-1991>.

31 Human Rights and Equal Opportunity Commission, above, pp. 301–302.

32 E Johnson, *Royal Commission into Aboriginal Deaths in Custody, National Report Volume 4* (1991), para 28.3.50, recommendation 213, <www.humanrights.gov.au/publications/racist-violence-1991>.

33 Johnson, *Royal Commission into Aboriginal Deaths in Custody*, para 28.3.34, <www.humanrights.gov.au/publications/racist-violence-1991>.

34 Australian Law Reform Commission, *Multiculturalism and the Law: Report No 57* (1992), p. 132–33, <www.alrc.gov.au/report-57>.

35 Commonwealth of Australia, Parliamentary Debates, House of Representatives, Tuesday 15 November 1994, p. 3336 (The Hon Michael Lavarch MP, Attorney-General).

36 For a useful commentary see S Rice, 'Charlie Hebdo attacks provide a false pretext for 18C debate', *The Conversation*, 16 January 2015, <www.theconversation.com/charlie-hebdo-attacks-provide-a-false-pretext-for-18c-debate-36248>.

37 *Creek v Cairns Post Pty Ltd* (2001) 112 FCR 352 (Kiefel J) cited with approval in *Bropho v Human Rights and Equal Opportunity Commission* (2004) 135 FCR 105.

38 See *Jones v Scully* (2002) 120 FCR 243; *Eatock v Bolt* [2011] FCA 1180.

39 *Kelly-Country v Beers & Anor* (2004) 207 ALR 421.

40 *Walsh v Hanson*, Unreported, Human Rights and Equal Opportunity Commission, Commissioner Nader, 2 March 2000.

41 *Bropho v Human Rights & Equal Opportunity Commission* [2004] FCAFC 16.

42 *Eatock v Bolt* [2011] FCA 1180. For academic commentary about this case and its impact on public debates, see K Gelber & L McNamara, 'Freedom of speech and racial vilification in Australia: "The Bolt Case" in public discourse', *Australian Journal of Political Science*, vol. 48, no. 4 (2013), pp. 470–84.

43 G Brandis, *Racial Discrimination Act*, Media Release, 25 March 2014, <www.attorneygeneral.gov.au/Mediareleases/Pages/2014/First%20Quarter/25March2014-RacialDiscriminationAct.aspx>.
44 Brandis, *Racial Discrimination Act*, Media Release, 25 March 2014, <www.attorneygeneral.gov.au/Mediareleases/Pages/2014/First%20 Quarter/25March2014-RacialDiscriminationAct.aspx>.
45 Freedom of Speech (Repeal of S.18C) Bill 2014.
46 Reported in 'Race hate: voters tell Brandis to back off', *Sydney Morning Herald*, 13 April 2014, <www.smh.com.au/federal-politics/political-news/race-hate-voters-tell-brandis-to-back-off-20140413-zqubv.html>.
47 University of Western Sydney, *Challenging Racism: The Anti-Racism, Research Project*, 2010.
48 S Rice, 'Race act changes are what you get when you champion bigotry', *The Conversation*, 26 March 2014, <theconversation.com/race-act-changes-are-what-you-get-when-you-champion-bigotry-24782>.
49 R King, *An Offence: The Politics of Indignation*, Scribe Publications, Melbourne, 2013, p. 219.
50 F Voltaire, *Candide, or Optimism*, Cramer, Marc-Michel Rey, Jean Nourse, Lambert, and others, France, 1759, p. 28.
51 Peters, *Courting the Abyss*.
52 E Burke, *On Taste; On the Sublime and Beautiful; Reflections on the French Revolution; A Letter to a Noble Lord*, Grolier Enterprises Corp, Danbury, CT, 1980.
53 Survey responses from the Australian Human Rights Commission's consultations as part of the National Anti-Racism Strategy in 2012 (unpublished).
54 National Congress of Australia's First Peoples, Australian Hellenic Council, Executive Council of Australian Jewry, Chinese Australian Forum, Chinese Australian Services Society, Armenian National Committee of Australia and Korean Society of Sydney, 'Community groups continue campaign for retention of law against race hate' Joint Media Statement, 12 February 2014, <www.ecaj.org.au/2014/community-groups-continue-campaign-for-retention-of-law-against-race-hate/>.
55 For a discussion of free speech protections in Australian legal and political culture, including restrictions on speech imposed by regulations concerning terrorism, protest, hate speech and corporations, see K Gelber, *Speech Matters: Getting Free Speech Right*, University of Queensland Press, Brisbane, 2011.
56 NSW Legislative Assembly Standing Order 72 'Offensive Words

Not to be Used'; Victorian Legislative Assembly Standing Order 119 'No Offensive Language against Other Members'; Queensland Legislative Standing Order 234 'Personal Reflections on Members'; South Australian House of Assembly Standing Order 121 'Irreverent use of the Sovereign's name or the Governor's name', 122 'Offensive words against either House', and 125 'Offensive words against Member'; Western Australian Legislative Assembly Standing Order 42 'Member Named for Disorderly Conduct'; Tasmanian House of Assembly Standing Order 179 'Offensive words against either House, or against Statutes' and 181 'Offensive words against a Member'; ACT Legislative Assembly Standing Order 54 'Offensive Words'; and Northern Territory Legislative Assembly Standing Order 62 'Offensive or Unbecoming Words' respectively.

57   *R v Strong* [2003] NSWCCA 123. The offensive language provisions fell under section 4(1)(b), which is now section 4A.

58   *Del Vecchio v Couchy* [2002] QCA 9. This case involved section 7AA *Vagrants, Gaming and Other Offences Act 1931* (Qld), which was replaced in 2005 by section 6 of the *Summary Offences Act 2005* (Qld).

59   *Semmens v Police* [1998] SASC 6868.

60   *Kim Anne Ahmed v Harbour Radio Pty Limited* [2013] NSWSC 1928.

61   *Gacic v John Fairfax Publications Pty Ltd (No 2)* [2014] NSWSC 738.

62   Berlin, 'Two Concepts of Liberty' in *The Proper Study of Mankind*, pp. 10–11.

4   CASUAL RACISM AND BIGOTRY

1   See for example, L Hyers, 'Resisting prejudice every day: Exploring women's assertive responses to anti-Black racism, Anti-Semitism, heterosexism, and sexism', Sex Roles, 56(1) (2007), pp. 1–12, as cited in VicHealth, *Review of bystander approaches in support of preventing race-based discrimination*, 2010, p. 9; F Aboud and A Joong, 'Intergroup name-calling and conditions for creating assertive bystanders', in S Levy & M Killen (eds), *Intergroup attitudes and relations in childhood through adulthood*, Oxford University Press, New York, pp. 249–60, as cited in VicHealth, *Review of bystander approaches in support of preventing race-based discrimination*, 2010, p. 9.

2   J Hirst, *Sense and Nonsense in Australian History*, Black Inc Agenda, Melbourne, 2006, p. 301.

3   N Bryant, *The Rise and Fall of Australia: How a Great Nation Lost its Way*, Random House Australia, Sydney, 2014; W Aly, 'Noisy bigots drown out silent bias', *Sydney Morning Herald*, 4 April 2013, <www.smh.com.au/comment/noisy-bigots-drown-out-silent-bias-20130404-2h900.html>.
4   M Smith, 'Alan Joyce pilots Qantas from turbulence to clear skies', *Financial Review*, 13 December 2014 <www.afr.com/p/business/companies/alan_joyce_pilots_qantas_from_turbulence_Ozo9pccKXJS5HZqh0hzS2K>.
5   S Lane, 'Trujillo's tirade: Australia has racist views and business is "a step back in time"', ABC Radio (AM), 26 May 2009, <www.abc.net.au/am/content/2009/s2580674.htm>.
6   Bryant, *The Rise and Fall of Australia*, p. 163.
7   Bryant, *The Rise and Fall of Australia*, p. 166.
8   M Sawyer, 'How racist are you?', *Sydney Morning Herald*, 12 June 2014 <www.smh.com.au/comment/how-racist-are-you-20140611-zs43h.html>.
9   See J Nelson and J Walton, 'Explainer: What is Casual Racism?', *SBS News*, 2 September 2014, <www.sbs.com.au/news/article/2014/09/02/explainer-what-casual-racism>.
10 A Markus, *Mapping Social Cohesion 2014: The Scanlon Foundation Surveys National Report* (2014) p. 24, <www.scanlonfoundation.org.au/wp-content/uploads/2014/07/mapping-social-cohesion-national-report-2013.pdf>.
11 A Ferdinand, Y Paradies & M Kelaher, *Mental Health Impacts of Racial Discrimination in Victorian Aboriginal Communities*, The Lowitja Institute, 2013, <www.lowitja.org.au/lowitja-publishing/L023>.
12 Markus, *Mapping Social Cohesion 2014*, <www.scanlonfoundation.org.au/wp-content/uploads/2014/07/mapping-social-cohesion-national-report-2013.pdf>.
13 J Baird, 'Hate speech should be shouted down', *Sydney Morning Herald*, 30 January 2015, p. 36 (also at <www.smh.com.au/comment/hate-speech-should-be-shouted-down-20150130-131owp.html>).
14 C Mills, *The Racial Contract*, Cornell University Press, Ithaca, 1997.
15 T Soutphommasane, *Don't Go Back To Where You Came From: Why Multiculturalism Works*, NewSouth Publishing, Sydney 2012, p. 68.
16 C Sams, 'A Current Affair breached code with 'All-Asian Mall' story', *Sydney Morning Herald*, 13 September 2013 <www.smh.com.au/entertainment/tv-and-radio/a-current-affair-breached-code-with-allasian-mall-story-20130913-2toio.html>; S Duck, 'Pauline

Hanson tries moonlighting as a journalist' <www.heraldsun.com.au/entertainment/celebrity/pauline-tries-moonlighting/story-e6frf96o-1226361571562?nk=51ea1eed2968acb31752a69eb2c0442e>.

17 Cited in H Vatsikopoulos, 'Whose Australian stories? Cultural diversity at the ABC', *The Conversation*, 23 July 2014, <www.theconversation.com/whose-australian-stories-cultural-diversity-at-the-abc-29481>.

18 See P Kalina, 'Diversity still out of the picture', *Sydney Morning Herald*, 1 March 2012, <www.smh.com.au/entertainment/tv-and-radio/diversity-still-out-of-the-picture-20120229-1u1jg.html>.

19 Ralph Bunche Centre for African American Studies at UCLA, *2014 Hollywood Diversity Report: Making Sense of the Disconnect* (2014).

20 R Coates, 'Covert Racism: Theories, Types and Examples' in R Coates (ed.) *Covert Racism: Theories, Institutions, and Experiences*, Brill Publishers, Leiden, 2011.

21 See P Kalina, 'Diversity still out of the picture', *Sydney Morning Herald*, 1 March 2012, <www.smh.com.au/entertainment/tv-and-radio/diversity-still-out-of-the-picture-20120229-1u1jg.html>.

22 Cited in H Furness, 'One in seven BBC presenters and actors to be black, Asian or ethnic minority under new Lord Hall pledge', *The Telegraph*, 20 June 2014, <www.telegraph.co.uk/culture/tvandradio/bbc/10914219/One-in-seven-BBC-presenters-and-actors-to-be-black-Asian-or-ethnic-minority-under-new-Lord-Hall-pledge.html>.

23 A Singh & H Furness, 'BBC staff take 'unconscious bias' course to encourage more diverse recruitment, *The Telegraph*, 28 April 2014, <www.telegraph.co.uk/culture/tvandradio/bbc/10794205/BBC-staff-take-unconscious-bias-course-to-encourage-more-diverse-recruitment.html>.

24 Australian Bureau of Statistics, 'Cultural Diversity in Australia', *Reflecting a Nation: Stories from the 2011 Census, 2012-2013*, 21 June, 2012, <www.abs.gov.au/ausstats/abs@.nsf/lookup/2071.0main+features902012-2013>.

25 Diversity Council Australia, *Capitalising on Culture: A National Survey of Australian Business Leaders*, 2013, p. 22.

26 A Booth, A Leigh and E Varganova, 'Does Racial and Ethnic Discrimination Vary Across Minority Groups? Evidence from a Field Experiment', July 2010, CEPR Discussion Paper No. DP7913, <ssrn.com/abstract=1640989>.

27 L Quillian, 'Does Unconscious Racism Exist?', *Social Psychology Quarterly*, vol. 71, no. 1, 2008.

28 C Frayling, *The Yellow Peril: Dr Fu Manchu & The Rise of Chinaphobia*, Thames & Hudson, United Kingdom, 2014; A Broinowski, *The Yellow Lady: Australian Impressions of Asia*, Oxford University Press, Melbourne, 1996.
29 Diversity Council Australia, *Capitalising on Culture*, p. 15
30 K Woo, Unpublished paper. For some corroborating academic evidence about negative discrimination and stereotypes about Asians in the US, see J Berdahl and J Min, 'Prescriptive stereotypes and workplace consequences for East Asians in North America' (2012) *Cultural Diversity and Ethnic Minority Psychology* 18 pp. 141–52.
31 K Woo, Unpublished paper. For some corroborating academic evidence about negative discrimination and stereotypes about Asians in the US, see J Berdahl and J Min, 'Prescriptive stereotypes and workplace consequences for East Asians in North America' (2012) *Cultural Diversity and Ethnic Minority Psychology* 18, pp. 141–52.
32 J Whelan, 'The myth of merit and unconscious bias', *The Conversation*, 16 October 2013, <theconversation.com/the-myth-of-merit-and-unconscious-bias-18876>.
33 G Frederickson, *Racism: A Short History*, Princeton University Press, Princeton, 2002, p. 31.
34 E Griffiths, 'Burka segregation in Parliament reversed by Speaker Bronwyn Bishop', *ABC*, 20 October 2014, <www.abc.net.au/news/2014-10-20/burka-segregation-is-not-the-best-says-mp/5825404>.
35 See, e.g., G Dyett, 'Businesses are resisting a social media campaign targeting them over Halal certification fees', *SBS News*, 12 November 2014, <www.sbs.com.au/news/article/2014/11/12/businesses-stay-strong-against-anti-halal-campaigns>.
36 See also M Grattan, 'Grattan on Friday: In Conversation with ASIO chief David Irvine', *The Conversation*, 15 August 2014, <www.theconversation.com/grattan-on-friday-in-conversation-with-asio-chief-david-irvine-30536>.
37 Australian Food & Grocery Council, 'Halal Certification', <www.afgc.org.au/about-afgc/our-policies/halal-certification/>.
38 RSPCA, 'What is Halal slaughter in Australia?', <www.kb.rspca.org.au/what-is-halal-slaughter-in-australia_116.html>.
39 T Blair, 'Inside Sydney's Muslim Land', *Daily Telegraph*, 18 August 2014.
40 Office of the Commissioner for Community Relations, *4th Annual Report – Community Relations Commissioner, 1979*, AGPS, Canberra, p. 3; Office of the Commissioner for Community Relations, *5th*

Notes to pages 171–188

Annual Report – Community Relations Commissioner, 1980, AGPS, Canberra, p. 3.
41   Australian Human Rights Commission, 'Racism. It Stops With Me: Bystanders', <www.itstopswithme.humanrights.gov.au/what-can-you-do/speak/bystanders>.
42   Stanford University, *Encyclopaedia of Philosophy* (at 4 May 2012) 'Toleration', <www.plato.stanford.edu/entries/toleration/#FouConTol>.
43   Stanford University, *Encyclopaedia of Philosophy* (at 4 May 2012) 'Toleration', <www.plato.stanford.edu/entries/toleration/#FouConTol>.
44   J Chait, 'Not a Very P.C. Thing to Say', *New York Magazine*, 27 January 2015, <http://nymag.com/daily/intelligencer/2015/01/not-a-very-pc-thing-to-say.html>.
45   AA Gill, *The Angry Island: Hunting the English*, Orion Books, London, 2010, pp. 163–64.

5   EMPATHY AND PRIVILEGE

1   D Hume, *A Treatise of Human Nature*, 1817, p. 106.
2   A Smith, *The Theory of Moral Sentiments*, Cosimo, New York, 2007, p. 10.
3   P Sheehan, 'You call this even-handed? Refugee series is strictly for the gullible', *Sydney Morning Herald*, 23 June 2011. At <www.smh.com.au/federal-politics/political-opinion/you-call-this-evenhanded-refugee-series-is-strictly-for-the-gullible-20110622-1gfav.html> (viewed 4 November 2014). I also discuss this example in my *Don't Go Back to Where You Came From: Why Multiculturalism Works*, NewSouth Publishing, Sydney, 2102.
4   See Australian Jewish News, 'SMH slammed on "anti-Semitic" cartoon', 31 July 2014, <www.jewishnews.net.au/smh-slammed-over-anti-semitic-cartoon-36678>.
5   See, e.g., M Devine, 'Left's race to call us bigots', *Daily Telegraph*, 15 October 2014, <www.blogs.news.com.au/dailytelegraph/mirandadevine/index.php/dailytelegraph/comments/the_lefts_race_to_call_us_all_bigots/>; G Henderson, 'Minority groups should engage in self-reflection, not victim mentality', *The Australian*, 4 October 2014; C Kenny, 'Hashtag for an imaginary backlash', *The Australian*, 17 December 2014, <www.theaustralian.com.au/opinion/columnists/hashtag-for-an-imaginary-backlash/story-fn8qlm5e-1227158594514>.
6   H Lee, *To Kill A Mockingbird*, J B Lippincott Co, Philadelphia, 1960, p. 30.

7   L Jamison, *The Empathy Exams: Essays*, Granata Books, London, 2014, pp. 3, 5.
8   Jamison, *The Empathy Exams*, p. 23.
9   J Haidt, *The Righteous Mind: Why Good People are Divided by Politics and Religion*, Penguin, London, 2012.
10 Quoted in S Manzoor, 'Rereading: Black Like Me by John Howard Griffin', *The Guardian*, 27 October 2011, <www.theguardian.com/books/2011/oct/27/black-like-me-john-howard-griffin>.
11 H Pilarczyk, 'Criticism of a New Racism Film: Journalist Goes Undercover to Discover Life as a Black Man in Germany', *Spiegel Online International*, 21 October 2009, <www.spiegel.de/international/germany/criticism-of-new-racism-film-journalist-goes-undercover-to-discover-life-as-a-black-man-in-germany-a-656569-druck.html>.
12 BBC News, 'New film uncovers racism in Germany', *BBC News*, 6 November 2009 <www.news.bbc.co.uk/2/hi/8347040.stm>.
13 J Dewey, *Democracy and Education: An Introduction to the Philosophy of Education*, Macmillan, New York, 1916, pp. 133–34.
14 B Anderson, *Imagined Communities: Reflections on the Origin and Spread of Nationalism*, Verso, London, 1983.
15 D Bromwich, *Moral Imagination: Essays*, Princeton University Press, Princeton, 2014, Preface, xii.
16 E Burke, *Reflections on the Revolution in France*, (1821), p. 171.
17 Bromwich, *Moral Imagination*, p. 7.
18 Dewey, *Democracy and Education*, p. 140.
19 A Smith, *The Essential Adam Smith*, W W Norton & Company, New York, 1987, p. 106.
20 C Taylor, 'The Politics of Recognition', in A Gutmann (ed.) *Multiculturalism: Examining the Politics of Recognition*, Princeton University Press, Princeton, 1994, p. 43.
21 For discussion, see Soutphommasane, *Don't Go Back To Where You Came From*; T Soutphommasane, *The Virtuous Citizen: Patriotism in a Multicultural Society*, Cambridge University Press, Cambridge, 2012.
22 'How Racist Are You? With Jane Elliott', Channel 4, <www.youtube.com/watch?v=6MYHBrJIIFU>.
23 P McIntosh, 'White Privilege: Unpacking the Invisible Backpack', p. 1, <www.isr.umich.edu/home/diversity/resources/white-privilege.pdf>.
24 See A DiAngelo, 'White Fragility', *The International Journal of Critical Pedagogy*, vol. 3, no. 3, 2011.

25 C Mills, *The Racial Contract*, Cornell University Press, Ithaca, 1997, p. 13.
26 Mills, *The Racial Contract*, p. 93.
27 In J Rothman, 'The Origins of "Privilege"', *The New Yorker*, 12 May 2014, <www.newyorker.com/books/page-turner/the-origins-of-privilege>.

6 FRIENDSHIP

1 For the most authoritative historical account of mateship, see N Dyrenfurth, *Mateship: A Very Australian History*, Scribe Publications, Melbourne, 2015.
2 R Ward, *The Australian Legend*, Oxford University Press, Oxford, 1958, p. 2. For trenchant criticisms of mateship's associations with racism and sexism, see respectively: H McQueen, *A New Britannia*, University of Queensland Press, Brisbane, 2004; M Dixson, *The Real Matilda*, UNSW Press, Sydney, 1999.
3 Dyrenfurth, *Mateship*.
4 Ward, *The Australian Legend*, pp. 258–59.
5 N Culotta, *They're a Weird Mob*, Ure Smith, Sydney, 1957, p. 204.
6 A C Grayling, *Grayling*, Yale University Press, New Haven, 2014, pp. 1–2.
7 R Bartlett & S Collins (trans), *Aristotle's Nichomachean Ethics*, University of Chicago Press, Chicago, 2011, p. 163.
8 Bartlett & Collins (trans), *Aristotle's Nichomachean Ethics*, pp. 164, 197.
9 Bartlett & Collins (trans), *Aristotle's Nichomachean Ethics*, p. 167.
10 Bartlett & Collins (trans), *Aristotle's Nichomachean Ethics*, p. 205.
11 Cicero, *On Living and Dying Well*, Penguin Group, London, 2012, pp. 82, 85.
12 Cicero, *On Living and Dying Well*, p. 90.
13 F Tönnies, *Community and Society (Gemeinschaft und Gesellschaft)*, P Loomis (ed.; trans), Michigan State University Press, East Lansing, 1957.
14 M de Montaigne, *The Complete Essays*, MA Screech (trans), Penguin, London, 2003.
15 L Stone, *The Family, Sex and Marriage in England*, Harper and Row, New York, 1977, p. 93.
16 See T Hobbes, *Leviathan: Or the Matter, Forme, & Power of a Common-wealth Ecclesiasticall and Civil*, Yale University Press, New Haven, 2010.
17 RW Emerson, *Essays: First and Second Series*, First Vintage Books, New York, 1990, pp. 114, 123.

18 CS Lewis, *The Four Loves*, Harcourt Brace & Co, New York, 1960, Introduction.
19 Lewis, *The Four Loves*, p. 65.
20 Lewis, *The Four Loves*, p. 65.
21 Lewis, *The Four Loves*, p. 58.
22 Lewis, *The Four Loves*, p. 66.
23 E Nussbaum, 'Difficult Women: How "Sex and the City" lost its good name', *The New Yorker*, 29 July 2013, <www.newyorker.com/magazine/2013/07/29/difficult-women>.
24 See C Lasch, *The Culture of Narcissism: American Life in an Age of Diminishing Expectations*, Norton, New York, 1979.
25 W Deresiewicz, 'Faux Friendship', *The Chronicle Review of Higher Education*, 6 December 2009, <www.chronicle.com/article/Faux-Friendship/49308/>.
26 Deresiewicz, 'Faux Friendship', <www.chronicle.com/article/Faux-Friendship/49308/>.
27 L Besser & S Nicholls, 'Ian Macdonald found corrupt by ICAC again', *Sydney Morning Herald*, 30 August 2013, <www.smh.com.au/nsw/ian-macdonald-found-corrupt-by-icac-again-20130830-2surh.html>.
28 M Whitbourn, 'SES Commissioner Murray Kear resigns following corruption finding at ICAC', *Sydney Morning Herald*, 12 June 2014, <www.smh.com.au/nsw/ses-commissioner-murray-kear-resigns-following-corruption-finding-at-icac-20140612-zs56z.html>.
29 MJ Sandel, *Democracy's Discontent: America in Search of a Public Philosophy*, Belknap Press of Harvard University Press, Cambridge MA, 1996.
30 LS Pangle, *Aristotle and the Philosophy of Friendship*, Cambridge University Press, Cambridge, 2003.
31 P Conrad, *At Home in Australia*, Thames & Hudson, London, 2003, p. 163.
32 'Big W joins Aldi in ditching "racist" T-shirts', *NineMSN* (online) 9 January 2014. At <www.news.ninemsn.com.au/national/2014/01/09/08/38/federal-government-approved-racist-tshirts>.
33 R Rorty, *Achieving Our Country: Leftist Thought in Twentieth-Century America*, Harvard University Press, Cambridge, 1999; T Soutphommasane, *Reclaiming Patriotism*, Cambridge University Press, Melbourne, 2009.
34 Australian Bureau of Statistics, The "average" Australian (2013) At <www.abs.gov.au/AUSSTATS/abs@.nsf/Lookup/4102.0Main+Features30April+2013#back3>.

35 See 'Chen, Kim, Singh are the new big names', *Sydney Morning Herald*, 25 January 201, <www.smh.com.au/national/chen-kim-singh-are-the-new-big-names-20120124-1qffe.html>.
36 A Markus, *Mapping Social Cohesion 2013: The Scanlon Foundation Surveys National Report* (2013), p. 34.
37 T Soutphommasane, *The Virtuous Citizen: Patriotism in a Multicultural Society*, Cambridge University Press, Cambridge, 2012, chapter 2.
38 For more detailed discussion of the connection between patriotism and civic responsibility, see Soutphommasane, *The Virtuous Citizen*.
39 WEH Stanner, *The 1968 Boyer Lectures: After the Dreaming* (1968).
40 R Dworkin, *Freedom's Law: The Moral Reading of the American Constitution*, Harvard University Press, Cambridge, 1996.
41 *Official Record of the Debates of the Australasian Federal Convention*, Third Session, Melbourne, 20 January–17 March 1898, p. 240.
42 R French, 'The Race Power: A Constitutional Chimera' in HP Lee & G Winterton (eds), *Australian Constitutional Landmarks*, Cambridge University Press, Cambridge, 2003, p. 181; and J Quick & R Garran, *The Annotated Constitution of the Australian Commonwealth*, 1910, p. 622.
43 Commonwealth, *Parliamentary Debates*, House of Representatives, 26 September 1901, p. 5233.
44 Expert Panel on Constitutional Recognition of Indigenous Australians, *Recognising Aboriginal and Torres Strait Islander Peoples in the Constitution: Report of the Expert Panel*, Report, Commonwealth, January 2013, p. xviii. The Expert Panel's proposed new section 116A reads as follows:
Section 116A Prohibition of racial discrimination
(1) The Commonwealth, a State or Territory shall not discriminate on the grounds of race, colour or ethnic or national origin.
(2) Subsection (1) does not preclude the making of laws or measures for the purpose of overcoming disadvantage, ameliorating the effects of past discrimination, or protecting the cultures, languages or heritage of any group.
45 M Davis & G Williams, *Everything You Need to Know About the Referendum to Recognise Indigenous Australians*, NewSouth, Sydney, 2015, pp. 106–107, 117.
46 M Davis & G Williams, *Everything You Need to Know*, pp. 109–112.
47 A Collins, 'Noel Pearson backs separate declaration of recognition for Indigenous Australians', ABC News (Online), 13 April 2015, <www.abc.net.au/news/2015-04-13/noel-pearson-backs-

declaration-of-recognition-for-indigenous/6388116>.
48 N Pearson, 'A Rightful Place: Race, Recognition and a More Complete Commonwealth', *Quarterly Essay*, vol. 55, 2014.
49 N Robinson, 'Spectre of bill of rights kills racism clause: MP', *The Australian*, 4 March 2015, p. 7.
50 Davis & Williams, *Everything You Need to Know*, p. 110.
51 Legislation that was previously enacted in reliance of the race power include: *World Heritage Properties Conservation Act 1983*; *Aboriginal and Torres Strait Islander Heritage Protection Act 1984*; *Native Title Act 1993*; *Corporations (Aboriginal and Torres Strait Islander) Act 2006*.
52 French, 'The Race Power: A Constitutional Chimera' in Lee and Winterton (eds), *Australian Constitutional Landmarks*, p. 206.
53 Davis & Williams, *Everything You Need to Know*, pp. 119–20.

AFTERWORD

1 Australian Bureau of Statistics, 'Overseas born Aussies hit a 120 year peak', 29 January 2015, <www.abs.gov.au/ausstats/abs@.nsf/latestProducts/3412.0Media%20Release12013-14>.
2 Close the Gap Campaign Steering Committee for Indigenous Health Equality, *Close the Gap Progress and Priorities Report 2015*, 2015, Sydney <www.humanrights.gov.au/sites/default/files/document/publication/CTG_progress_and_priorities_report_2015.pdf>.
3 J Kidd, 'Over-representation of Indigenous Australians in prison a catastrophe, says Mick Gooda, the Aboriginal and Torres Strait Islander Social Justice Commissioner', *ABC News Online*, 5 December 2014, <www.abc.net.au/news/2014-12-04/number-of-indigenous-australians-in-prison-a-catastrophe/5945504>.
4 N O'Brien, 'Controversial Islamic group Hitzb ut-Tahrir accused of inciting hatred against Jews', *Sydney Morning Herald*, 25 February 2015, <www.smh.com.au/national/controversial-islamic-group-hitzb-uttahrir-accused-of-inciting-hatred-against-jews-20150225-13odro.html>; V Alhadeff, 'Hizb ut-Tahrir leader's speech reveals our peaceful values are taken for granted', *The Australian*, 2 March 2015, <www.nswjbd.org/default.aspx?ArticleID=687>. The rising occurrence of anti-Semitism is documented in J Nathan, *2014 Report on Antisemitism in Australia: 1 October 2013-30 September 2014*, Executive Council of Australian Jewry, Sydney.
5 P Keating, '20th Anniversary of the Racial Discrimination Act', speech delivered 9 June 1995, <www.pmtranscripts.dpmc.gov.au/transcripts/00009625.pdf>.

6 P Cosgrove, 'Address on the occasion of conference marking the 40th anniversary of the Racial Discrimination Act', speech delivered 19 February 2015, <www.gg.gov.au/speech/conference-marking-40th-anniversary-racial-discrimination-act>.

INDEX

Abbott Government 99–100, 121–22, 243
Aboriginal and Torres Strait Islander peoples
  arguments about Aboriginality 36
  Constitutional recognition 237–41
  Freedom Ride (1965) 33
  impact of British colonisation on 18–19
  land rights and native title 78–79
  legalised racism towards 53–54
  policies to exclude and destroy 18–19, 53–54
  referendum (1967) 33
  regular experience of racism 150
  stolen generations 32–33
  white-settler narratives and 37
Aboriginal Deaths in Custody Royal Commission 116
AHRC *see* Australian Human Rights Commission
ancestry 14, 42
anti-Muslim sentiment 166–69
Aristotle 218–21, 231
asylum seeker policy
  racism in 37–39

Australia as racist *see* racism in Australia today
Australia Day 13
Australia Day T-shirts 205–6, 233
Australian Constitution
  immigration power 28
  proposed prohibition of racial discrimination 239–41
  proposed recognition of Aboriginal and Torres Strait Islander peoples 237–43
  race power 28, 238–39
  racial discrimination provisions 54–56, 237–38
  referendums 33, 243
Australian Human Rights Commission 69
Australian identity and nationhood *see also* multiculturalism; White Australia
  concern with racism 1, 5–6, 13–14
  cultural diversity and 234–35
  exclusion of Aboriginal people 236
  ideology of racial unity 13, 30, 92
  mateship 214–15
  patriotism 232–35
  sense of anxiety 11

Index

unwritten cultural rules 39–42
Australian Labor Party 30
Australian Law Reform
 Commission 116–17
The Australian Legend (Ward) 214

Bailey, Karen 2, 142
Barton, Edmund 238–39
Berlin, Isaiah 101–4, 135–36
bigotry
 religious 165–69
 right to express 98–99, 130,
  210 (*see also* Freedom of
  Speech (Repeal Section
  18C) Bill)
Black Like Me (Griffin) 191–92
Black on White (documentary film)
 192–93
'Blue Eyes–Brown Eyes'
 experiment 193–95, 199–200,
 202
Bolt, Andrew 99, 120–21
Bonner, Neville 64
Border Protection Act 2001 37
border protection rhetoric 37–39
Bradman, Don 41
Brandeis, Louis 106–8, 111–12
Brandis, George 98, 121–22
Bringing them home Inquiry 32
British colonisation 16–19
Bryant, Nick 11, 147
The Bulletin 27
Burke, Edmund 195–96
bystander effect 143

casual racism
 bystander resistance 142–43,
  170–71, 180
 versus everyday racism 148–50
 examples and characteristics
  46, 145–48, 176–82
 harm caused by 151–52

 standing up to 176–82
CERD see *International
 Convention on the Elimination
 of All Forms of Racial
 Discrimination*
Chaney, Fred 64
Charlie Hebdo 4, 90, 96, 99–100,
 119–20
Chinese immigration
 opposition to 21–25
Cicero 220–21
civic friendship
 Aristotle on 230–31
 and Constitutional reform
  237–43
 and multiculturalism 216,
  234–35
 and patriotism 232–35
civility 85, 91–92, 95–97, 173–74
clientelism 230–31
colonisation 16–19
Community Relations
 Commissioner 67, 68–69
conciliation of complaints 48–49,
 70–74
 agreements reached 49, 70–74
 conciliation mechanism 49,
  70–74
Connick, Harry Jr 146–47
corruption 230–31
Cosgrove, Sir Peter 252–53
criminal offences 49, 70, 71–72
Cronulla race riot xv, 6
cultural relativism 198–99
A Current Affair 154

Davis, Megan 240
Deakin, Alfred 28
defamation 134
Deresiewicz, William 229–30
Dewey, John 194, 197
dictation test 29, 34

dignity *see* human dignity
Dodson, Mick 32–33

Eatock v Bolt 120–21
education
    and human rights advocacy 82–84
    promoting empathy through 188–91, 193–95, 199–202
    promoting tolerance through 170
Elliott, Jane 193–94, 199–200, 202
Emerson, Ralph Waldo 223
empathy
    concept 185–86
    conditions of 188–93
    experiencing through impersonation 191–93
    obstacles to 197–202
    personality traits for 191, 202
    privilege as barrier 202–7
    through education 188–91
    through experience, thinking and imagination 193–97
    through impersonation 191–93
    withholding of 186–88
The Empathy Exams (Jamison) 189–90
Enderby, Kep 61, 65–66
Enlightenment thought 16, 222

The Footy Show 153–54
Fraser Government 94
freedom, two concepts of 101–4
freedom from racial vilification 109–14
freedom of speech
    absolutist arguments 127–32

classic liberal defence 105–9, 130
as counter to hate speech 127–31
limited by other rights and values 106, 114–15, 132–36, 212
under *Racial Discrimination Act* 115, 120–21
and right to express bigotry 121
US Constitution 105–6
Freedom of Speech (Repeal Section 18C) Bill
    deficiencies 123–27
    main proposals 121–22
    'ordinary reasonable person' test 124–25, 137–41
    public opposition 122–23, 131
French, Robert 78
Friends 226–28
friendship
    classical notions 217–21
    clientelism and 230–31
    contemporary notions 226–30
    modern notions 221–25

Gaze, Beth 75
Gibbs, Sir Harry 77
Gill, AA 174–75
Go Back to Where You Come From 186–87
Gobineau, Arthur 20
Goodes, Adam 2–3, 83, 147
Grant, Stan 155
Grassby, Al 34, 67, 170
Greenwood, Ivor 65
Griffin, John Howard 191–92

Hage, Ghassan 40
Hanson, Pauline 94, 120, 154, 245

Index

harm caused by racial vilification 110–14
hate speech 2, 88–91, 126, 128, 142, 210, 252 *see also* racial vilification
Hey Hey It's Saturday 146
Higgins, Henry Bournes 28
Holmes, Oliver Wendell 106–8
Home and Away 156
Howard, John 64, 71–72, 94
Howard Government suspension of RDA 80
human dignity
    harm caused by non-recognition of 60–61, 114
    in international law 56–57
    meanings 57–58
    Waldron on 58–59
Human Rights and Equal Opportunity Commission 69
Hume, David 186

ICCPR *see* International Covenant on Civil and Political Rights
Immigration Restriction Act 1901 29–30, 37, 238–39
Indian indentured labour 21
Indigenous Australians *see* Aboriginal and Torres Strait Islander peoples
International Convention on the Elimination of All Forms of Racial Discrimination 34, 51, 57, 115
International Covenant on Civil and Political Rights 56–57, 114–15
Islam *see* anti-Muslim sentiment

Jamison, Leslie 189–90
jingoism 232–33

Joyce, Alan 146

Keating, Paul 76
Kenneally, Christine 15
Kirby, Michael 79
Koowarta v Bjelke-Petersen 77, 78–79

Lane, William 24
Lavarch, Michael 117
Lewis, CS 224–25
liberty *see* freedom; freedom from racial vilification; freedom of speech
Living with the Enemy 200–201

Mabo v State of Queensland (No. 1) 78–79
Manne, Robert 39
Martin Place siege 7, 167
McGuire, Eddie 147
McIntosh, Peggy 202–3, 206
media, structural racism in 152–58
Migration Act 1958 34
Mill, John Stuart 24, 107
Mills, Charles W 204–6
Montesquieu, Charles de 16
moral imagination 195–97
Moss, Irene 116
multiculturalism
    antagonism to 94
    cultural relativism and 198–99
    as new national vision 34, 36, 93–95, 215–17, 234–35
    patriotism and 216, 234–36
    public support 68
    role of civility and civil friendship 91–97, 216, 234–35
Multiculturalism and the Law (report) 116–17

I'm not racist but ...

Murphy, Lionel 61
Muslims *see* anti-Muslim sentiment

National Anti-Racism Strategy 82–83
National Inquiry into Racist Violence (report) 116
National Life and Character: A Forecast (Pearson) 25–27
Native Title Amendment Act 1998 80
Neighbours 156–57
Northern Territory Intervention 80–81, 240

offensive language 133–34
O'Grady, John 215
Oliver, John 11
One Nation party 94, 120, 245
'ordinary reasonable person' test 124–25, 137–41

Pacific Island Labourers Act 1901 28–29
Parkes, Henry 23
patriotism 216, 232–36
Pearson, Charles 25–27
Pearson, Noel 19, 241
Perkins, Charles 33
political correctness 174
Post and Telegraph Act 1901 30
power inequality 201–2, 211–12
privilege 202–7

Quantum Leap 183–84

race
    and ancestry 15, 208–9
    as civic principle 23–27
    concept 14–16, 42
    in Enlightenment thinking 16

genetic aspect 15
links with religion 165, 168–69
notion of European superiority 16–20, 238–39
recognition of racial differences 244–48
and self-identification 208–13, 244–48
structural notions 204–6
Race Discrimination Commissioner, office of
    functions 69, 82–83, 265–66
Racial Discrimination Act 1975
    amendments 68–70
    civil character 49, 70, 71–72, 118
    complaint-handling process 48–49, 70–74, 81–82
    constitutional validity 78
    excerpts 255–66
    forces behind 51–52
    human dignity as basis 56–58
    impact on native title 78–81
    impact on prejudice and attitudes 82–87
    litigation under 70–71, 81, 118
    main provisions 49–50, 61–63, 66
    parliamentary debate 61–66
    sections 18C and 18D (see *Racial Discrimination Act 1975* (Part IIA))
    significance 50, 67, 76–81, 252–54
    suspension of 79–81, 240–41
Racial Discrimination Act 1975 (Part IIA)
    case law involving 115–16, 119–21

Index

conciliation mechanism 118–19
exemptions (section 18D) 70, 117, 119–20
excerpts 263–64
and free speech 121, 211
prohibition of racial vilification (section 18C) 70, 85, 115, 117
proposal to repeal section 18C 98–99, 121–27
as response to racist violence 116
Racial Hatred Act 1995 69
Racial Hatred Bill 1994 72, 117
racial identity 208–13, 244–48
racial vilification see also *Racial Discrimination Act 1975* (Part IIA)
absolute freedom of speech as remedy 105–6, 127–29
as curtailment of freedom 113–14
health effects 110–13, 124
public support for legal protections 123–24
racism *see also* casual racism; racial vilification; structural racism
casual racism 46
as civic harm 3, 44, 47
concept 42–43, 44
health effects 110–13, 124
public acts of 2–3, 176–82
as restriction on freedom 113–14, 131
sources 44–46
standing up to 2–3, 88–91, 96–97, 176–82
racism in Australia today
denial of 5–6, 43, 46–47, 64, 65, 178–80, 246–48
international images 11–12

personal encounters with 8, 149–50, 176–82, 246–48
sensitivity to allegations 1, 5–6, 13–14
'Racism. It Stops with Me' campaign 83–84, 170–71
racist violence 116
RDA *see Racial Discrimination Act 1975*
referendum (1967) 33
Rice, Simon 74, 125

Sawyer, Mark 147
Seinfeld 226–28
Sex and the City 227–28
Sheehan, Paul 187
Sheil, Glen 63
Smith, Adam 186, 197–98
Stanner, WEH 236
stolen generations 32–33
structural racism
advancement into leadership positions 159–63
entry into employment 160
parliamentary representation 159
public service leadership 159–61
responding to 163–64
television 152–58

Taylor, Charles 103
'Team Australia' 41–42, 99
television drama 155–57
They're a Weird Mob (Culotta) 215
Thornton, Margaret 75
To Kill a Mockingbird (Lee) 188
Toben, Frederick 126
Today Tonight 154
tolerance 171–74
Torres Strait Islander people 150
Trujillo, Sol 11–12, 146

295

US Constitution 105–6
Waldron, Jeremy 58–59
Wallraff, Gunter 192–93
Ward, Russel 214–15
Warren, Samuel 111–12
White Australia
   anti-Chinese sentiment and 21–25
   'border protection' rhetoric and 37–39
   dismantling 33–34, 36, 50
   and European ethnic exclusion 30–31
   intellectual and popular influences 24–28
   international reaction 30–31
   legacy 35–43
   legislative expression 28–30
   public and political support 31–32, 238–39
   relevance to Indigenous Australians 31–32
Whitlam, Gough 67, 76
Whitlam Government 34
   see also Racial Discrimination Act 1975
Williams, George 77, 240
Wilson, Sir Ronald 32
Wood, Ian 64
Wyatt, Ken 241

www.ingramcontent.com/pod-product-compliance
Ingram Content Group UK Ltd.
Pitfield, Milton Keynes, MK11 3LW, UK
UKHW041302180426
11947UKWH00009B/622